WHEN WOMEN RAN
Fifth Avenue

Also by Julie Satow

The Plaza

WHEN WOMEN RAN
Fifth Avenue

Glamour and Power
at the Dawn of
American Fashion

Julie Satow

Doubleday
New York

Jacket design by Emily Mahon
Front-of-jacket photograph © Trunk Archive
Book design by Betty Lew

Library of Congress Cataloging-in-Publication Data
Names: Satow, Julie, author.
Title: When women ran Fifth Avenue : glamour and
power at the dawn of American fashion / Julie Satow.
Description: First edition. | New York :
Doubleday, [2024] | Includes index.
Identifiers: LCCN 2023039182 (print) | LCCN 2023039183 (ebook) |
ISBN 9780385548755 (hardcover) | ISBN 9780385548762 (ebook)
Subjects: LCSH: Department stores—New York (State)—
New York—History. | Fashion—New York (State)—New York—
History. | Women executives—New York (State)—New York.
Classification: LCC HF5465.U64 S367 2024 (print) |
LCC HF5465.U64 (ebook) | DDC 381.1410973-dc23/eng/20231130
LC record available at https://lccn.loc.gov/2023039182
LC ebook record available at https://lccn.loc.gov/2023039183

MANUFACTURED IN THE UNITED STATES OF AMERICA

1   3   5   7   9   10   8   6   4   2

First Edition

To My Parents

Female shoppers and saleswomen crowd around a counter
at the Siegel-Cooper department store in 1897.

Buying and selling, serving and being served—women. On every floor, in every aisle, at every counter, women. . . . Down in the basement buying and selling bargains in marked-down summer frocks, women. Up under the roof, posting ledgers, auditing accounts, attending to all the complex bookkeeping of a great metropolitan department store, women. Behind most of the counters on all the floors between, women. . . . Simply a moving, seeking, hurrying mass of femininity, in the midst of which the occasional man shopper, man clerk, and man supervisor, looks lost and out of place.

—RHETA CHILDE DORR, 1910

Contents

Window-shoppers at Bonwit Teller in 1930.

Prologue

As ice gathered several inches thick on the Hudson River and the mercury plummeted below freezing, Hortense Odlum stepped from her chauffeured car onto the Fifth Avenue sidewalk. Gripping her felt hat to her auburn updo, she stared at the Art Deco skyscraper looming above her, at the two-story entryway made of filigreed bronze and glass and the words "BONWIT TELLER" etched prominently into the limestone facade. A morning rush of passersby leaned against the gale, men lugging briefcases as they trudged toward glass-walled boardrooms and women in nubby woolen coats ready for a day serving coffee and taking stenography. It was the height of the Great Depression, but even the ranks of the jobless seemed purposeful, huddling against the tall buildings to shield themselves from the biting cold, their bare hands outstretched in the hopes of a Christmas coin.

Hortense pulled her fur coat around her and stepped gingerly through the revolving doors. At once, the scramble and blizzard outside fell away as an atmosphere of hushed grandeur and a blast of warm air enveloped her. She looked about the store's main floor, with its maze of glass counters and mirrored columns, the clacking of high heels against marble echoing through the vast space as a handful of early morning shoppers wandered the aisles. Eyeing the bank of elevators sitting along the far wall, Hortense walked toward them, clasping her purse nervously as she asked the operator for the eleventh floor. She exited into a reception area, behind which were a series of doors where Bonwit Teller's management had its offices. The secretary showed her to a nearby couch. Moments later, an elderly gentleman, dressed nattily in a three-piece suit with a shock of silver hair, stuck his head from behind one of the large wooden doors and waved her inside.

Paul Bonwit, the seventy-year-old merchant, gestured for Hortense to sit across from his imposing, presidential desk, and she took her seat with a small, polite smile. Mr. Bonwit, who had come from Germany in his youth and founded his store four decades earlier, had spent countless hours charming wealthy housewives with his old-world manners and continental accent. But as he launched into his standard line of questioning, asking after Hortense's trip into Manhattan and how her children were faring, his typical ease faltered and the air between them became stiff and awkward.

Bonwit Teller had been one of New York's most exclusive, well-appointed department stores. But three years into the Great Depression, its rows of mink coats and shelves of Baccarat glass sat unsold, and, teetering on the cusp of bankruptcy, Mr. Bonwit had been forced to sell. The new owner, Floyd Odlum, was a Wall Street tycoon and one of America's richest men. So far, Mr. Bonwit had managed to keep Floyd at bay, holding on to his large, carpeted office and his position as store president. But now Floyd's wife had made a sudden appearance, and Mr. Bonwit was confounded by the arrival of this forty-one-year-old mother of two. While she had shopped plenty, Hortense had never worked—and certainly not in a store. "There's a small office down the hall, Mrs. Odlum, where I hope you'll be comfortable," Mr. Bonwit finally ventured. "And by the way, my secretary will be glad to take your dictation when you need her."

Hortense's face reddened. She didn't want to be there any more than Mr. Bonwit wanted her to be. But her husband had asked her to make the rounds of the store and report back on her impressions. And while she had little idea how to proceed, Hortense was willing to try nearly anything to please Floyd. "What would I do in an office?" she replied, nervously. "I wouldn't know how to act in an office, and I wouldn't have the faintest idea of what to say to a secretary."

As their meeting concluded, Mr. Bonwit may have felt relief at Hortense's ignorance of the corporate world. But as he took his guest by the elbow and gently guided her toward the door, he had little way of knowing that Hortense's inexperience belied an instinctive business acumen. That by the following year, their roles would reverse, with Hortense occupying the corner office at Bonwit Teller, sitting at the stately desk as her secretary took dictation, supervising more than one thousand employees, and directing a store that boasted record-breaking sales. Hortense was setting herself on a path that would thrust her into a career that she had never intended, that would challenge her notions of womanhood and force her to confront difficult truths. It was the start of a journey that would lay the groundwork for an evolution of the grand department store and a metamorphosis of American fashion.

In the early twentieth century, department stores were a land of glamour and possibility. In a single afternoon, you could have the details of a wedding (or funeral) planned; find out the dates for the civil service examinations; send a telegram at a Western Union outpost; drop your baby at the nursery to have a leisurely lunch at the tearoom, followed by an appointment at the hair salon; arrange for the express delivery of an ermine fur wrap to your home; buy refrigerated steaks; or order a pair of rare green parakeets from the Seychelles Islands. There were stores with miniature zoos and fishponds and mechanical boats, those with emergency hospitals and trained nurses, and even one store, in Oklahoma City, that sponsored a "baby week," offering nine infants for adoption, with six lucky tykes finding permanent homes. There were window displays featuring works by Georgia O'Keeffe and Salvador Dalí, as well as those with elaborate Christmas trains and towers of delicate Easter eggs.

While department stores were palatial wonderlands where a nearly boundless array of objects and services could be purchased or arranged, for women they offered something even greater. From their very inception, department stores were uniquely female universes, where women commanded power in ways that were often unattainable elsewhere. Here, female customers held sway over male clerks and managers whose jobs it was to serve them. Here, at a time when it was considered impolite and even dangerous for women to walk alone in public, department stores provided cover, enabling them to stroll and congre-

A rendering of Le Bon Marché and its grand staircase
in 1872, by the artist Hubert Clerget.

gate on their own, to peruse store windows or purchase needed items.
It was here, at the department store, that women could earn a living
and, even more, receive the education and training to transform their
jobs into lasting careers.

Le Bon Marché in Paris, opened in 1838, is often credited as the
world's first department store. Its enormous plate glass windows, featuring mannequins dressed in the latest fashions, were astonishing, as
was the fact that any person could freely enter, with no obligation to
buy, just for the joy of running their hands along a display of silk shawls,
or to try parasols in rainbow colors, or smell the aromas wafting from
the perfume counters. In America, the Marble Palace stunned onlookers when it opened in 1846, a majestic four-story galleria on Chambers
Street in Manhattan boasting novelties such as a "Ladies' Parlor," where
women could preen in front of Parisian-imported full-length mirrors.
In 1862, the founder of the Marble Palace, Alexander Turney Stewart,
an Irish-born immigrant who would become the nation's third-richest
man, after William Astor and Cornelius Vanderbilt, opened an even

larger and more opulent shopping mecca. The new cast-iron Palace was the largest store in the world, boasting a roster of well-heeled customers including Mary Todd Lincoln, whose compulsive clothes-buying habit was so severe that she ran up a tab that equated to $500,000 in today's dollars over the course of a single summer. Her husband, President Abraham Lincoln, could not repay it.

Located on Broadway, between Ninth and Tenth Streets, A. T. Stewart's cast-iron Palace became the cornerstone around which an entire shopping district sprouted. Ladies' Mile ran from Astor Place to Madison Square Park, earning its moniker from the crush of mostly white middle- and upper-class women who appeared there daily, partaking in the new national pastime of window-shopping. These early stores were a visual feast, with merchandise constantly refreshed, the newest, most aspirational items displayed in arresting fashion, tempting eyes and wallets. The ground floors had soaring ceilings and grand staircases, with sunlight shining through atriums and stained glass, and long counters with rotating stools where shoppers could try on cosmetics and leather gloves. Some featured confectioneries with an array of sweets, and notions areas with piles of ribbons and lace. There were bargain basements where kitchen maids and factory workers rummaged for discount dishware and winter coats sold on clearance, and upper floors where wealthy women in wasp-waisted gowns examined silk bedding and porcelain china patterns. In 1896, more than 150,000 women attended the grand opening of the Siegel-Cooper store, angling to see hundreds of grand pianos, the largest photography gallery in the world, and a pet department that went far beyond the typical dogs and cats, offering monkeys, lions, and even panther cubs for sale. These were elaborate, fantastical places. At Macy's in Herald Square, shoppers could explore the world's largest rug collection across its twenty-two acres of selling space, choose to ride on one of thirty-three hydraulic elevators or four escalators, and wonder at the pneumatic tube system that shot cash and sales slips along a web of cylinders affixed to the ceiling.

New York City did not have a monopoly on large department stores. There was the Loop neighborhood in Chicago, for instance, which boasted several large retailers, most notably Marshall Field's, with

A. T. Stewart's opulent cast-iron Palace was
for a time the world's largest department store.

Women working in the accounting department
at the Siegel-Cooper department store in 1906.

seventy-six elevators, thirty-one miles of carpeting, and a Tiffany dome made from 1.6 million pieces of glass. Its founder's famous mottoes included "Give the lady what she wants" and "The customer is always right," and any item purchased there could be returned for a full refund, at any time, with no questions asked. In San Francisco there was Market Street and Union Square, with stores like the White House, the Emporium, and I. Magnin, while Boston had Jordan Marsh and Filene's. In the late nineteenth and early twentieth centuries, department stores proliferated, from Wanamaker's and Strawbridge & Clothier in Philadelphia, to Kaufmann's and Horne's in Pittsburgh, and from Rich's in Atlanta to Famous-Barr in St. Louis.

Peeling back the glossy layers of these stores, unseen by the crowds, were the army of harried saleswomen checking the stockrooms in the hopes of satisfying impatient customers, and the girls known as wrappers furiously folding sweaters into boxes and tying ribbons with amazing dexterity. As women increasingly entered the workforce, department stores became a refuge, where ambitious employees could receive instruction and support and the opportunity to rise through

The tearoom at Marshall Field's in Chicago in 1909.

the ranks. Amid the buzz of activity, upstairs in a warren of offices, dozens of female bookkeepers toiled among rows of filing cabinets and mountains of paper records, while the powerful female fashion buyers sat at their desks planning their next visit to the Paris couture shows, and the handful of copywriters of both sexes contemplated the next crackerjack ad copy for that Sunday's newspaper.

While growing numbers of female workers were being employed at department stores, their numbers thinned out considerably at the upper levels, with few female managers and even fewer female executives. It wasn't until the Great Depression that the first woman ascended to the presidency of a major department store. Hortense Odlum, a sub-urban mother and wife, took the helm of Bonwit Teller despite never having held a paying job before, embracing her lack of experience and transforming the ailing Fifth Avenue establishment into a profitable powerhouse, at a time when many competitors were facing ruin. Yet Hortense never intended to have a career, and she remained ambivalent about her status as a businesswoman. In later years, she came to rue her time at Bonwit Teller, blaming it for her personal hardships and eventually forsaking her legacy.

While Hortense was taking over at Bonwit Teller, a determined, steely-eyed Dorothy Shaver was rising through the ranks at Lord & Taylor. The career-minded Dorothy eschewed romance to singularly pursue her ambition, and her merchandising and marketing genius was pivotal in giving rise to the American fashion industry. In 1945, when Dorothy was appointed president of Lord & Taylor, she became one of the highest-paid female executives in the country's history, *Life* magazine labeling her "America's No. 1 Career Woman." In the ensuing years, she leveraged her platform to influence politics and current affairs, visiting the Stalin-era Soviet Union, discussing freedom of thought with Edward R. Murrow, and honoring figures as varied as Albert Einstein and Agnes de Mille.

And finally, just as Dorothy was nearing the end of her tenure at Lord & Taylor, the theatrical and brilliant Geraldine Stutz, a thirty-two-year-old former fashion editor at *Glamour* magazine, took control of Henri Bendel. In the swinging 1960s and disco mania of the 1970s, Geraldine ruled over New York's chicest shopping destination, promoting cutting-edge designers and drawing customers like Jackie O and Mick Jagger. In 1980, Geraldine bought a piece of Bendel's, becoming the first woman owner of a major New York department store. But as the decade progressed, and a craze for shopping malls and chain stores gripped the nation, Geraldine would lose everything that she had built. One fateful decision not only would lead to the demise of Henri Bendel but would become a harbinger for the downfall of the industry.

Department stores have long been overshadowed by the men who founded them, figures like R. H. Macy, Edward Filene, and the Bloomingdale brothers. But these establishments were truly female-centric worlds, where women were freed from many of the societal constraints they faced outside the store. The history of Hortense, Dorothy, and Geraldine has been overlooked, but while they were establishing their lives and careers decades ago, their experiences remain immediate and relevant, their challenges shockingly familiar, many of the biases and structural sexism they faced still in place. These were strong, complex women, figures with interlocking yet varying fates, pioneers of their eras whose efforts contributed to the contours of American fashion and helped pave the way for women today.

Hortense Odlum in an
undated photograph.

Part 1

‡———‡

I'm no businesswoman. The only career
I ever wanted was in the home.

—*Hortense Odlum*

Chapter 1

Hortense Goes Shopping

Hortense could never forget the first dress she bought in New York City. It was the ugliest outfit she ever wore, black chiffon, costing $10, purchased in a bargain basement of a department store that was worlds away from the grandeur of Bonwit Teller and Fifth Avenue. "It was horrible. I was twenty-five and it made me look fifty," she recalled. This was in 1916, when Hortense had been in the city for barely a month, living with her husband and infant son in a cramped apartment in Brooklyn, filled with cheap vinyl furniture and a roommate to help them cover the rent. Floyd was working as a junior clerk at a white-shoe law firm in Manhattan. His paycheck was small, but the position had career potential and was a step forward for the ambitious young couple.

The new mother spent her days in Brooklyn caring for her baby, Stanley, and keeping house on a small budget while Floyd worked long hours. "Every way I could, I saved money," said Hortense, who wasn't new to the idea of watching every penny. Growing up in a pioneer town, surrounded by the harsh desert canyons of southwestern Utah, Hortense had always scrounged for necessities; her mother ran a guesthouse to support her children, and the family raised chickens and scratched out a spindly garden in the parched soil. Here, Hortense didn't grow her own food, but she did buy hamburger meat instead of steak and used scraps of gingham and percale to sew herself house-dresses. She mended Floyd's shirts "until he would refuse to wear them 'just one more time,'" then used the discarded fabric to sew Stanley's baby clothes.

Hortense embraced her role as homemaker. "I loved caring for my baby and doing my housework. It gave me tremendous satisfaction to know that as my husband was doing his job well, I was helping him by doing mine well," she wrote years later in her autobiography, adding that it gave "dishwashing and floor scrubbing dignity and meaning." But Hortense's domestic bliss was disrupted when, a few weeks into their time in New York, a colleague of Floyd's asked the couple to his home for Thanksgiving dinner. Hortense had few friends and no family in Brooklyn, and there was little occasion to socialize. This outing, however, would render her simple, homemade wardrobe far too conspicuous. Refusing to appear at a business dinner in a housedress, Hortense argued with Floyd. "We can't go," she told him. There was no one to watch Stanley, and even worse, "I haven't anything to wear," she cried. Floyd tried to pass on the invitation, telling his colleague that they could not find a babysitter, but his friend refused to take no for an answer and invited Stanley too. Hortense, unwilling to tolerate such embarrassment, felt she had no choice but to allocate some of the family's meager budget to buying herself a new dress.

The following morning, Hortense put Stanley down for a nap and rushed out the door and into the subway. "I started for a department store in Manhattan that someone had told me had good, inexpensive clothes," she said. Arriving there, Hortense was discouraged by the sight of dozens of bargain bins and clothing racks chaotically stuffed with a variety of items in different sizes and styles. The dresses were nearly all made of inferior fabric, cut in unflattering shapes, and smothered in ribbons, buttons, or beading that was meant to make them appear elegant but only made their cheapness all the more obvious.

Desperate to be home before Stanley awoke from his nap, Hortense approached a saleswoman for help. But when she said that her budget was $10, the saleswoman gazed past her in boredom, waving vaguely to a section where the least expensive dresses were on display. Hortense hurried over and grabbed several that seemed promising, taking them into the dressing room. As she tried them on, Hortense was increasingly deflated, each one looking worse than the last. As the minutes ticked by, she finally grabbed the least offensive of the lot, a simple black chiffon, hoping that the dress might look better once she had tried it on in the quiet of her bedroom. "I knew really that it was all wrong for me, but I was nearly reduced to tears, and I had to have something," she said.

Hortense rode the subway back to Brooklyn and, after giving Stanley a bottle, tried on the new outfit. To her dismay, "it looked as bad in my bedroom mirror as it had in the store. Maybe worse." For Hortense, this experience of being a young mother with limited time and money, of the saleswoman who treated her with total disregard, and of the dearth of dresses that were both flattering and affordable would be seminal. Years later, after she was comfortably ensconced in her presidential office at Bonwit Teller, that day would fundamentally inform her approach.

Hortense grew up far from Fifth Avenue and the world of department stores. Her childhood was spent in the province of the Western cowboy, of hardscrabble living, and of devotion to the Church of Jesus Christ of Latter-day Saints. She had little exposure to lavish lifestyles and urban bustle, or to conspicuous consumption and the extravagances of Ladies' Mile. Hortense's grandparents were early converts to the Mormon church, following Brigham Young from Scotland and England across the ocean to the promised land in the desert. Arriving in America in the mid-nineteenth century, they were among the first white settlers in St. George, a dusty, sun-drenched outpost carved into the Mojave Desert, in the valley where the Colorado Plateau and the Great Basin converge. There, her grandparents erected tents and slept in wagon boxes, subsisting on a diet of corn bread and molasses as they dug wells for water and planted crops. Hortense's parents were among the first generation of white transplants to be born in St. George, her father, Hector, standing a commanding six feet one, with dark, curly hair and a deep voice, while Ella was petite, with serious eyes and finely boned features. They had six children, and the family lived in a small adobe home that they built by hand and repaired each spring after the rains.

Hector could never quite settle down, flitting between stints as a blacksmith, a lumberjack, and a farmhand and spending long stretches away from the family, searching for gold in the Nevada mines or for construction work on the streets of Los Angeles. In the 1910s, roads around St. George were improving and cars were becoming more prevalent. The dramatic scenery of the surrounding area, eventually part of Zion National Park, with enormous boulders precariously perched atop craggy mountains, deep mazes of sandstone canyons, and bursts of cottonwoods and Utah daisies, was gaining fame as a tourist draw. While Hector was gone, Ella began supporting her brood by taking in visitors, running a guesthouse out of their home. When Hortense was a teen, Hector fell in with a gang that was selling bootlegged whiskey to Indigenous Americans on a nearby reservation. He was caught and held on $600 bail, the equivalent of $19,000 today. After a year, the case was dismissed for lack of evidence, but Ella had had enough. She filed for divorce and eventually remarried, while Hector, who later had a leg amputated after he ignored his doctor's advice and left hospital care prematurely, remained estranged from Hortense and her siblings.

Hortense was born in the middle, and while she described her three sisters as beautiful, she called herself homely, with "a stringy straight red mane that no amount of brushing or combing could make neat, and an impish freckled face." Hortense cared deeply for her appearance and was exceedingly well groomed, dressing as fashionably as she could in St. George, cutting out dress patterns to sew. As she grew older, Hortense followed a strict diet, smoked to curb her appetite, and subscribed to the latest beauty crazes, like repeatedly slapping her thighs to decrease cellulite. Hortense and her siblings were close but competitive, angling for attention from their hardworking mother. They made up games and fashioned toys from wood and bits of cloth and decorated their walls with art made from yarn and even strands of human hair, which they wove into wreaths and fanciful flowers. The siblings were known for their theatrical productions, performing in the granary behind their house. Hortense often played the role of Mad Maude the Lunatic, dressing in discarded lace curtains and falling back onto a sofa made from grain bags in a dramatic stage death.

Hortense could be willful and temperamental, a self-described prob-lem child. "I had, and have to this day, a complete inability to take things lightly or to do things by halves," she said. "I had a curiosity that was never satisfied and a restless urge to experience, to discover new worlds." When she was fighting with her siblings or feeling sorry for herself, she retreated to the attic, where she had fashioned a refuge in a corner under the eaves, making curtains from old fabric scraps, a sofa from cast-off rugs, and a table from packing boxes. Hortense spent hours up there reading, playing with dolls, or daydreaming, contemplat-ing revenge against her latest enemy or envisioning escape routes out of the small town. She was inspired by her grandparents' tales of how they had traversed an ocean and crossed thousands of treacherous miles over wildlands to establish their vision of paradise. "Theirs was no namby-pamby way of life," Hortense said, their pioneer stories still "very close to us children, very much a part of our living present." Hortense had that same fearlessness and desire as her forebears, but it was St. George that she wished to escape, and her utopia was big-city living.

Hortense, aimless and unsatisfied, left St. George before she finished high school to move in with her older sister, Zella, in Salt Lake City. There, she continued to feel desultory, as if "nothing presented itself into which I seemed to fit," Hortense later wrote. Before long, she moved again, this time to Provo, where she took classes at Brigham Young High. But Hortense's sense that she was "only marking time" lingered. It wasn't until the winter of 1912, when she was twenty-one, that Hortense found direction, after falling in love with a car salesman who lived in Los Angeles. Floyd Edward Manges was two years older than her, with light hair that was beginning to recede, blue eyes, and that most attractive of qualities—a residence outside Utah. On Christ-mas Eve, the couple married at the Mormon temple in St. George, the local paper describing the bride as "a popular young lady whose many friends wish her much happiness." A month later, Mrs. Hortense Manges decamped from her childhood home and moved to L.A.

There are few records of what happened next, but at some point the relationship with Floyd Manges fell apart. By 1915, Hortense was sin-gle once more, a twenty-three-year-old divorcée without a high school

degree, and under pressure to figure out her life's trajectory. One evening, she went with her sister Zella to a dinner party in Salt Lake City,
where she was introduced to a young lawyer. Floyd Odlum was not
like Floyd Manges. Handsome, with sandy hair and an athletic, wiry
frame, Floyd Odlum was ambitious and clever. The son of an itinerant Methodist minister, the youngest of five, Floyd was game for most
anything, if he perceived that it would propel him toward success. Born
in Union City, Michigan, he held a series of colorful jobs growing up,
from piling scrap lumber in a mill yard ten hours a day, to racing an
ostrich named Tom on a half-mile track at an amusement park in Grand
Rapids. Floyd attended the University of Colorado in Boulder, working
his way through in three years, waiting tables and stacking books in the
library. He then attended law school, passing the state bar exam with
the highest marks of anyone else that year. In Utah, Floyd was working
as a law clerk at a public utility company.

Floyd had a cowboy's embrace of hard work, and while he didn't
speak much, when he did, it was often with understated humor.
Hortense was charmed by him. In Floyd she found a kindred spirit—
an outsider, and a striver who, like her, longed for far more than the
world he had been born into. They shared not only a desire to make
something of themselves but also a willingness to work for it, a trait
that would bond them for years as they traveled east and raised a family. Floyd's paycheck was $50 a month, or about $1,500 today, and he
worried about supporting Hortense on his small salary. But she did not
care, confident that Floyd was fated for success, sure that his paycheck
would soon grow. "I was determined that I would not reject or postpone
that life which I had waited for so eagerly," Hortense said. So, on April
Fools' Day 1915, Hortense married for the second time.

The newlyweds moved into a two-room apartment in Salt Lake City,
not far from Zella, and almost immediately Hortense became pregnant.
A little over ten months after their wedding, Stanley was born. And
when he was just three months old, Floyd arrived home from work one
evening nearly hysterical with excitement. Brandishing a sheet of paper,
Floyd, using Hortense's nickname, cried, "Tenny, we're moving! We're
moving to New York!" Floyd had been offered a junior position with a
famous Manhattan law firm. New York was more than two thousand

miles away, Hortense was a new mother, and she had never been so far from home. Yet despite her trepidation, she felt a surge of burning excitement. A few weeks later, Hortense found herself holding Stanley tight to her chest as she sat in a sweaty, crowded train car, barreling toward Grand Central Terminal.

—»•«—

Chapter 2

Dorothy Arrives "Home"

In the waning months of 1918, Dorothy Shaver stepped out of the 20th Century Limited and into the bustle of Manhattan. She was twenty-five and single, tall with long, shapely legs, her brown hair pulled back to show off her angular face and aquiline nose. Standing on the crowded pavement outside Grand Central, she had the overwhelming sense that even though her surroundings were not in the least like the tiny Arkansas town where she was raised, New York was her home. Dorothy hadn't arrived alone; she had her sister Elsie in tow. Weighing just ninety pounds with a mop of bright red waves that fell loosely about her face, Elsie was two years younger and far more circumspect about this trip. The siblings were constant companions and a study in contrasts: Dorothy with a practical business mind and a knack for numbers, and Elsie a daydreamer who wrote children's stories and painted fanciful watercolors. Dorothy had felt the pull of the big city, and though Elsie preferred trees and open spaces, the older sister always led and the younger always followed.

The Shaver sisters had bought their train tickets on impulse, a lark after Elsie had been sent a surprisingly large check for illustrations that she had made for a children's catalog for Marshall Field's. It was a windfall for the young women, who had been living in Chicago without much money while Elsie studied at the Academy of Fine Arts and Dorothy attended classes at the University of Chicago. After manically celebrating their winnings, they had calmed down, and Dorothy had pulled her younger sister aside. "Now," she told her conspiratorially, "we have had a pretty hard time and I think we need a change. How about our going to New York City for just a weekend?" Their parents back in Arkansas would have been furious, but the young women took the L to LaSalle Street Station anyway and bought two tickets, splurging on a sleeper car replete with its own drawing room.

The sisters arrived in the Big Apple with a single piece of luggage between them. With little knowledge of hotels, and even less knowledge about New York, they made their way to a dingy hostel on Twenty-Third Street. The room was cramped and filthy, and they pushed the furniture against the door frame before falling asleep, afraid of intruders.

When the weekend was finished, Dorothy pleaded with Elsie, "Let's stay a little while longer."

"But Mother and Daddy, what will they think?" Elsie asked.

"I am writing them that we are staying over for a little longer."

"But the money."

"If we are careful, we can manage for a few more days," Dorothy assured her.

Dorothy wrote to their parents, who were back in Mena, a small town sandwiched between the Ouachita National Forest and the Oklahoma border. When their mother discovered that her daughters had absconded to New York and were hoping to stay there, she wired them money, then called a cousin who lived there and begged him to check in. The cousin obliged and, seeing the state of the girls' lodgings, took matters in hand. He helped them find more suitable quarters, on the second floor of a brownstone on East Thirty-Eighth Street. It was owned by a kind, elderly couple who also allowed Elsie to use a spare, sun-filled room on the third floor to paint. Money, however, remained an issue.

"We were here exactly one week and a few days when we went broke," Elsie recalled. Grasping for how they might support themselves, Dorothy reminded her sister of her recent triumph at Marshall Field's. In Chicago, their parents had sent them a small stipend, but while it was enough for food and board, there wasn't much left over to take advantage of the city's many wonders. Neither sister had any intention of ever living in Mena again, and as Elsie said, "It was sink or swim and we decided to swim."

It was common practice among Elsie's friends at art school to traipse around Chicago with their portfolios, visiting advertising agencies and department stores looking for illustration work. Elsie had followed suit, and one day she ventured into the enormous Marshall Field's, where its in-house advertising department hired her to illustrate its children's catalog. Hoping that New York stores would do the same, the sisters strolled up Fifth Avenue, where the better department stores were clustered. They walked into the first one that looked promising. It was Best & Co., and the advertising department reviewed Elsie's work and hired her for a small job. Dorothy negotiated her sister's pay. With Elsie situated, Dorothy then looked for her own work. What she found was acceptable, if not her calling: a position editing movie programs for a film company, earning some $30 a week. They were finding their way, and after their mother sent one last check, "From then on, we were earning on our own," Elsie said.

Dorothy and Elsie arrived in New York just as World War I was ending and a wave of single, young women were converging on big cities across the country in the hopes of carving out careers. A new female archetype, the flapper, was emerging in the national consciousness: glamorous, sexually uninhibited, and financially independent, she represented previously unimaginable freedoms for young women. The summer after the sisters arrived in New York, Congress held its monumental vote approving the Nineteenth Amendment, which would guarantee women's suffrage. The Progressive Era was in full swing, and universities were opening their doors to more female students, increasing their course offerings in areas deemed socially acceptable, such as social work, teaching, and nursing. Meanwhile, women who had been hired during the war in jobs vacated by men who were drafted, such as laborers in munitions and textile factories, or as stenographers and bookkeepers, refused to give up their gains even as soldiers returned from the front. "The time has come now when we women have a right to ask that we shall be free to labor where our labor is needed, that we shall be free to serve in the capacity for which we are fitted," declared the suffragette Anna Howard Shaw. At the same time, New York was growing wild as Prohibition took hold, and the city teemed with smoky speakeasies, dangerous bootleggers, and illegal bathtub gin.

For Dorothy and Elsie, it was a heady time to be in Manhattan, and while drawing department store illustrations and copyediting movie programs was certainly a start, they were hungry for more. Up late one night discussing their situation, Dorothy recalled an article that she had read about Rose O'Neill, the artist who had invented the Kewpie cartoon. She had reportedly earned $50,000 by turning her illustrations into the wildly popular Kewpie doll toys. "Make a doll! Something original, different," Dorothy urged her sister. "You design it, and I'll promote it, and we'll make enough money to stay in New York."

As Elsie pondered her sister's suggestion, she turned for inspiration to stories their grandfather had told them while growing up in Mena. Their home was a railroad boomtown, situated on the Kansas City Southern line, at the midpoint between Fort Smith and Texarkana. Their father, James, had moved to Mena from the even smaller Center Point, just "a little wide place in the road," in the hopes that it would offer him greater opportunities. A lawyer and later a judge, James was tall and dark-haired, like Dorothy, while their mother, Sallie, resembled Elsie, a petite, well-mannered southern belle, with smooth skin and large violet eyes. The family was well-off by Mena standards. James was on the school board and a director at the local bank, but they weren't rich, and like all their neighbors they often bartered for services and goods. "The farmer paid his legal fees by his produce, just as the doctor took care of the lawyer and the lawyer took care of the doctor," Elsie said. "Paper money I do not remember seeing, silver yes, and people spoke of '2 bits or 6 bits.'"

The Shavers, including Dorothy's two older brothers, lived in a large, rambling house with Grecian columns, a wraparound veranda, and a big backyard marked by an enormous oak tree. There was a fruit orchard with grapevines, a small vegetable garden, and a stable with two ponies. James, who built his children a tennis court in the pine grove that grew behind the house, was well read and kept a large library that he insisted his children frequently explore, stocking it with books by Charles Dickens and Sir Walter Scott and travelogues by John Lawson

Stoddard. He encouraged his children to engage in debates over the dinner table, and the family often argued politics and current affairs.

The Shaver children, who had a "colored mammy" they called Pop (and who, to their endless amusement, married a man named Gun), were a rambunctious lot. Dorothy, in the middle, played baseball and tennis with her brothers and captained her school's basketball team. She was smart, graduating as high school salutatorian and accepted at the University of Arkansas. Dorothy was also spirited, with a quick temper and prone to tantrums. One infamous family story involved Dorothy, called Didi, being reprimanded when she was young over some mishap, and rushing into the kitchen, grabbing a fistful of butter, and smearing it all over the wallpaper in their dining room. No matter how many times Sallie repapered it, a stubborn oily spot would reappear.

The Shavers had deep roots in Arkansas. Dorothy's maternal grandfather owned and edited *The Arkansas Gazette* and famously dueled the editor of the competing *Arkansas Banner* after calling him a coward in an editorial. (Her grandfather misfired his gun and was shot, although his adversary quickly rushed to his side to stem the bleeding; after the incident, the foes became lifelong friends.) Dorothy's paternal grandfather, Robert "Fighting Bob" Shaver, earned renown in the Battle of Shiloh against Ulysses S. Grant where two horses were shot out from under him, and he survived an exploding shell that left him unconscious for several hours. When the South surrendered, Fighting Bob and his regiment were said to be the last organized Confederate force to abandon the battlefield.

In the aftermath of the South's defeat, Fighting Bob had a bounty on his head, and he fled on his warhorse to New Orleans; his family followed behind in a riverboat. They escaped capture and absconded to British Honduras, hiding for four years deep in the jungle, sleeping in huts made from palm fronds, with a constant threat of snakebites and starvation. By 1875, Fighting Bob's allies were back in power and soon ushering in the discriminatory laws known as Jim Crow. Fighting Bob, who was welcomed home a hero, was appointed county sheriff. He also joined the Ku Klux Klan, where he bragged of a seat on its grand council and of commanding a force of ten thousand men. Like for other white southerners, the Civil War was a humiliating, painful memory for the Shavers. James, who was a small child while in British Honduras, urged his daughters, "We must be charitable and make allowances for Father because of what he must have suffered," adding, "His life was one war after another." Years later, Elsie insisted that despite her grandfather's virulent racism her father "had no patience with intolerance of any sort," frequently admonishing his daughters, "Everyone has the same right to live as you two."

The town where the Shavers lived had had a deplorable race record, and there was little doubt Dorothy was exposed to hateful rhetoric while growing up. When she was eight, an African American, John Blake, boarded a train in Mena and was violently thrown off as it barreled down the tracks at full speed. That same year, Peter Berryman, a thirty-six-year-old Mena resident described by locals as mentally unwell, was lynched after he'd been arrested for reportedly kicking and injuring a twelve-year-old white girl. His first night in jail, masked men broke into his cell and dragged him outside. Mr. Berryman's body was found in the morning, hanging from a tree; according to a witness, he'd "been shot, his skull fractured, and his throat cut." The body was left hanging so that the townspeople could view it, and "hundreds of curious citizens" did so. Despite a reward, no one was ever brought to justice. The Black community took the hint: in 1900, there were 152 Black people living in Mena, and by 1910 there were just 16. By 1920, there were only 9 Black residents in the entire county, and by 1937 the last one had died. Mena was a "sundown town," so called because its citizens prohibited African Americans from being inside its city limits after sunset, enforcing the rule with intimidation, harassment, and violence. Beyond Mena's border, a sign was posted warning, in no uncertain terms, "N—— Don't Let the Sun Go Down on You in Mena."

Dorothy never spoke publicly of her grandfather's racism, and while it is difficult to know exactly how it shaped her own views, her choices later in life give some indication. As her power and influence grew, she became a vocal advocate for racial equality, and in the era of Senator McCarthy and his House Un-American Activities Committee she vociferously defended free thought and decried conformity. Elsie, meanwhile, saw the plight of white southerners primarily through a familial lens. After the war, Fighting Bob "had nothing, nothing," she wrote. "At that time in the South, it was difficult for most everybody—no one could get blood out of a turnip." When he was older, Fighting Bob moved in with the family in Mena, and "somehow, we used to get grandfather mixed up with God," said Elsie. "Grandfather sitting in his old rocking chair with his white beard so mellowed in the sunlight was just the way we thought God must be sitting up there in his rocking chair too with his white beard flowing in the clouds."

Fighting Bob was a storyteller, and he loved to unspool fantastical yarns to the delight of his grandchildren. As Elsie heeded her sister's advice, thinking up a toy that might mimic the success of the Kewpie doll, she began recalling those stories, particularly her favorite, about the Land of Never Wuz. This was a magical place, ruled by the kindly Princess Olie-ke-wob. "Elsie and I loved her tenderly and protectively, because the princess had a great problem," Dorothy said. "In all the fairy stories we had read, princesses had tiny, pretty feet. But Princess Olie-ke-wob had big feet, which she was always trying to hide." Revisiting these tales, Elsie began sketching imaginary companions for Princess Olie-ke-wob.

Before long, Elsie created a series of characters that she called the Five Little Shavers. In addition to the Princess, there was Thomas Squeelix, "the juvenile member" of the family, with "no Mother Phelix nor Daddy Delix," and who wanted "a home, a little bit of love and some adoption." There was also Ketsy Piper, a scaredy-cat who liked "to be held very close," and Baby Olie-ke-wob, who used to be just a plain old sofa pillow until, "one night, when no one was looking, a head popped right out on my shoulders and the next night two feet kicked straight out in front of my eyes, and over I rolled, and the third night I found two arms to wave and a voice to gurgle and so I came to be." The fifth doll, Patsay Doola, had a "Hindoo" mother and an Irish father, "and that's why I smile, have blue eyes and red hair—and don't give a care!" The dolls had soft, cream-colored bodies stuffed with silk moss, hair made of yarn in striking colors like canary yellow and henna red, and hand-painted faces with round, rosy cheeks and wide black eyes.

Elsie placed each doll in a painted cardboard box, along with rectangular postcards on which she wrote their unique origin stories in a cutesy, bubbly cursive.

One Sunday, Elsie had just finished making the prototypes of her dolls and the sisters were having tea and toast for lunch, when the doorbell rang. Standing in front of them was a tall, dapper man with gray hair, a high hat, a cutaway coat, and striped trousers. Standing by his side was an equally dolled-up woman.

"Good day. I am Mr. Reyburn, and this is Mrs. Reyburn. And which Miss Shaver are you?"

Dorothy gave her name and politely invited the couple in. At first puzzled as to who they were, she then recalled that her mother had mentioned her third cousin who lived in New York and who planned to stop by. Dorothy served the Reyburns tea, and the foursome began to chat. But there wasn't much that the young women and the older couple had in common, and they soon exhausted the topic of family. Dorothy, searching for a new subject, struck on the idea of the Little Shavers. At her urging, Elsie ran upstairs to fetch the dolls, and when she saw them, Mrs. Reyburn was charmed, admiring their artistry. Mr. Reyburn took each one in hand and examined them carefully, asking questions about their production and how much they hoped to charge for them. After the Reyburns left, the sisters wondered at his intense interest in their little project.

The next morning, they found their answer when the doorbell rang and four men were standing at their door.

"We're from Lord & Taylor," one said. "Mr. Reyburn told us about your dolls. Would you mind showing them to us?"

"Mr. Reyburn . . . ?"

"Mr. Reyburn—the president. You know, the president of Lord & Taylor?"

Dorothy had never asked what her mother's cousin did for a living, but she was delighted when she found out. She invited the men in, including the head of Lord & Taylor's toy department, and by the time they left, the Five Little Shavers had received their first order.

Elsie got to work sewing and painting, and a few weeks after the Reyburns had visited, Lord & Taylor featured the Little Shavers in its

The Little Shavers were all the rage, the handmade dolls featuring
hair made from yarn and soft bodies stuffed with silk moss.

Fifth Avenue Christmas windows. That first day, 110 dolls were sold,
with no advance advertising. Their popularity grew, and the *New-York
Tribune* soon ran a two-page spread on the toys, calling them "a new
race of dolls for young and old." Elsie told the paper that her creations
were meant to be "odd" and "eccentric" and explained how she hoped
to give children "the appreciation of the absurd." The Little Shavers
were all the rage among the elementary school set, with children stroll-
ing the sidewalks of New York happily swinging the dolls, which hung
from their wrists by large loops attached to the dolls' heads, like purses.
Even businessmen were buying them, their silly humor adding a touch
of gaiety to their otherwise staid office decor. The newspaper called
Elsie "young and modest to the point of being bashful," while Dorothy
"should not be overlooked" as "the practical one in the family," adding that "while Elsie created the Little Shaver dolls, it is to be doubted
whether the Fifth Avenue world would ever have met any of them if it
hadn't been for Dorothy."

The dolls became so popular that the sisters received offers to license
the manufacturing of the toys, in exchange for royalties on sales. But
Dorothy and Elsie declined the deals, choosing instead to manage the
growing business themselves. They leased a space on Forty-Seventh
Street, just off Fifth Avenue, and opened the Little Shavers Shop. Dorothy worked at the front of the store, handling customers and depart-

ment store orders, while Elsie oversaw the workroom in the back, where a team of seamstresses helped her sew. In 1919, it was notable for two young women to have such a successful, independently owned endeavor. "They are building up a most lucrative business and are making a name for cleverness in a city already full of clever folks," marveled their hometown paper, *The Mena Star*. Through their creativity and business sense, Dorothy and Elsie had managed to find a way to stay in New York.

Maggie Walker's New Venture

On a spring day in April 1905, just before the Easter holiday, the St. Luke Emporium opened in the bustling heart of Richmond, Virginia's shopping district. Hundreds swarmed the department store as a frenzy of shoppers wandered past the shoe department, the towering shelves of dry goods, and the racks of stylish, ready-made dresses. With an electric sign out front and colored wax figures in the windows, the St. Luke Emporium was a new type of store, founded by African American women and aimed at African American customers. Opening in the former Confederate capital, a city in the midst of instituting prejudicial and discriminatory Jim Crow laws, where gerrymandering was forcing the erasure of its majority-Black political district, where poll taxes were disenfranchising Black voters, where Black principals were being fired, and railroads and streetcars were being segregated, the store was a monumental achievement.

The entrepreneur and community activist Maggie Walker founded a women-led, African American department store.

If times were hard for wage-earning white women during this era, then they were doubly hard for women of color. The St. Luke Emporium was the latest salvo by one of Richmond's best-known African American business leaders, Maggie Lena Walker, to create opportunities within her community. The department store was a chance for Black women to earn enough to be financially independent and to enjoy fulfilling careers, and for Black consumers to have a store all their own. The African American press embraced the endeavor. "The St. Luke's Emporium opened up with the most flattering promise and every department is receiving liberal patronage," reported *The New York Age;* its saleswomen, "though new to the business, have gotten down to it like veterans." The store "contains everything that a woman could want," declared the New York *World,* admiring its "immense up-to-date business block of four stories in the very heart of the most fashionable business section of the city."

Maggie's rise had been unusual. Born to a formerly enslaved mother who worked as a paid servant for Elizabeth Van Lew, the noted unionist spy and abolitionist, her biological father was an Irish immigrant and Confederate soldier who impregnated her mother when she was just sixteen. When Maggie was a teenager, she joined the Independent Order of St. Luke, an African American benevolent association, and when she was forced to quit her job as a schoolteacher after getting married, as was the rule, she became active in the organization, taking on several high-ranking positions. Maggie started an African American newspaper, an insurance company for women, and in 1903, two years before the St. Luke Emporium, she opened the St. Luke Penny Savings Bank to promote savings among young African Americans. Maggie was the first Black woman to charter a bank, and the first female Black bank president. The St. Luke Penny Savings Bank eventually merged to become Consolidated Bank and Trust and was the longest-running Black-owned bank in the country until it was sold in 2005.

"If the white man insists that we must have separate cars, churches, schools, hotels, parks and places of social meeting then why not separate banks and stores?" Maggie declared. "Why do we insist on pushing ourselves where we are not wanted?" She was speaking to a crowd, urging them to support her new department store. "Spend your money with us. Help us to help ourselves."

After the flurry of excitement following its grand opening, the St. Luke Emporium struggled to stay afloat. The Black community flocked to the St. Luke Penny Savings Bank, but it failed to show similar support for the St. Luke Emporium. "You know the stores from which you bought your hats, shoes, and clothing," Maggie said, "the white woman is there. You know how it is where your wife and children bought their hats and dry goods. The white woman is there." The white woman, she said, "is in many of the places that she is because your money, your influence, your patronage keeps her there, while your own women, flesh of your flesh, blood of your blood, are left to shift for themselves as best they can." The store provided Black women with well-paying jobs, and support from the community was critical to its success. "The St. Luke's Emporium has been very largely the work of our women. If we have united and struggled and have gotten to the point which we have, deep down in your heart don't you feel that you ought to spend your money with us?"

The lack of Black patronage at the department store might have been a result of the community's limited spending capital, or perhaps it was the notion that white-owned stores had higher-quality or more fashionable goods. Nonetheless, Maggie was facing more than just lackluster support from Black residents of the city. She was also battling outright harassment from Richmond's white residents, particularly other merchants. For two years, Maggie worked surreptitiously to buy the land in Richmond's shopping district where she planned to open the store. But when she was found out, white merchants offered her $4,000 above the sales price, or $128,000 in today's dollars, if she sold them the property. "If it is worth that much to them, it is as valuable to us," Maggie told her partners, refusing to sell. The white retailers then increased their bid to $10,000, or more than $350,000 in today's dollars, but once again Maggie rebuffed their offer.

Maggie continued with her plans, and when the St. Luke Emporium finally opened, the white store owners banded together to form the white Retail Dealers' Association, vowing to put it out of business. "Now, for what purpose have they done this?" asked Maggie. "Simply to crush out those Negro merchants who are objectionable to them because they compete with them and get a few dollars which would otherwise go to the white merchant." The white shop owners sent warning letters to every wholesaler who conducted business with the St. Luke Emporium, threatening a boycott if they continued supplying the store. They didn't just limit their missives to local businesses; wholesalers as far away as New York received such letters. Some vendors began insisting that the St. Luke Emporium pay its outstanding bills immediately and refused to sell it items on credit. Others stopped doing business with the department store entirely, making it almost impossible for it to restock its shelves.

"St. Luke's Emporium, the negro department store in West Broad street, conducted exclusively by and for the colored race, is having its troubles," reported the Richmond *News Leader* in an article titled "Creditors Are After St. Luke's Emporium." The story detailed how one wholesaler was suing the St. Luke Emporium for $960, or $33,000 in today's dollars, for unpaid bills. Maggie bemoaned the pressure campaign. "The white man doesn't intend to wait until the Negro becomes a financial giant," she said, "he intends to attack him and fetter him now, while he is an infant in his swaddling clothes, helpless in his cradle."

Despite its many challenges, the St. Luke Emporium stayed open for seven years, until January 1912, when its financial plight became so severe that it was finally forced to close. "If confidence and forethought could have led the way, there would be today a great business monument to the Negro's ability to be willing to pay the price for business and success," Maggie reflected. In its first year, the Emporium had made almost $33,000 in sales, or more than $1 million in today's dollars, but by the time it closed, its sales had plummeted by more than 60 percent. "We felt, as Negroes, we should at least have the opportunity to learn how to buy and sell to and for ourselves," Maggie said, but "the St. Luke store could not meet the competition on either side of it; the members of our race failed to give proper support." It was a bitter moment. "We close our eyes, we heave a sigh, we drop a tear over the birth, life, and death of this undertaking," she said.

—»•«—

Chapter 3

Dorothy Discovers Art Deco

After several years of running their Little Shavers Shop on Forty-Seventh Street, Elsie became increasingly frustrated with the endeavor, bored of having to produce the same dolls, on repeat, with no end in sight. She wanted to pursue her painting and told her older sister that she wished to close the store. At first, Dorothy balked, and Elsie grew so upset that she started tossing boxes of dolls into the garbage. "I believe in eliminating," she declared. Dorothy was so furious at her younger sister and her outburst that the two didn't speak for two weeks. But Dorothy couldn't make a go of the Little Shavers without Elsie, and so even as orders continued pouring in, they shuttered their shop.

Mr. Reyburn, their mother's cousin, who had given Dorothy and Elsie their start by ordering the Little Shavers for the windows at Lord & Taylor, welcomed this turn of events. He was impressed with Dorothy and her management skills, at how she had steered her profitable doll business, and wanted her to work for him at the department store. The sisters had already been advising him unofficially, but now Mr. Reyburn offered Dorothy full-time employment on the store's management track. But she wanted something more than working at Lord & Taylor. Dorothy was hoping this could be an entryway into a new career, a departure from retailing, possibly into publishing. Mr. Reyburn, however, was persistent, and on his fourth try Dorothy finally acquiesced.

In 1924, Dorothy came aboard at Lord & Taylor to supervise the store's powerful comparison-shopping department. In this era, department stores were locked in fierce rivalries, and corporate espionage was a basic tenet of how the industry conducted its business. Comparison shoppers were store employees who posed as regular customers and "shopped" at rival stores, spying to discover what style of gloves was selling best, or what competitors were charging for Parisian evening gowns, or which items were headed for the clearance piles. Stores went to great lengths to conceal the identities of these comparison shoppers—not only from other stores, but from their own employees as well. This was because comparison shoppers were just as frequently tasked with surveilling their colleagues, wandering through various departments, and inconspicuously grading fellow staffers on friendliness and knowledge, then writing their findings in reports that provided the basis from which managers doled out bonuses or docked pay. "I know one store that has a concealed entrance for its shoppers," a contemporaneous source recounted. "Ladies simply go up to the business office and are taken in to see the adjustment manager, presumably to register a complaint. He lets them out another door that leads through a hidden passage to a little room equipped with typewriters. They nip in there and get their assignments in the morning and leave their sheets there in the evening."

In New York, Macy's boasted the most notorious comparison-shopping department. The store, founded by the former Nantucket sailor Rowland Hussey Macy in 1858 in the heart of Ladies' Mile, was famous for its unbeatable discounts. Its slogan, "It's smart to be thrifty," coined by the advertising maven Bernice Fitz-Gibbon, was almost as well known as the store's red star logo, which was taken from a tattoo on Rowland Macy's hand. "When, in a moment of desperation, a competitor cuts under a Macy price, we immediately cut under his price," declared a sign at the store's soap counter one spring day in 1919. The sign had been pasted to the cash register in the wake of a bitter price war with Hearn's over peroxide soap. The item typically sold for eight cents, but after comparison shoppers discovered that Hearn's was selling the same item for seven cents, Macy's cut its price to six. By the end of the day, Macy's was selling fifteen soap cakes for one cent, while Hearn's sold fourteen cakes. The next morning, Macy's went even further, advertising a sale of eighteen cakes for one cent.

"Long lines of people stormed the soap counters which were in the basement of both stores," reported *Women's Wear*. "Yesterday afternoon about 150 women were counted standing in line at Hearn's, this morning there were nearer 300." While both stores lost money in the war—their actual cost was five cents per soap cake—Macy's more than made up for it by holding on to its reputation. In fact, Macy's became so famous for its unbeatable discounts that Gimbels subtly referenced its competitor in its slogan, declaring, "Nobody but nobody undersells Gimbels!" (Bernice Fitz-Gibbons, the advertising executive who had come up with "It's smart to be thrifty" also thought up the Gimbels tagline; apparently, she was agnostic when it came to shopping for a bargain.)

In these years, comparison shopping was a key tool used by stores, in part because so many Americans were flush with cash and looking to spend. As the Roaring Twenties stock market surged upward, consumers harnessed historic purchasing powers to snatch up goods from radios to automobiles, and clothing to jewelry. Department stores were thrust into a manic competition to lure customers, by any means necessary, from spying, to new building improvements, to unfurling an astounding array of amenities. Suddenly stores touted escalators that could transport as many shoppers in a single hour as forty elevators, revolving doors rather than swinging doors so more people could enter their premises at once, and wider aisles to ease traffic flow. Lord & Taylor, in 1924, the year that Dorothy arrived, announced the opening of a new French salon offering only the most exclusive Parisian haute couture designs; a gift-suggestion service that was directed at the often clueless male shopper; a new span of rooms running along its sixth floor that included a sun parlor, a breakfast nook, and a library with a constantly rotating set of interiors, as well as a newly widened Fifth Avenue entrance.

During this period, the ranks of saleswomen expanded as changing national attitudes toward female workers were reflected in miniature in the department stores. Since the days of the old dry goods shops and general stores, retail clerking was a predominantly male occupation. But at the turn of the century, attitudes began to shift. In 1880, for instance, America counted eight thousand saleswomen; a decade later, by 1890, that figure had ballooned to more than fifty-eight thousand. By 1920, there were more than half a million women working in sales, or 10 percent of the nonagricultural labor force. The Boston department store owner Edward Filene was amazed by the feminine takeover of his eponymous business. Surveying the scene one afternoon, gazing at the dozens of saleswomen stationed behind counters and dozens more female customers wandering the aisles, Filene deemed his store an "Adamless Eden."

Owners like Filene considered the vast armies of women who worked for them important representatives of their store. Many were working class, leading to occasionally antagonistic interactions with the middle- and upper-class customers whom they served. Saleswomen were expected to be ambitious and hardworking, yet also genteel and sophisticated. It was a difficult balance, and acrimonious encounters abounded. "A fat well-dressed woman would come to the counter to buy and treat me as if I were her servant," recalled one saleswoman, in a typical gripe. "The great majority of women who visit the store make life miserable for us. They don't know what they want, and they expect us to teach them, and when we try to do so they resent it."

To minimize tensions, store owners instituted broad training programs for their staff, hiring educators to conduct classes on practical topics like selling techniques and arithmetic, as well as softer skills, such as proper etiquette and housekeeping methods. The appearance of the saleswomen was paramount, and while they didn't have to be beautiful, they needed to present themselves in ways that would appeal to their customers. As such, department store owners opened lunchrooms to provide staff with discounted meals to ensure they didn't look too skinny and offered exercise classes to prevent them from getting fat. It wasn't unusual to have in-house doctors, dentists, even chiropodists to care for saleswomen's tired, aching feet. Many had recreation areas set aside for employees, and the largest stores even purchased resorts and campgrounds in rural areas so that they could offer their employees free or low-cost vacations. There were also mutual aid societies, where employees paid into funds that would provide sick pay and death benefits.

Even with such perks, a saleswoman's job was not easy. The female staff worked long hours; most shifts began before 8:00 a.m. and ended after the store closed at 6:00 p.m., with only a single thirty-five-minute break for lunch. Some worked six or seven days without a break and stayed late on Saturdays, when stores had extended hours, remaining at their posts until after 10:00 p.m. On Sundays, many department stores were closed. Most saleswomen were prohibited from sitting, even when there were no customers around to see them, and they were made to wear starched white shirtwaists daily, which meant that after a long shift at the store they had to spend their evening hours laundering their clothes for the next morning. Pay could be less than factory work, and fines for infractions such as tardiness and chewing gum were frequent. Most of the largest stores required that their saleswomen speak grammatically correct English, so many hires were native-born, and few were knowingly hired who weren't white. While African Americans were rarely hired as saleswomen or supervisors, they were employed by department stores in relatively large numbers behind the scenes, toiling in the kitchens, handling the warehouse stock, and working in maintenance.

Staff in each department often formed their own insular groups, and the saleswomen could be close-knit and collaborative, even as they jostled and competed against one another for advancement. They had their own slang, words like "crepe-hanger," which referred to a saleswoman who talked a customer out of buying an item after she had already set her mind on purchasing it, and phrases like "Oh, Henrietta," to notify colleagues that a customer was impossible to please. They maintained customs, like a single tap of a pencil to warn that a supervisor was on his way, or two taps to indicate the arrival of a high spender. Perhaps the issue that most unified saleswomen was "the stint." If a saleswoman exceeded the stint and sold too much merchandise, she was called "a grabber," and her colleagues would be furious, since it made them look lazy. But if she couldn't make the quota and sold too little, that was just as bad, since it would bring unwanted scrutiny on the department

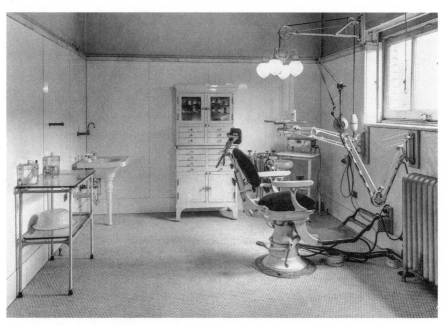

An employee dentist office at Lord & Taylor in 1919.

Graduates from Lord & Taylor's employee training program in 1923.

from the supervisor. The stint was the measure by which the sales team succeeded or failed, and it was jealously guarded: a woman who deviated from it risked being shunned by her colleagues and shut out of sales.

Most stores employed women in the sales ranks, but their supervisors were still largely male. While the worst of these managers harassed and abused the saleswomen, even the best treated their female underlings with condescension and paternalism. At Filene's, for instance, saleswomen were required to refer to male bosses as "dad," while at Marshall Field's employees were prohibited from frequenting dance halls, gambling houses, or any place that served alcohol. It was even worse for those employed at the Siegel-Cooper store, which readily admitted to spying on its staff. "You would be very much surprised if you knew the trouble and expense we go to, to find your character and habits," it warned in one company-wide missive. "Detectives you don't know are often detailed to report all of your doings for a week."

In the 1920s, as progressive values, muckraking journalists, and societal reformers became increasingly influential, a new breed of female investigators grew interested in studying the phenomenon of women workers. Frances R. Donovan, a sociologist and teacher, spent two summers working undercover in various roles at New York department stores. She published her findings in *The Saleslady*, a book reminiscent of Jacob Riis's *How the Other Half Lives*, which came out just weeks before the 1929 crash. "The employment department of the store I shall call McElroy's, woman's section, is crowded with 'girls'—for in a department store every woman is a girl—girls of every type and of every age," Donovan wrote. There were "girls who are under seventeen, with and without working certificates; girls who are graduates of the high schools or grammar schools of Manhattan and its environs; girls who have worked many seasons in department stores; girls who have never held any kind of job." Young and old, there were brides seeking employment until they became mothers, even "girls who are grandmothers left without means of support" and "girls who are widows by grass or by sod whose husbands have died without leaving insurance or from whom alimony cannot be collected."

At "McElroy's," Donovan was hired as a saleswoman in the dress department. On her first day, she was handed a sales book and ordered

to fill out a check after each sale. This was a deceptively simple requirement, because sales checks required that she memorize complicated
procedures and codes. "My first sale completed," she recalled, "I make
out the check, tear off the triplicate as I have been instructed, and, as
it is a 'Cash taken,' send it merrily up the compressed air shute [sic]
in a gray carrier, at the same time handing over the merchandise to
Flossie, the bundle-wrapper, my customer standing the while beside the
desk waiting for her package and her change." With incredible rapidity,
Flossie, a seventeen-year-old whirling dervish of a pixie, with bobbed
hair and fast-moving hands, "stuffs the frock with tissue paper, flips the
sleeves into position, folds the skirt, grabs a box, bends it into shape,
inserts the flaps that hold it together, binds it with a string, japs the
string with a knife, makes marks with a blue pencil, a few hieroglyphics
upon the cover, crams the triplicate check in at the edge, snatches my
gray carrier which has just catapulted down upon the desk, and starts
to hand me my change, but—around the carrier is a red rubber band."

"That's a premium!" snapped Flossie, using a term that signified a
saleswoman incorrectly filled out her check and that whoever spotted it
was to be paid an extra ten cents. With her sharp eye and even sharper
tongue, Flossie earned a small fortune. "As a customer I had considered
the making of a sales check mere child's play," Donovan wrote. "After
twenty-four hours of experience, I wondered how any clerk could ever
get one right." The process was nearly impossible, she said. "I had
to make out my sales checks with my book resting on an edge of the
merchandise desk, with half a dozen girls knocking my elbow, shoving
dresses at Flossie, chopping tickets, and grabbing carriers, while my
right elbow was seized by a lady with a distressed face who demanded in
a distressed voice that I sell her a frock to wear to her husband's funeral,
a second lady was nudging into my left elbow the information that she
must attend a wedding at four, a third was dangling over my shoulder
three or four frocks, suspended from hangers, and all this while I was
trying to remember whether the amount of the sale or the number of
the customer's account belonged in a certain little rectangle."

While sociological studies such as Donovan's *Saleslady* were largely
positive portrayals, in the decades leading up to the book's publication,
some moralists took a dimmer view of the department store industry.

For progressives who closely hewed to Protestant values of thrift, frugality, and moderation, department stores were a plague on society, emphasizing consumerism and material goods, morally compromising those who worked there. These activists, many of whom were women and suffragists, spread the narrative that saleswomen were overworked and underpaid and that corrupt, profit-maximizing department stores were coercing them into prostitution and lives of crime and were responsible for fostering a morality crisis in American cities.

"To the very poor, especially the very poor shopgirls who work in the big stores with all their atmosphere of spending and pleasure, the urge of life is particularly keen," wrote General Theodore Bingham, a former New York police commissioner, in a sensationalist essay in *Hampton's Magazine*, raising alarm in his readers. The department store "is a regular stamping ground for the cadet," he wrote, referring to pimps. "He picks out the attractive girl, scrapes up an acquaintance with her, and if he finds that she is without protection, so much the easier for him. He takes her to the theater, to Central Park, to Coney Island. He commiserates her poor circumstances, and he points out to her handsome women dressed in costly gowns, riding in their motor cars. He tells her these were all wage-earning women who discovered an easier way of life. Gradually the poison sinks into her mind, and soon there is another moth singeing its wings."

The notion that young women with low-paying jobs in department stores and elsewhere were being lured into nefarious activities was part of what became known as the "white slave scare," a misguided attempt to compare southern plantation owners' enslavement of African Americans to industrialists' exploitation of white employees. Quasi-governmental groups such as the Chicago Vice Commission and New York's Committee of Fourteen sent investigators into stores to uncover such plots, but their discoveries were almost uniformly disappointing, the most salacious scoops lewd language or rumors of staff being "kept" by wealthy customers. "Sales girl aged 17, reported to have had improper suggestions made to her by floorwalker; complaint to superintendent of department was laughed at," read a report by an undercover investigator embedded at Macy's. "Millinery department, ruined by store buyer; salary $10. Became prostitute." Headlines such as "Women Forced to Underworld by Low Wages" were common.

In the 1920s, when Dorothy arrived at Lord & Taylor, the hand-wringing over department stores and moral vice had mostly dissipated, and the industry was more focused on the battle for customers than defending their practices to the public. Lord & Taylor was one of America's oldest and largest department stores, and it was founded nearly one hundred years before Dorothy arrived. In 1826, the twenty-three-year-old English-born merchant Samuel Lord opened a small dry goods outpost on Catherine Street, near the chaotic East River waterfront, squeezed between shoe shops, tin shops, cloak shops, crockery shops, and pawnbrokers. The store was lit with whale-oil lamps and kept warm with a wood-burning stove, and each morning Lord lugged his purchases from the nearby market, removed the heavy wooden blinds that covered the windows, and laid out his wares. Lord was soon joined in business by his wife's cousin, George Washington Taylor, and the men enjoyed a strong partnership. "Mr. Lord had an aptitude for buying and selling; Mr. Taylor had a clear head for figures and could carry the whole business of the young firm, to a penny, in his memory," wrote *The New York Times*.

By 1853, Lord & Taylor was doing well enough to move to a larger building on Grand and Chrystie Streets. It would move twice more before settling into its fifth and final location, in 1914, on Fifth Avenue between Thirty-Eighth and Thirty-Ninth Streets. The location had been the former Murray estate, the scene of a pivotal Revolutionary War battle. Made of granite and limestone, the Italian Renaissance Lord & Taylor building featured several architectural feats, including fireproofing and a vacuum heating and cleaning system. The move uptown to this final location had cost Lord & Taylor more than it had anticipated and more than it could afford. A consortium of banks extended a loan to the store, and as part of its restructuring it installed Mr. Reyburn, Dorothy's relative, as its treasurer. Mr. Reyburn was a banker by training and had previous experiences reversing the fortunes of troubled busi-

Dorothy in her office at Lord & Taylor.

nesses. He did so well that two years after arriving, in 1916, Mr. Reyburn was appointed the store's president.

By the time Dorothy was hired, Lord & Taylor had twenty-two hundred employees and was on much stronger footing than when Mr. Reyburn had first taken over. There was an employee cafeteria, hospital rooms, and a dentist's office. Saleswomen could take free courses at New York University in topics such as interior decorating and retail merchandising. And staff could play sports on a recreational roof and enjoy both classical and popular music on constant replay from a player piano. But while Lord & Taylor was one of New York City's leading department stores, when Dorothy arrived, she would shake things up even further.

For her first day at the store, Dorothy settled on a no-nonsense uniform that lent her an air of authority and discretion, and over the ensuing decades she would hardly vary it. Dorothy wore a conservative, dark suit skirt, typically black or navy, small gold earrings, and closed-toe pumps. Her one feminine flourish was a sheer white linen handkerchief that she always kept tucked into her sleeve. From the very start, she had told Reyburn exactly what she thought. The store was "too man-made," she wrote him in one memo, adding that he had failed to "merchandise yourself into the heart of the woman. You have given her the things she *needs* and not the things she *loves*." Reyburn didn't begrudge Dorothy her criticisms, and often rallied behind them. A rare figure for the time, Reyburn embraced the idea of female careerists, cheerleading women in the workplace. "I believe homes would be better taken care of and children would benefit from having their mothers in business," he said in a speech to fellow retailers the year he hired Dorothy. "There is physiologically nothing outside of the heaviest physical labor, such as war itself, that women cannot do."

Within weeks of being hired to supervise the comparison-shopping department, Dorothy wrote Reyburn an unsolicited report arguing that the department should be disbanded. "The idea of 'comparison' struck me as ridiculous," she later said. "We should spend less time finding out what other shops were doing and pay more attention to developing our own business." Instead of comparison shopping, she wrote that Lord & Taylor should create a bureau of fashion stylists. Her idea was to employ women who understood fashion and could move between departments, advising customers how to match these gloves with this hat and that suit, and help buyers identify coming trends. It was the first iteration of what would be known as personal shopping, a core service at Lord & Taylor for decades to come and a concept that was widely copied by competitors. While Reyburn liked her idea of a bureau of stylists, he didn't agree that the comparison-shopping department should be abandoned. Instead, he just added this new area to Dorothy's growing list of responsibilities. In fact, it was only the beginning of a tenure that saw repeated promotions and title changes. In her second year at Lord & Taylor, the thirty-three-year-old Dorothy became its director of fashions and interior decorations, and in her third year she was appointed to the store's board of directors—one of only two women to hold the position.

In her fourth year, in 1928, Dorothy made her biggest splash yet. She spent six months traveling back and forth to Europe, visiting art galleries, touring showrooms, and scouring flea markets, carefully curating items for an exhibit that would establish her as the industry's most promising young executive. That winter, flappers dressed in sequins and fringe and men in top hats and tails shivered as they walked a red carpet that had been laid out before the Fifth Avenue entrance to Lord & Taylor. There was Paul Claudel, the French ambassador to the United States; Frank Crowninshield, the editor of *Vanity Fair*; and Otto Kahn, the financier. Long-stemmed roses stood in vases and a spotlight roamed the crowd as doormen politely ushered the city's glitterati up to the seventh floor, where Dorothy had positioned herself, dressed elegantly in a white column gown, to welcome the guests.

Dorothy's *Exposition of Modern French Decorative Art* was the largest collection of Art Deco furnishings ever shown in America. Over the next month, more than 300,000 visitors flocked to see watercolors by Picasso, lacquer pottery by Jean Dunand, and sculptures by Chana Orloff. The store's seventh floor was transformed into an art gallery, with salons displaying a boudoir by Vera Choukhaeff made of Baccarat glass, a suspended hammock by Pierre Chareau made of palisander wood and hung from the ceiling by handwrought-iron fixtures, and a polished walnut bed by Francis Jourdain featuring ebony inlay and an attached nightstand that could also serve as a breakfast table.

The demand for tickets was so great that the show was extended, twice. "Ambitious in scope, imposing in execution and authoritative to the last detail," raved *Women's Wear Daily*. "A magnificent exposition of French originals exceeding in number, variety, and beauty anything which heretofore has been seen of this new work in the United States," exclaimed *The Christian Science Monitor*. After visiting the show, the Swiss modernist architect William E. Lescaze penned a fan letter to Dorothy, thanking her "for having had the courage and the strength to conceive it and to carry it out," while Edna Woolman Chase, the editor of *Vogue*, wrote, "Surely this will bring you great acclaim." Dorothy called the expo "an expression of the age in which we live," maintaining that even though the items had come from France, the Art Deco aesthetic, with its "simplicity, frankness and directness," was quintessentially American. Her goal in presenting these works was to inspire American creativity, "to help guide a new movement in this country," she told *The New York Times*. She hoped to convince domestic artists that they could "be leaders rather than onlookers." It was such a success that Grover Whalen, who had not yet seen the exhibition, sent Dorothy a note asking for a favor. "Look, I have to be up on dinner conversation," he told her. "Everyone is talking about the show. Please tell me enough about it to carry on table talk." Presumably she did.

While the show burnished Dorothy's personal reputation, it also brought profits and recognition to Lord & Taylor. To piggyback off the expo, the store had manufactured a line of its own Art Deco furnishings, and as visitors swarmed the exhibit, the Art Deco pieces sold briskly; within months, 20 percent of all the furniture that Lord & Taylor sold was in this modernist style. And Dorothy's effect was not limited only to the store. In the show's wake, several large galleries began importing and selling Art Deco pieces, from furniture to artwork, and magazines published features on the modern aesthetic, widely praising it and reporting how it had become the in-demand decor among America's most fashionable crowds. Dorothy's efforts blurred the lines between art and commerce, managing to be both aesthetically beautiful and profitable. Dorothy had proved that department stores could rival galleries, and even museums, as cultural arbiters, and she had cemented her position as a visionary capable of going beyond simply serving her customers' needs and wants; she could actually shape their tastes.

Chapter 4

—▸—◂—

Hortense's First Job

Hortense stared out the tall windows of her home, watching a light snow fall outside. The house was stately, its facade made of stone and dark wood half-timber framing, with a rounded turret and a steeply pitched roof that made it look like a medieval castle towering over the grass lawns and clean white sidewalks of the residential enclave. It was the winter of 1932, and Floyd, having succeeded at growing his paycheck, as Hortense knew he would, had moved the family out of Brooklyn and into leafy Forest Hills, an affluent part of Queens, on the border with Long Island. Turning her gaze inside, Hortense studied her den, enjoying the glow from the fireplace, noting its imposing marble mantel and large oil painting above, the smell of Christmas pine still lingering from the tree. It was a world apart from the dry desert hills and adobe bricks of her childhood, and she savored this feeling, appreciating the perfection of life's appearance. "I had done my share in making it beautiful and peaceful," she thought of her house. "Everything that happened in it, that involved the people who lived in it, was my pleasant concern." She was, Hortense told herself, "a woman who had found that rare and elusive thing—happiness."

Her quiet idyll was interrupted by a shrill ring; Floyd was on the phone to tell her he would be bringing several business colleagues home for dinner. Then Bruce, her ten-year-old son, rushed in, slumping into his favorite chair—an old disreputable piece of furniture that she'd kept despite her decorator's beseeching—and began unspooling details of his ice hockey win. A gust of wind and Stanley was also home, her

The Odlum home in Forest Hills, Queens.

eighteen-year-old eldest bragging of his own exploits at an afternoon tea dance.

Then her younger sister Anne phoned. The two had always gotten along, but they had grown closer in recent years, ever since Anne's husband, Boyd, had accepted a job working with Floyd, and the couple had relocated from Utah to a house down the street. The brothers-in-law would be together for dinner, Anne told her, so why not "come along and have your dinner with me? Let the men have an exclusively masculine evening." Before she set off for her sister's, Hortense checked in with the help, directing the cook to make roast beef for Floyd and his colleagues, instructing the butler which wines to pair with the meal, sitting with Bruce as he scarfed down a burger, and helping Stanley with his bow tie for an evening formal. Finally ready, Hortense walked down her front steps and out into the dark, quiet neighborhood.

At Anne's that night, the two sisters fell into conversation over a mutual friend. The woman had claimed that she was bored with her domestic life and had decided to start an interior decorating business.

"I can't understand it," Hortense said. "I never think of being bored by my life. Do you?"

"No, not bored exactly," Anne replied. "But I don't think that just running a house is enough to keep a woman interested. You've got to have some outside interest."

"But surely, you don't have to become a businesswoman to get variety and interest in your life?" Hortense asked, pushing back. "Why, the days are too short for me to do all the things I'm doing now and there are countless things I want to find time to do." Her image of a working woman was tough, unfeminine, "calculating, hard," Hortense told her sister. The women would eventually move on to other topics, but in later years Hortense looked back on the conversation with wonder, given what would follow.

As Hortense and Anne were having dinner, world history was at a tipping point. The economy was in shambles, and businesses from banks to factories were failing in domino fashion, leaving millions of Americans out of work. That year, the Dow Jones Industrial Average reached an all-time low of 41, unemployment surged to nearly 24 percent, and twenty-five hundred "hunger marchers" swarmed the Capitol. Franklin D. Roosevelt trounced the incumbent, Herbert Hoover, in a landslide election, while in Congress the wets argued for the repeal of Prohibition, trotting out experts like a Yale University professor who presented test tubes filled with alcohol to prove that daily highballs were a health tonic. In Germany, fistfights broke out in the lobby of the Reichstag as Nazis and communists battled one another with brass knuckles, while Hitler gathered support in a bid for the chancellorship. In New York, blocks from Bonwit Teller, makeshift encampments were springing up in Forgotten Men's Gulch, a dusty six-acre expanse that had once been the Central Park reservoir, while shantytowns like Hardlucksville, with its 850 cardboard-and-tin shacks, lined the banks of the East River. Hortense was largely insulated from this reality, but as she drove around in her chauffeured car, she couldn't help but notice the breadlines stretching for blocks, the sidewalks crowded with former businessmen hawking apples, and the out-of-work laborers wearing placards pleading their need for a job.

With so many men unemployed, backlash against female job seekers was inevitable. In the 1930s, women workers were finding themselves largely in the same place that they had been at the turn of the century, as sexism and a lack of government support chipped away at the modest gains they had made during the Progressive Era of the previous decade. This phenomenon, in which women's work was intermittently celebrated and condemned, would repeat in subsequent decades. Not until the late 1960s and the women's liberation movement would this cult of domesticity begin to erode, ushering in a paradigm shift that would bring wider cultural acceptance of female wage earners.

As the Great Depression continued, women employed outside the home were increasingly described in the popular press as impertinent interlopers who stole jobs from more deserving men. Single mothers who toiled at the mill to feed their children, for example, or daughters who worked on the factory lines to support their out-of-work fathers were swept up in rhetoric that portrayed them as selfish, even immoral. The liberal journalist and editor Norman Cousins wrote of the assault on female laborers in his essay "Will Women Lose Their Jobs?" In it, he tidily summed up the opposing view: "There are approximately 10 million people out of work in the United States today. There are also 10 million or more women, married or single, who are jobholders. Simply fire the women, who shouldn't be working anyway, and hire the men. Presto! No unemployment. No relief rolls. No Depression."

Educated women were also under pressure to dampen their career ambitions and stay home. "Is it necessary for you to be gainfully employed?" asked Dean George W. Mullins, addressing the graduating class of the all-women's Barnard College in 1931. "If not, perhaps the greatest service that you can render to the community and to the nation at this time, when countless thousands are out of work, is to have the courage to refuse to work for gain." Publications that had once led the charge in supporting women workers turned their backs on the cause. In 1893, the liberal magazine *Forum*, for instance, published "The Condition of Wage-Earning Women," an exhortation against poor labor laws and the wretched living conditions of many female workers, written by the researcher and labor investigator Clare de Graffenried. But by 1930, it ran articles that called upon "our job-bent women to return to the eighteenth-century tradition and be true ladies of leisure by cultivating the graces of civilization."

In 1932, *The Forum* published "You May Have My Job: A Feminist Discovers Her Home." It detailed a writer's transformation from a freewheeling flapper, "one of those girls about whom Mr. Fitzgerald alarmed parents," to a devoted homemaker. "I burned my candle at both ends; cut my wisdom teeth on a gin bottle; declared myself for all the fashionable emancipations," wrote the author. But a chance meeting with an old college friend changed all of this. This friend was a career woman, and over the years she had become "swift, hard," all the joy and liveliness gone from her life. Fearful she might soon become like her friend, the author quit her job and embraced the paradise that was stay-at-home motherhood. "I had contempt for women who embroidered, made lace, preserved pickles, cultivated gardens," she wrote. "But I have discovered an immense snobbery in that attitude, a misconception of the creative features of those jobs, an underestimation of their requirements." According to her view, staying home and prioritizing married life "is simply too big for too many women; they blink at the challenge and cry out 'oppression—slavery—double standard!'" And instead, "they retreat to evasions, complaints, and the shibboleths of feminism."

Despite such narratives, in these years the reality was that many women were their families' sole breadwinners. In fact, fully one-third of married women who worked were entirely responsible for supporting their families, while one-half shared the responsibility with others. Widowed, separated, and divorced women made up one-quarter of the female workforce. But the New Deal programs that were established to prop up the unemployed rarely focused on these women wage earners. Some policies even targeted them. It began in the private sector, as businesses facing layoffs chose to fire married women first, rationalizing that they had spouses to support them. Then some businesses barred the hiring of married women and in several cases required that those who had been hired earlier be fired. These exclusionary policies were soon codified on the national level, in the federal Economy Act of 1932. It dictated that federal agencies that were downsizing first fire wives if they were married to men who also held government jobs. Within a year, more than sixteen hundred female federal employees were let go. The country's school systems, one of the largest employers of women, followed suit. Nearly 80 percent of public schools barred hiring wives, and roughly half of them fired female teachers who were married.

A few months before Hortense and Anne had their dinner, *Good Housekeeping* ran a series of articles exploring various perspectives on female wage earners, with titles such as "Do You Need Your Job?" and "Marriage or Career?" With few exceptions, the consensus was that women needed to make a choice. In "Marriage or Career?," several prominent women were interviewed, including the portrait painter Cecilia Beaux. "Art is the most jealous mistress in the world and will endure no rival," she told the magazine. "A painter and a homemaker at once? No." A single Red Cross nurse, Clara D. Noyes, who organized hospital units during World War I, said, "One thing is certain—a career is all engrossing." Some interviewees were more philosophical, such as Annie Jump Cannon, a Harvard astronomer who developed a classification system for stars that is still used today. "Happiness is within yourself," she answered. "Let the ambitious young scientist undertake both marriage and a career if she really desires both. The day has come, I believe, when she need not renounce either."

For Hortense the decision whether to work or stay home was never much of a consideration. While she happily raised Stanley in their Brooklyn apartment, Floyd quickly distinguished himself at work, out-shining the other junior lawyers. One client, a public utility affiliated with General Electric, was so impressed with Floyd's skills that less than eighteen months after he had arrived from Utah at the New York law firm, it hired him away. Floyd spent the next dozen years at the company, a rising star who was steadily promoted until he became one of its top executives, earning $100,000 a year, or $1.7 million in today's dollars. By the 1920s, Floyd was wealthy enough to move his growing family into the large home in Forest Hills. The family also bought a retreat in Logan Canyon, Utah, a scenic area in the Wasatch Mountains north of where Hortense had grown up. She often took the children there for the summer months while Floyd stayed in New York to work, joining them for shorter periods. While there, the family hiked in the woods, fished in the mountain rivers, and spent hours swimming in their large pool.

As his wealth grew, Jazz Age Wall Street speculation was at a frenzy, and Floyd decided to invest some money in the roaring stock market. He and Hortense pooled $40,000, or about $685,000 in today's dollars, with another couple to play the market. By the following year, their investments were doing so well that Floyd persuaded his brother-in-law Boyd to relocate from Utah and help him manage the money, forming a fund, which they called Atlas. It became so enormous that Floyd also quit his job to direct its investments.

In 1929, Atlas boasted $6 million in assets, or $100 million in today's dollars. That September, just as the market was cresting to its precrash peak, Floyd admitted hundreds of new investors into Atlas, raising an additional $9 million, or roughly $150 million today, more than doubling its size. Then Floyd switched tacks. He later claimed that he had a sense of foreboding that the market was shifting, and rather than reinvest this new money back into stocks, Floyd presciently kept it in cash. Even more fortunately, he sold half of Atlas's other stock holdings, keeping those proceeds in cash, too. On Black Monday, when Wall Street faced total ruination, Atlas emerged relatively unscathed, with an astounding 80 percent of its assets safely outside the market. While nearly all other investors were grappling with bankruptcy, Atlas boasted a war chest of $14 million, or the equivalent of $240 million in today's dollars.

When the Great Depression arrived, Floyd greeted it as one of America's ten wealthiest men, according to some estimations. He used this vast cash reserves to vacuum up troubled entities, from undervalued Hollywood studios to bankrupt national airlines to risky uranium mines, earning monikers like "Octopus of the Depression" and "Fifty Percent Odlum" for his ability to snatch up businesses at fifty cents on the dollar. Atlas's strategy was to purchase large holding companies on the cheap, then sell off their underlying subsidiaries at steep profits. Among its investments were RKO Pictures, Transcontinental Airlines, and Greyhound. It also acquired a holding company that included, among its many subsidiaries, a nearly bankrupt Manhattan department store, Bonwit Teller.

❧·❧

When Hortense returned from dinner at her sister's, she found Floyd, Anne's husband, Boyd, and their work buddies deep in conversation. Hortense didn't usually involve herself in Floyd's work, so after she checked in on the men, she was heading to bed, when a colleague of Floyd's suddenly spoke up.

"Mrs. Odlum, come in and sit down a minute," he urged. Hortense looked to her husband for an explanation. But Floyd merely nodded for her to take a seat. "I can't imagine how I can help if it's business," Hortense responded, perching on a nearby settee.

Floyd explained they were discussing Bonwit Teller, the department store in which they were now large investors. "It's on the rocks, and we don't know what to do with it. None of us knows anything about women's shops—what makes them successes or failures—why women go to some and won't go to others," he said. "What do you think of Bonwit Teller? Why hasn't it kept up with the parade? Why don't women shop there anymore?"

Hortense wasn't sure how to answer. She didn't know the store, and she admitted as much to the group.

"There you are! That's what we want to get at," said one of the men. "Why haven't you ever gone into Bonwit Teller?" Hortense racked her brain, then finally admitted the obvious. "I suppose I never heard anything about it that made me think I'd find what I wanted there."

From that point, the conversation turned from Bonwit Teller to the vexing issue of what women wanted in a department store. The men bemoaned how choosy a woman could be, and Hortense, finally feeling as if she had something of value to add, grew more animated. "Clothes mean much more to women than to men," she said. "They often mean the difference between success or failure. When she knows she's well dressed she can be sure of herself," she added.

The men nodded in approval. "Why don't you go to Bonwit's and wander around a bit? See if they're any worse than any other store?" said one. The others, including Floyd, agreed.

❧·❧

Hortense had no way of knowing that Floyd might have had an ulterior motive in asking her to check in on Bonwit Teller. Since earlier that year, Hortense's husband had been carrying on an affair with a brash, twenty-six-year-old blonde. Floyd wanted to be with his girlfriend, and if Hortense was occupied with the store, perhaps it would provide enough distraction to ease the pain of a separation.

How Floyd first met his girlfriend is up for debate. According to Hortense's longtime hairdresser, it was Hortense herself who was the unwitting cause of the tryst. The hairdresser, Sydney Guilaroff, was a stylist at Antoine's, the fashionable salon at Saks Fifth Avenue, where society women like Hortense were regulars. One day, Hortense arrived for her appointment, and because it was near closing time, the salon was empty of clients, save for Sydney and the manicurist, whose name was Jackie Cochran. Hortense was usually quite reserved, but she had a comfortable rapport with Sydney, and in the quiet salon she began absentmindedly chatting as her hair was styled and her nails painted. As she prattled on, Hortense mentioned in passing that Floyd was working so hard he had decided to take a cruise to Miami alone, in order that he might get some much-needed rest.

When Sydney was finished styling Hortense's hair, he walked her to the elevator and her waiting car. Upon returning to the salon, Sydney found Jackie on the telephone. He was surprised, because it was strictly against salon policy to make personal phone calls, but when he heard whom she was talking to, he was shocked. Jackie was on with Furness Bermuda Line, booking a ticket for the very same voyage that Floyd was taking.

"I know what you're up to," Sydney cried, aghast at her bald ambition. "You're going to go after her husband!"

"It's none of your goddamn business," Jackie reportedly snapped.

Sydney, who recorded this story in his autobiography, *Crowning Glory: Reflections of Hollywood's Favorite Confidant*, also claimed that this betrayal was the basis for Clare Boothe Luce's hit Broadway play *The Women*, later an MGM movie starring Joan Crawford, in the role of Jackie. The story centers on a loyal, well-mannered wife who is devastated when she finds out her wealthy husband is having a torrid affair with a gold-digging seductress salesclerk. There's even a secret phone call that changes the trajectory of their lives. "While the playwright was herself among my regulars and apparently borrowed much of her bitchiest dialogue by eavesdropping on my other customers, she changed my character to a woman," wrote Sydney of Clare Boothe Luce. "As a salute to my connection with the story, however, [Louis B.] Mayer ordered that the salon in the film be named Sydney's," he added, referring to the MGM honcho, "with the set designs based on Antoine's actual look."

For her part, Jackie always claimed a different meet-cute with Floyd. In her telling, she had been sent down to Miami by Antoine's to service the salon's wealthy clients who moved south for the winter months. Jackie, who had a curvy figure, with big brown eyes and luminous skin, was a good dancer and was invited to a nonstop round of Miami dinner parties to serve as a partner for unaccompanied men.

One night at the Surf Club, Jackie was paired with Floyd. He hadn't wanted to go to the dinner, despising insufferable, drunken party talk, but the host had convinced him by promising one of the guests would be a pretty working girl. Jackie was the antithesis of the typical bridge-playing housewives Floyd usually met. She had grown up shoeless and illiterate in a sawmill town in the Florida Panhandle. Seated next to

Floyd and Jackie arriving home
from a trip to Europe in July 1938.

Floyd at the dinner, Jackie fascinated him, regaling her seatmate with stories of life as a traveling salesgirl, hawking dress patterns from the back of her Ford Model T. In her southern twang, she told him how she had saved up to buy the car and then learned to fix its engine herself because she couldn't afford a mechanic.

Floyd was enthralled, and according to Jackie, two nights later, he hosted his own dinner party and invited Jackie as his guest of honor. The following morning, however, Floyd returned to New York without saying goodbye. He needed time to think, and Jackie was distraught. When she herself got back to New York, Jackie told the manager at Antoine's that although it was against salon policy, if Floyd phoned, she insisted on speaking with him. She waited the rest of that cold winter, and into the spring. But on a day in May, which she later claimed was her birthday, Jackie finally got the call she'd been hoping for.

Bonwit Teller, the store that Floyd had just purchased, was, like so many historic New York department stores, born in the era of Ladies' Mile. It was founded by Paul J. Bonwit and a silent partner, Edmund D. Teller, in 1898, and was Mr. Bonwit's third attempt at being a merchant. Born on a farm in the German countryside, Mr. Bonwit immigrated to America when he was twenty-one, and after a short stint out west, where he'd gone to be an actor, he returned to New York and began working in the city's burgeoning retail industry. His European sensibilities imbued him with an exotic charm, and he quickly earned a legion of loyal female shoppers.

When he was thirty-three, Mr. Bonwit, now married with a child on the way, decided to strike out on his own. He opened a store on Eighteenth Street, and then a second location a few blocks north. But he was too confident, and his brisk expansion proved unsustainable. He was forced to close both businesses, but undeterred, he then partnered with Teller to reopen on Twenty-Third Street, as Bonwit Teller. The department store became known for its well-curated coat selections, its variety of dresses imported from Paris, and its well-appointed, elegant merchant-owner. As the twentieth century got under way, Mr. Bonwit bought out his partner, and as retailers abandoned Ladies' Mile to follow New York's wealthy set uptown, Mr. Bonwit relocated to midtown. And when the better retailers began congregating around Fifty-Seventh Street, Mr. Bonwit, ever conscious of the latest fads, once again followed the herd. In 1930, just as the Great Depression's vise was tightening its grip, he set his sights on a new, opulent flagship store.

The new location was ideally situated at the corner of Fifth Avenue and Fifty-Sixth Street, and was the former home of Stewart & Co.—no relation to A. T. Stewart's cast-iron Palace—a fashionable department store that had collapsed in the crash. Designed by Warren & Wetmore, the architect behind Grand Central Terminal, the twelve-story tower was made from "severe, almost unornamented limestone climbing to a ziggurat of setbacks," wrote *The New York Times*, culminating at the top with ornamental bas-reliefs of two naked female figures, their rounded curves barely covered by scarves that appeared to ripple in the wind. The entrance, meanwhile, was "like a spilled casket of gems," with decorative platinum and bronze, hammered aluminum, glazed ceramic, and tinted glass that, when lit from the inside during the evening hours, glowed like an elongated jack-o'-lantern. It cost $7.5 million, or $130 million in today's dollars, to construct. The ill-fated Stewart & Co. opened in its grand, new home on October 16, 1929, celebrating with a flashy gala attended by numerous celebrities, including Eleanor Roosevelt. But only a dozen days later, Black Monday fell like a hammer, crushing the stock market and flattening the department store.

Disregarding the warning signs, Mr. Bonwit proceeded to lease the entire building for a costly sum and spent lavishly on a redesign of the practically new structure. Hiring the architect Ely Jacques Kahn, he pared down the more decorative elements and transformed the store's elaborate entryway into a simplified, Art Deco masterpiece of geometric patterning made from metal and glass. On September 15, 1930, Bonwit Teller opened in its new home. But, as the merchant should have expected, sales lagged, and the store's costly new lease ate away at what revenues it was able to generate. Mr. Bonwit paid his top employees high salaries, which, when times were flush, meant a deep bench of expert sales staff and loyal managers, but now added to his financial duress. Most disastrous for Mr. Bonwit was his decision, made just before the crash, to issue Bonwit Teller shares on the stock exchange, transforming his privately held store into a public company. As the Depression dragged on, the store's once-soaring stock imploded, and Atlas, a vulture investor ever on the lookout for fresh targets, swooped in and took a large chunk out of the distressed company.

It was somewhat of an accident that Floyd ended up with Bonwit Teller. Atlas was looking to purchase the holding company that owned the store, and in fact, when it was researching the acquisition, Atlas deemed Bonwit Teller so unprofitable that it appraised the store at zero value and intended to close it. Floyd dispatched his brother-in-law Boyd to deliver the news to the Bonwit Teller staff, but when Boyd arrived to inform the employees of their grim fate, he balked. "Jobs were hard to get at that time and when employees came to the meeting, they were stiff with fear," Floyd later wrote. Closing the store would put hundreds out of work, and during the Great Depression that could mean months without income; it might even lead to destitution and starvation. Boyd went back to Floyd to see if there wasn't some way to keep the struggling store open, and that's why the Atlas leadership was gathered in Hortense's den that fateful night, to debate how they might possibly save Bonwit Teller. Eventually—and fortuitously—they turned to Hortense for answers.

While Floyd might have had private reasons for wanting his wife to go to Bonwit Teller, Hortense likely had her own secret motivation. There is no evidence that she knew of Floyd's affair with Jackie, but Hortense may have hoped that spending time at Bonwit Teller would give her an opportunity to bond with her increasingly disengaged husband over the very thing that he seemed most passionate about—work. Maybe, too, she wished to prove her worth by excelling in the arena where her husband had always dominated.

Hortense waited a few days, until Floyd had left on another one of his many business trips, before she visited the store for the first time. When she emerged from that first awkward meeting with Mr. Bonwit, Hortense felt bewildered and overwhelmed, with a nagging fear that she may be in over her head. After leaving his office, Hortense had wandered the store for several hours, observing.

Later that night, back in Forest Hills, she sat with her feet up, eating dinner off a tray, thinking back to how sad and morose the atmosphere was at Bonwit Teller. These were the darkest days of the Depression, and the furnishings were shabby, the saleswomen looked tired, and the clothing racks seemed nearly empty of inventory, particularly for women on a budget. While the situation was grim and Hortense was at a loss as to how she might fix it, her can-do pioneer spirit and stubbornness wouldn't let her give up. She never liked to do anything halfway; it was the attitude that had first bonded her to Floyd and how the pair had risen above their humble stations to become one of the richest couples in America. So, with a renewed focus, Hortense woke the following morning and returned to the store, resolved to go there daily until she had solved the problem.

As Hortense visited Bonwit Teller day after day, she grew emboldened to confront the staff and point out problems. She would not be cowed by Mr. Bonwit or by the listless shopgirls who stared at her irritably, she thought. Her role may be only that of an unpaid adviser, but Hortense had Floyd's authority and backing. "There isn't a dress in that department that a well-dressed woman would want to wear," she told Mr. Bonwit. "I've never in my life seen so many Christmas-tree ornaments on clothes. And there's not a big enough selection nor enough salespeople." The store had "insufficient stock, poorly selected," not to mention an "insufficient sales force badly in need of help and encouragement." Hortense told the store president that his employees were "apathetic and dull-eyed" and scolded him for "the low morale," which, she said, "was suggesting itself to customers on every floor and in every department."

Hortense didn't only criticize. She recommended improvements, but Mr. Bonwit and his staff were not swayed. "I suppose it does seem possible to an outsider, Mrs. Odlum, but it can't be done," one told her when she made a suggestion. "It's just not possible!" said another after she expressed her view. The Bonwit Teller management knew far more than she did, they argued. Mr. Bonwit, for goodness' sake, built the store from the ground up and ran it successfully for decades. Hortense, on the other hand, had no experience as a merchant and had come aboard merely as a consultant. In letters to friends, Mr. Bonwit expressed outrage, referring to Hortense and Floyd dismissively as "those people," even calling them "Machiavellian." In one letter to Gladys Tilden, an editor at French *Vogue* and sometime buyer for the store, Mr. Bonwit bemoaned, "I never did anything as clever as those people conduct their affairs," noting his "constant worry what those people will do next."

But Hortense gained confidence the more time she spent at Bonwit Teller. She began caring less about what had been done before, because it obviously wasn't working, and grew more interested in what she could do to ameliorate matters. In the 1930s, hats were a necessary component of a complete outfit, as much a requisite as underwear or shoes. And Hortense was convinced that the millinery department, which Bonwit Teller had buried in an obscure corner of an upper floor, should be prominently displayed and easily accessed by shoppers. Hats were relatively inexpensive items, impulse buys, a gateway purchase made "out of the spirit of adventure or as a tonic on a dull day," she thought. "How many times had I heard a woman say, 'I felt so low today that I went in and bought a hat and I felt like a new woman?'" Hortense told everyone who would listen—a limited audience—that hats were a key accessory to convert a window-shopper into a paying customer. To be sure, if a shopper was dedicated to purchasing a hat, she would find it no matter if it was six flights up and pushed into a corner. "But why not make it easier for her to indulge her harmless whimsies?"

Mr. Bonwit, of course, did not agree. But Hortense proceeded anyway. "I consulted the buyer, I interviewed the architect, I talked to workmen," she recalled. At night, after the store had closed, the workers began whirring saws and hammering nails, building new display tables and shelving. Finally, Hortense's remodel was finished, and one weekday morning Bonwit Teller opened, and a new hat department was unveiled.

Hortense was sure that her gamble would pay off. That first morning, she stationed herself nearby to wait for customers, and before long a throng was buzzing around the hat displays, fingering the merchandise, and trying them on. Soon enough, Bonwit Teller's hat sales had tripled. "The benefits of its location have been spread floor wide," wrote *Women's Wear Daily.* "Women come in for a handbag or an article of jewelry and purchase a hat as well. Or they may have the last named only in mind and leave with other items in addition." Hortense had pushed ahead despite the naysayers, and she had prevailed. Now the question became, who really was in charge at Bonwit Teller?

Bessie Harrison Becomes a Buyer

The week that Bessie Harrison entered high school, her mother gave birth and her father fell ill. It was 1904, and Bessie lived with her family of eight in three rooms above a warehouse in the Mission District in San Francisco. Her father was a tailor, earning $10 a week and spending one week's wages every month for rent. But then he pricked his finger and it became infected. As he lay in bed for weeks, and then months, his hand and arm swollen, his mind often delirious with fever, Mrs. Harrison gave birth to her seventh child. She took a single week to recuperate before she began taking on sewing jobs to fill the gap left by the loss of her husband's wages, and to cover his growing medical bills. She had always hoped that Bessie, her oldest daughter, would graduate from school and become a teacher, earning double what her father made. But it was soon clear that the sixteen-year-old would need to chip in and find a job.

A logical place for a young girl in search of employment was Union Square. There, several large new shopping meccas were opening their doors, stores like City of Paris, which boasted a seventy-foot replica of the Eiffel Tower on its roof, and the Emporium, with a glass arcade and soaring dome. "I remember the morning well," Bessie recalled. "There was a mist driving in from the bay as I walked to a great department store in Market Street to answer a 'help wanted' advertisement."

Bessie approached the department store's employment desk and stood, one among dozens of applicants, awaiting her turn for an interview. Bessie was much younger than many of them, and she quietly observed the hiring agent who sat at the head of the room. "This man had great power over the fortunes of girls, yet he was no melodrama villain," she thought. "In place of a leer, his face had a mature, kindly look." When it was finally Bessie's turn, the hiring agent gently inquired of her schooling and asked her to describe her home life and the reason she was searching for work.

Bessie, who was small and timid, her dark hair worn loose, looked barely more than twelve. After she answered his questions, the agent sent her to the chinaware department, where she was given a job dusting shelves for $4 a week. Bessie's supervisor had once been a cash girl, one of the lowest ranks next to her own position as dust girl, yet she had somehow surpassed those humble beginnings. As soon as Bessie had appeared on the floor, this supervisor whisked her aside with a stern warning. "Every little butter-dish in this store is accounted for," she hissed. "There's not going to be any missing, either from knocking them off the shelves or—" And the supervisor reached toward a twelve-inch soup tureen and motioned as if she were hiding it under her apron. "If there is, you go home—provided you have one." Bessie was offended at the insinuation, but also frightened. "Those piles of dishes looked so topply and so fragile," she wrote, in an autobiographical essay for *The Forum* in 1917. "My nervousness wore off, but I never relaxed my industry from eight-thirty in the morning until five-thirty at night, except at lunch hour."

Bessie's department was in the basement of the store, next to the machinery room, where the loud pumping of the cool-air system provided a constant drumbeat, and near the elevators, where the motors banged and hissed each time an elevator car was called. "There were whirring, clicking cash-carriers and big truck-loads of crockery and china," Bessie wrote, and "the basement air defied ventilation systems. It was a noisy, stuffy, crowded, wearing place." She was one of nearly a hundred employees who worked down there, including a dozen floorwalkers, whose job was to supervise the saleswomen, and a team of bundle wrappers who packaged the items that had been sold. As she worked amid the chaos, Bessie couldn't help wondering how a dusting girl like her might one day become a saleswoman. She considered how her boss was promoted from a mere cash girl, yet it felt overwhelming, as there were still so many layers of managers and supervisors above her. While at first Bessie held to her mother's dream of becoming a teacher, gradually, and despite the obstacles, "my mind formed an ambition to rise in this store business."

Like many high-end shops at the time, Bessie's department store featured a large room on one of the upper floors where staff could eat their lunch and get hot coffee or tea while on break. It was in this recreation room that Bessie made friends with her co-workers. "Most of them, I found, intended to get married as soon as possible. The store did not permit flirting, but there was always a string of boys waiting around the corner from the employees' entrance at closing time." Those who wore engagement rings often neglected their duties, too busy thinking of their upcoming nuptials and the fact they would soon quit the workforce. "I hope you're not going to 'get married soon,' Bessie," her supervisor said one day. Bessie responded with a rigorous shake of the head. "Then we'll make something of you," the supervisor replied with a smile.

During that first Christmas season, when the store was inundated with holiday shoppers, Bessie got her chance to do more than just dust. Shortstaffed, her supervisor assigned Bessie to a small table in one of the aisles where she was tasked with selling saltcellars and pepper shakers for ten and fifteen cents apiece. The following morning, Bessie arrived with her face shiny and pink from scrubbing, dressed in her best white shirt, her long hair a near match to her ankle-length black skirt. "I had spent all my spare time studying my stock and fingering my sales book to get the knack of the carbon slips," Bessie wrote. "When I got my first little rush, it flustered me, and I forgot about my stock. Some of my sales slips came back for correction and one or two women made sneering remarks about service." But her friends from the recreation room told her not to worry. "I'll bet those folks that put on airs are in debt to the grocer," one colleague quipped. Bessie's performance improved, and by the end of the week she was doing a brisk business in saltshakers. Her abilities won her a promotion to salesgirl. In her new position, Bessie saw her paycheck doubled, and she gained access to more of the inner workings of the store. She began interacting with supervisors, including the stock clerk who assisted the chinaware buyer. One day, Bessie and the stock clerk were chatting, and he complained of how much time he had to spend with each salesgirl, explaining the various items they were to sell.

"If I didn't lose so much time with them, I'd be a buyer by now," he said.

"Do buyers make much money?" Bessie wondered.

"Do they? Just ask me. And a trip to New York twice a year and London and Paris once in a while."

Bessie had never traveled beyond Oakland, and armed with this new information, she now longed to become a buyer. She came up with a strategy for accomplishing this, and the next time the stock clerk came around, Bessie asked him if he could please buy some better dishes for her department. Rather than just plain white porcelain plates, she wanted dishes with a gilt band. When he refused, insisting that plain dishes were good enough for working-class customers from the Mission District, Bessie persisted.

"They're entitled to just as good as their money will buy," she said, "and if they want gilt band dishes, they ought to have them."

The stock clerk finally agreed to do as she wished, and a few weeks later not only had Bessie sold out the stock of gilt-banded dishes, but the higher-priced merchandise had translated into greater profit for her department. The achievement drew the attention of the buyer, Edelson, who sent for Bessie. After interviewing her, he offered Bessie a job as his assistant.

Bessie was overjoyed that her ploy to sell better merchandise had translated into a job offer with Edelson. But a few days later, Bessie's world, as well as those of her neighbors, was irrevocably transformed. The Great 1906 Earthquake and the deadly fire that followed killed 3,000 people, left as many as 250,000—out of a population of 400,000—homeless, and destroyed 80 percent of San Francisco's buildings. Bessie and her family were luckily unharmed, but the department store where she worked was rubble. Several weeks later, the store tried to regroup, reopening as a small lean-to near the ruins of what had once been its building. Bessie was rehired as a saleswoman, but she gave up any hope of working as an assistant buyer for Edelson. "I saw some of the rich women who had annoyed me," she recalled of those difficult days. They were now "at the knick-knack table buying cheap dishes to resume housekeeping. The fire had taken all they had."

Several weeks into working at the temporary shack as a saleswoman, Bessie was shocked when Edelson returned. He was rebuilding his business, he told her, and he still wanted Bessie's help. She leaped at the opportunity. "In that little box of an office on Van Ness Avenue, with a ruined city in sight from the window, I commenced to learn more about business and human nature than I ever had dreamed of," Bessie wrote of this period. She observed her boss as he negotiated with wholesale houses, bargained with jobbers eager to unload merchandise, and navigated unscrupulous salesmen who promised imported goods from Paris but swapped them with bric-a-brac from

Ohio. Bessie stayed with Edelson for three years, gradually promoted until she was earning a salary of $40 a week, or about $1,340 in today's dollars.

Bessie was in her early twenties, and doing well enough that she moved her family out of the cramped Mission District and into a geranium-hedged neighborhood in Berkeley, across the San Francisco Bay. She helped her father open his own tailor shop, and she kept her focus on her career. Bessie's personal life, however, was not a priority. "Salesmen sometimes brought me flowers and candy. Occasionally one would invite me to luncheon," she wrote. But "Mother had schooled me to rigid conduct, and I followed her training with daily admonitions." Bessie remained aloof from any relationship, even though she believed that "most men are gentlemen," noting, "An independent girl can keep them in their place."

But despite her increased paycheck, Bessie was still working under Edelson, and not a buyer in her own right. She wanted that promotion, and she realized that meant she must emerge from beneath Edelson's shadow, as her boss had no plans to retire anytime soon. Bessie felt stuck until one day, a newly married buyer in the needlework department announced she was quitting. Bessie knew nothing about embroidery, despite her father's job as a tailor, but she interviewed for the post anyway. When she voiced her insecurities to the hiring boss, he quickly reassured her that "you know business methods and store policies" and the rest could be easily learned. Bessie was awarded the buyer position, and with it her income soared to $10,000 a year, or about $230,000 in today's dollars.

"I started at $4 a week when I was sixteen, and now I am twenty-eight," she wrote. "I own the home we live in and have been able to help my parents and brothers and sisters. I spend several weeks abroad every year. I am still young enough to marry should I wish." For young, ambitious women such as herself, Bessie assured readers, they couldn't do much better than apply for a job at a department store.

Chapter 5

President Hortense

A flurry of reporters descended on Bonwit Teller in October 1934 as the first woman president of a department store officially took her place at the helm. Hortense, attractive and trim, dressed in a snug wine-red sheath that skimmed her five-foot-two frame, was trailed by the gaggle peppering her with questions as she took the elevator to her eleventh-floor office. There, sitting behind the large desk, its surface covered by a telephone, a silver-trimmed calendar, and a cigarette box, to which she frequently helped herself, Hortense began answering their queries. Yes, she had "never held a job before" and "never earned a penny in my life." Yes, her husband was supportive. It was Floyd, in fact, who had pushed her to take the job, telling her, "Women know what women want in a store." As for her plans for Bonwit's future? Well, they'd just have to wait and see.

The hungry pack of journalists ate up her performance. "A woman of vivacity and alertness, with an expression that alternates quickly from a pleasant smile to firmness of decision," raved *The New York Times*. Hortense "combined the candor and 'breeziness' of the Westerner with the poise and smartness of the East," gushed *Women's Wear Daily*. Most appraised the forty-three-year-old's appearance. "A small woman, with the figure of a debutante and the personality of a favorite actress," one noted, "she THINKS just like a man," a dubious compliment.

For these reporters, and their readers, a female president of a business was an exotic concept. Almost all women workers in these years toiled in entry-level, junior positions. More than a decade after Hortense ascended to the presidency, in 1947, for instance, the percentage of employed women who worked in managerial or administrative positions was a paltry 5 percent. Thirty-one years later, in 1978, that figure had barely budged, increasing to just 6 percent. Parity arrived painfully slowly in the world of business. It wasn't until 1972, in fact, that the first woman would be named the CEO of a Fortune 500 company, when Katharine Graham, the widow of Philip Graham, was named chief executive of *The Washington Post*. And not until 1987 was a female-owned company, the Lillian Vernon Corporation, listed on the American Stock Exchange.

Hortense had little inclination to stand out, to be a rule breaker or fight the status quo. Undoubtedly, the fact that her position was so utterly unique was a key factor in why she chose to consistently play down her achievements. Despite the success of her Bonwit Teller debut, Hortense adopted a mantle of modesty, playing the role of the naïf. Years later, writing of her feelings that first morning at the store, she recalled, "I didn't feel like a president. I felt like a frightened woman!" This tactic, of diminishing her business accomplishments in a bid to retain her feminine bona fides, was one that Hortense frequently embraced over the ensuing years.

As for Mr. Bonwit, *The New York Times* reported that the seventy-two-year-old store founder had "retired because of ill health." Over his decades-long career, he had weathered dips and even financial panics, but relocating Bonwit Teller to an expensive new location at the very inception of the Great Depression had been a major misstep, one that proved impossible to recover from. At the same time, Mr. Bonwit had been contending with personal troubles. His wife of forty years was suffering a protracted illness, and when she died in January 1934, a heartbroken Mr. Bonwit had to face a mountain of medical bills and a depleted bank account. That spring, he took a leave from the store and went on an extended trip to France. In Nice, he rented a room in an apartment owned by an elderly couple, the three of them sharing cooking duties and expenses. Mr. Bonwit spent his days taking long walks and writing mournful letters to friends, detailing his loneliness as a new widower and his despair at watching his namesake store be transformed beyond recognition.

Mr. Bonwit returned from France, and to rooms at the Hotel Gladstone on East Fifty-Second Street, where he lived quietly for four more years. In 1939, he caught a fatal case of pneumonia. There were three hundred mourners at Mr. Bonwit's funeral, and while Hortense attended—and also closed the store for the day in his honor—she was not particularly admiring of her predecessor. Hortense told anyone who asked that when she had arrived, the store "was, literally, a morgue. It was positively lonesome. The faces of the salespeople were woebegone. Oh! How I longed to bring that place to life."

Hortense's greatest shortcoming as store president was her utter lack of experience, but, she realized, it was also her hidden strength. Her knowledge of running a business was limited, and her understanding of Bonwit Teller came only from the many months she had spent there, observing, as well as her insights as a woman and a shopper. She wasn't completely ignorant, of course, having lived with Floyd for years as he went from being a junior lawyer to a wealthy business magnate. But when it came to balance sheets and purchase orders, she was green. "There was nothing to do but frankly admit I didn't know anything about business," she said. "I brought to my new job a fresh point of view and what I liked to believe was plain common sense, both of which seemed to me to be sorely needed in the business world." In its advertising campaign in *The New York Times*, Bonwit Teller doubled down on the inexperience of its new female president, touting Hortense's "fresh take" on business. "Let's be unprofessional and do things that were never done before," the ad proclaimed. "Let's be feminine and follow our hunches." Another advertisement leaned into Hortense's gender, emphasizing "a woman's sixth sense" and touting how Bonwit was being "guided by a woman president's womanly intuition."

Hortense was also painfully aware that the more time she spent at Bonwit Teller, the less time she was available at home. "I worked, I think, twenty-four hours a day, for even in my sleep I dreamed about the store and its problems," she said. In those initial months on the job, Hortense began keeping notepaper and a pencil on her bedside table. "I never knew when suddenly in the middle of the night I'd start wide awake with an idea I'd want to try, or remember something that had to be attended to in the morning." While Stanley was away at boarding school, Bruce was home, and her younger son "began to complain that he never saw me any more and that I never talked about anything but Bonwit Teller," she said. "I had made up my mind when I accepted my job that I would not let it absorb all my interest, that I would not allow it to take all my energy so that I had nothing left when I joined my children. . . . I refused to become a career woman at the price of the happiness of my family."

To free up time for her children, and to focus on areas of the store where she was most impactful, Hortense needed help. She wanted to hire a general manager, someone who could shoulder some responsibilities, particularly the more technical aspects of the job. William Holmes was a merchant in Milwaukee that Floyd had heard of, and he flew to meet him, hiring Holmes on Hortense's behalf. Long after Holmes left his position at Bonwit Teller, in fact, he continued to work for Floyd. "With Mr. Holmes to divide with me the problems which confronted us," Hortense said, "to assume the responsibilities which I was not qualified to handle, I was freed to attack some of the weak spots in the organization which I wanted badly to correct."

Hortense compared her position as store president to her role as a housewife hosting dinner parties. This was as much to give her a familiar road map as she navigated her new role as to make palatable the fact of her working—that she was now the very career woman she had once feared and dismissed. "To be a charming and successful hostess means much more than just being a good conversationalist or having a pleasant personality. It means being sensitive to people's likes and dislikes, conscious of small details that would perhaps be easy to overlook," she said. "Was there such a great difference, then, between the job of a woman as wife and mother and her job as president of a woman's specialty store?" she asked rhetorically.

One of Hortense's chief priorities, from the moment she had begun spending time at the store as an unpaid adviser, was to win over Bonwit Teller's staff. Many of them had a strong allegiance to Mr. Bonwit, who had hired them and for many years paid them exceedingly well. Hortense recognized "the average human being's aversion to radical change," noting, "Unfamiliar ways, new methods are almost always greeted with suspicion." Soon after taking over, Hortense gathered the store's six hundred employees and assured them they wouldn't be fired, easing their fears. She also endeavored to make herself better known to them. "Day after day I wandered through the store, smiling at this salesgirl, asking questions of that one, passing the time of day with the elevator boys, inquiring after the health of a porter's child." While earning their loyalty was "a slow and often bitterly disappointing task," she said, "little by little I was rewarded for the hours I had spent endeavoring to get those people to like and trust me." Hortense also took an interest in their personal concerns. Far from seeing interoffice conflict as petty squabbles, she directed everyone, no matter how junior, to come directly to her office with their issues. "My office is a court of justice and politics is not played," she said. Employees streamed onto the eleventh floor, divulging their problems with bosses, dramas with colleagues, arguments over commissions, and scheduling complaints.

Hortense thought she would try a similar tack with the store's somewhat anemic customer base. She wanted every unhappy customer to be sent directly to her office, she told her employees. It was an unusual directive, but Hortense figured that it was the best way to learn Bonwit Teller's weak spots. She also perceived that if the staff knew their boss was going to hear directly from customers who were unhappy, they might step up their performance. In addition, Hortense was well aware that among a certain subset of female customers, the reputation of a store was critical. "I had spent all my free time at luncheons and bridges, and I know what most women talk about," she posited. "If they are pleased, they are a store's best advertisement . . . and vice versa." So her initial months at the store were spent listening to complaints from saleswomen and floorwalkers, cashiers and telephone operators, as well as a steady stream of disgruntled customers. "I did little else during store hours but listen to complaints," Hortense said. When this policy became too much, she began what she called a Consumers' Advisory Committee. "If I were at home and wanted to see my friends and acquaintances, if I wanted to keep in close touch with what they were doing and thinking, I'd ask them to lunch," Hortense rationalized. So, on the first Wednesday of every month, a handful of regular customers were randomly chosen to join her at her office for an informal lunch, and over platters of sandwiches and pitchers of lemonade she would listen to their suggestions.

Hortense also thought back to how it felt when she herself was a customer. Specifically, she recalled the somewhat traumatic experience of being a young mother, new to New York, and on a tight budget, trying to find a suitable dress for Floyd's colleague's Thanksgiving dinner. Hortense figured that, particularly in the Depression, there must be countless women in similar positions, with modest clothes budgets who still wanted something stylish to wear. "There was an enormous market waiting for any merchant who would take the time and trouble," she reasoned.

In the 1930s, department stores had seen a flood of poorly made, mass-produced dresses. Seventh Avenue had by then grown more efficient, as new assembly-line production methods quickened the pace of manufacturing, helped along by the popularization of synthetic fabrics, such as rayon, a cost-effective alternative to silk that worked particularly well with the era's bias-cut, drapey styles. But Hortense didn't want more of these cheap, mass-produced dresses. She gathered several garment manufacturers in her office to explain her idea: she wanted them to produce for Bonwit Teller a range of simple, well-made dresses in quality fabrics, rather than what they had been sending her, which were dresses that looked expensive but on closer inspection were covered in gimmicks to hide their poor quality. She didn't want another young mother to go through what she had, unable to find something flattering and affordable. "There are sign posts on every dress that shriek 'cheap' or whisper 'chic,'" she told them. "And the signs that shriek the loudest are buckles and bows and pins and clips that have no more purpose than to attempt to make up for lack of quality by needless ornamentation." She wanted well-cut clothes "that made no pretensions to being more than they are."

The grizzled old manufacturers, who had worked in the garment trade for decades, were dismissive. "Look, Mrs. Odlum, I've been making and selling an inexpensive line of dresses for twenty years. The women who buy those dresses don't want the kind of clothes you'd buy," said one. "You don't understand the difference between customers who buy inexpensive dresses and the ones who buy in your custom dressmaking department," said another. But Hortense did understand. And she insisted, telling them, "I'll prove it to you." She requested that they make her the dresses just as she had ordered—tailored and seemly, festooned only with the occasional belt or simple, well-made collar— and she would sell so many of them that the garment manufacturers and the store would profit handsomely. To that end, she opened two new clothing departments, Rendezvous, targeting young matrons, and Debutante, catering to a younger, fashion-forward customer. Several months later, as crowds flocked to the new areas in the store, she was proven exactly right.

Despite the depressed economy, Hortense envisioned a store that served the young, harried mother on a budget, as well as the well-heeled wives who played bridge, and she settled on a new slogan, "High class but not high hat." As part of this rebranding, she decided she had no choice but to spend some money on much-needed renovations. While the building was only a few years old, Mr. Bonwit, so strapped for cash, had ignored basic upkeep, and the heavy foot traffic from shoppers had taken its toll. "I knew I was criticized for spending money in what seemed to be a lavish fashion on the remodeling. But it just seemed common sense," she said. Hortense opened a beauty salon at the store, importing Monsieur Leon, a famed hairdresser, directly from Paris; she hired the designer Fira Benenson, known professionally as Countess Illinska, to supervise the new Salon de Couture, which boasted original dresses as well as imported Parisian designers, and she created the Travel Fashion Shop, which featured yacht-style portholes as windows and an arresting display that included a life-sized boat.

Hortense also established the 721 Club, named for the store's Fifth Avenue address. An all-male escape, it was directed at husbands and boyfriends who could sip scotch and smoke cigars free "from a crowd of frantic, elbowing women" and privately gaze at attractive models strutting by decked out in lingerie, bathing suits, and evening wear. Entered by a red lacquered door on the fourth floor, with a small sign above declaring, "For Men Only," habitués considered it "the only place you can get a decent drink on Fifth Avenue." Opened during the Christ-mas holiday season, it was ostensibly meant to assist male customers pick gifts for the ladies in their lives, and women shoppers were urged to leave their wish lists there. The club's most popular event was its annual Christmas party. Reminiscent of the Victoria's Secret fashion shows decades later, the 721 Club's event was attended by hundreds of men who slipped through the store's private side entrance to watch an elaborate runway performance; one year, the designer Elsa Schiaparelli oversaw the production, its showstopper a $3,000 gold lamé hostess coat lined in red velvet.

Hortense made other modernizing improvements, such as install-ing air-conditioning, which was still a novelty and a technological feat. It used 550 horsepower to melt 400 tons of ice every day, pumping 1,550 gallons of cold water every minute through 150,000 cubic feet of tubing. Hortense turned the air-conditioning into a publicity stunt, inviting the press and ceremoniously releasing a lever attached to an eight-foot thermometer to turn the system on. "In a jiffy cooled per-fumed air was wafted throughout the store!" marveled *Women's Wear Daily*. Bonwit Teller's ad campaign, titled "Our Mercury Goes *Down* So Spirits Go *Up*," ran in the dead of summer. "Maybe it's our pioneer blood, or maybe it's merely because we're women, but it seems to us that the thing to do at this moment is to put the chin in the air and go to work," it read. "*Bon air* to Manhattan—the greatest resort of them all."

Hortense also sought publicity to build Bonwit Teller's reputation, utilizing book publishing in particularly ingenious ways. In 1937, Bonwit Teller's head of advertising and fashion promotions, Sara Pen-noyer, published a novel, *Polly Tucker: Merchant*. The book, which was a bestseller and enjoyed eight printings, unspooled the tale of a plucky Philadelphia teenager who dreamed of a career at a department store. Polly parlays a first summer job as a bookkeeper for a fruit wholesaler on Front Street into a position at the fictitious, posh New York City department store Halliday's and eventually into a coveted job as an assistant buyer in ready-to-wear. Along the way, the heroine experi-ences doomed romance, friction with friends, and a family tragedy. It concludes with Polly excitedly winning a spot on the coveted executive track at Sperry's, the equally fictitious Manhattan department store, and smitten with a marriage-minded, handsome beau. The novel was a brilliant piece of marketing, inspiring young women to consider a career in retail while simultaneously establishing Bonwit Teller as a popular brand for the younger generation. "Polly Tucker is the ideal merchandising girl—the kind for whom alert modern stores are crying," Sara said in an interview just as her book was being published. "The making and selling of feminine clothes is now the fourth greatest industry in the country and the one in which women have the best opportunity of reaching the top. It is all terribly new, you see."

Polly Tucker: Merchant expertly wove industry wisdom and an insider's guide to the fashion and retail world of the time, with scenes of girlish drama, of Polly and her friends vacationing at a summer lake house or enjoying late-night outings at the Kit Kat Klub. In one episode, Polly rides with her mentor Lyda, the advertising manager at Halliday's, in the backseat of a taxi, to a fur showroom on Seventh Avenue. As traffic ensnarls the car, Polly gazes out the window, reading the words painted on the sides of delivery trucks double-parked on the narrow, chaotic side streets. "Lids for Kids," Lyda tells her, is the maker of children's hats, while "Cinderella Dresses" is a manufacturer of gowns. Lyda (or really, Sara) seizes the moment to give Polly (or really, the reader) a concise history of the Garment District, followed by an inviting tour of a fur showroom, where Polly sees models bundled in Persian lamb coats and blue fox capes, twirling around the large space as buyers admire and critique the styles from their seats in discreet, wood-paneled booths.

At another point, Lyda explains how profit margins work, and at another she bemoans the physical toll it takes standing all day on a selling floor. Sara also uses the novel to answer questions like "But tell me, Lyda, what chances have I of getting ahead—of really going places someday?" Lyda responds, "Lots of chances or none at all. It's up to you." A store job, she adds, is "natural for a woman because it appeals to all her feminine instincts. It has color, glamour. A big store adds such a lot of glitter and fun to the prosy business of everyday living."

Toward the end of the novel, there is a pause in the tale of Polly Tucker as several real-life, prominent fashion industry insiders offer their own sage advice. Bernice Fitz-Gibbon, the advertising phenom behind Macy's famous tagline, begins, "Don't you have to be dazzlingly clever to be a success in advertising? You don't. You don't have to be a great literary light. You don't have to write deathless prose," she advises. "Anybody—practically anybody—can learn to write advertising."

Polly Tucker: Merchant became much more than a book. Bonwit Teller produced a complementary line of clothing for the many Polly Tuckers out there, offering dresses, hats, and coats at affordable price points, "designed to play a dual role for the young career girl, whose busy schedule takes her from office to dinner table." The store also used royalties from the book, and profits from the Polly Tucker clothing line, to create a Polly Tucker scholarship to help aspiring young employees. The scholarship could be for "any night course in any school, the possibilities ranging from secretarial work to costume designing, to private lessons in conversational French," and was available to both men and women. Among its recipients was Ira Neimark, a young bellhop at Bonwit Teller, who used the funds to attend Columbia Business School and eventually worked his way up to president of Bergdorf Goodman.

Hortense wrote the foreword to *Polly Tucker*, and while she would later switch course and reverse herself, she used the character as an opportunity to urge young, female readers to consider retailing as a career. "She has her own specialized bailiwick," she wrote, "a field in which she does not have to compete at any disadvantage with men. She has no reason to feel defensive or hoist banners or talk of equal rights for women workers. She can't complain that men are better paid. They aren't, in retailing. She enters not only on an equal footing with men, but with the odds all her way. And it is up to her and her own ambition just how far she will go."

Two years after the success of *Polly Tucker*, Hortense followed up by writing her own book. An autobiography that spanned nearly three hundred pages, *A Woman's Place* was a glorified retelling of Hortense's childhood in St. George, her arrival in New York, and her appointment to Bonwit Teller's top job. The book, which was misleading in parts, omitting certain truths, never sold as well as *Polly Tucker*, although it did garner decent coverage in some papers, including *The New York*

Times, which called it "an interesting book for women to read" and "an unusual kind of success story."

Another of Hortense's notable initiatives were the "Tonic Sessions." These multiday conferences were held in the ballrooms of hotels like the Plaza and the St. Regis, and customers bought tickets to hear talks given by Bonwit Teller's experts. Countess Illinska, for instance, told audiences that "fashion is a frame of mind," and "this year women are dressing to be admired by men, not primarily to look chic." The buyer for corsets revealed the most flattering undergarments, while the travel bureau chief unveiled the best outfits for transatlantic journeys. There were lectures on "how to dress to please husbands" and "how to slim down a size forty figure with becoming costumes." One of the most widely attended sessions was a reading of the book *Ladies, I Give You— the Way to His Heart.* The title proved irresistible, and women flocked to hear it, although inexplicably the performer read while sitting behind a screen, hiding his identity. He was also the only male speaker at the conference. These Tonic Sessions became so highly attended that on one day, more than a thousand un-ticketed women had to be turned away. "Attempts are being made by the store to get larger quarters for a continuance of the series next week," reported *The New York Times.*

Another year, Bonwit Teller sponsored a contest with the magazine *Mademoiselle* called "Make the Most of Yourself." Essentially a beauty pageant held in reverse, the winner was the contestant deemed the least attractive: this "ugly duckling" would be transformed by the ministrations of a crack team of Bonwit Teller stylists. The hapless winner, chosen from among two thousand applicants, was twenty-four-year-old Kallie Foutz of Salt Lake City, harshly dubbed "America's Ugliest Girl." Kallie won after sending in a photograph of herself, along with the following text: "I have a proboscis that would make Jimmy Durante look to his laurels. . . . My hair is dun-colored . . . my hands are like hams. . . . My underpinnings brought out the remark, 'Best watch out, gal, or you'll be arrested for no visible support.' . . . And I'm something that looks like Bull Montana with a hangover."

Kallie was sent to New York City for two months, where she visited a dietitian, was styled with an entirely fresh wardrobe and new hairdo, and even met with a plastic surgeon. On her first morning in New York, Kallie was whisked away to the Medical Arts Building, where at 8:00 a.m. doctors measured her metabolism and at 10:00 a.m. "the surgeon went to work on her nose." *Women's Wear Daily*, which had assigned a journalist to follow Kallie, helpfully reported that she measured five feet, five inches, with a twenty-five-inch waist, a thirty-five-inch hip, and a thirty-two-inch bust. For those not satisfied with such details, it dutifully added that her head was twenty-one and a half inches, her shoes were a size 5, and she weighed 103 pounds. "Bonwit representatives sadly reported this morning she had no appetite at all and had bumps in the wrong places," the paper wrote in its initial dispatch.

The contest was a publicity bonanza, and Bonwit Teller revealed Kallie's transformation at the finale of a Tonic Session. The event introduced Kallie to an adoring crowd, and following a Q&A, there was a screening of a film documenting her journey, aptly titled *Ugly Duckling into Swan*. For those who missed the live showing, the film was screened several more times throughout the conference. Bonwit Teller also ran a series of newspaper advertisements touting Kallie's metamorphosis. They featured a close-up image of Kallie "before," a snapshot of her in profile that emphasized her prominent nose. It was juxtaposed with the "after" shot, which showed a woman who was nearly unrecognizable, glancing down seductively, her mouth pouty, her eyes nearly closed, wearing a formfitting, low-cut dress that revealed ample décolletage. "She's had plastic surgery and five weeks at the hands of Bonwit's," the ad copy read. "Her skin and hair have been revitalized in our Beauty Salon. Her figure and posture improved in our Salon of Body Sculpture . . . Kallie Foutz, now Karol Faust, is here to tell you about her metamorphosis." Yes, she also changed her name—a Faustian bargain, to be sure.

In the end, the publicity drummed up by ploys like the "Make the Most of Yourself" contest, and innovations such as air-conditioning and affordable-dress departments, would transform Bonwit Teller nearly as fully as Kallie Foutz. Though Bonwit Teller had once been a sagging business, it was now embraced as one of New York's chicest, most desirable shopping destinations. When Hortense was appointed president,

Bonwit Teller had a staff of six hundred and annual sales of $3.5 million, or $76.5 million in today's dollars. In her first year Hortense increased its sales figures by 27 percent, in her second year she doubled them, and in year three she tripled those numbers. In 1938, even as the Depression dragged on, Hortense steered the business to a store record, with annual sales totaling $9.5 million, or $197 million in today's dollars, beating its previous record, reached a decade earlier at the height of the Roaring Twenties.

By the time Hortense retired, she oversaw fifteen hundred employees and a business with annual sales that topped $10 million, or more than $200 million today. "We have been building within and without," Hortense said, relishing her successes. "We sought to build confidence and we have." *The Boston Daily Globe* wrote a feature titled "Woman Saved Store When Men Failed," marveling at her business acumen and wondering how she had accomplished so much while still remaining "essentially feminine, presenting none of the traditional appearance of the typical successful business woman." Hortense's achievements were unsurpassed, and even future executives would struggle to approximate her milestones. Yet Hortense would eventually disavow her career success, voicing deep regret for her working life.

Dorothy signs documents in her office
at Lord & Taylor in April 1946.

Part 2

I'd far rather have a brilliant career
than a humdrum married life. There's
nothing so dreadful as being bored.

—*Dorothy Shaver*

Chapter 6

Dorothy's American Look

In the spring of 1944, a fashion stylist hosted a luncheon at the St. Regis Hotel where he presented eight oversized hats. These elaborate concoctions were not merely large. Their wide brims were enormous, overstuffed with colorful ribbons, folded felt, straw, satin, and tulle, so overflowing with a profusion of materials that it looked as if a wearer's neck might buckle under the weight. The hats were supposedly created by the most famous haute couture houses in France and were smuggled out of occupied Paris via Spain. Within days, a select group of New York women, those who prided themselves on embracing cutting-edge looks, no matter if they flattered, were seen around town, balancing the ungainly hats on their heads. Within weeks, several Fifth Avenue shops had churned out collections featuring the look. The sudden proliferation of these hats was strange, but it became even stranger when fashion magazines that no one had ever heard of began flooding the mailboxes of fashion editors, stylists, and department store buyers, their pages chock-full of models sporting these same hats. The first publication to appear was *Plaire*, or "to please" in French, boasting 154 pages of thick, expensive paper, quickly followed by two more magazines filled with similar designs, setting insiders abuzz about this new fashion direction.

But while some industry gatekeepers took these new styles seriously, others doubted their provenance. The hats looked "like something dragged out of grandmother's trunk in the attic . . . an embodiment of the German hausfrau's idea of elegance," wrote one critic. "If these are truly French creations all I can say is that art has been killed by misery," quipped another. When it was pointed out that the types of fabrics and amounts of yardage used on the hats violated wartime rations, suspicions were further heightened. The War Production Board and the FBI were notified and began investigating whether the hats were an elaborate Nazi ruse manufactured by Germans, as a salvo meant to draw American fashionistas into buying enemy creations. Because the hats relied on scarce, rationed materials, they were likely meant to injure the Allies' war effort. It was a "daring propaganda plot executed like a well-planned store promotion," said Sara Pennoyer, the Bonwit Teller executive, "a blow against American women dumb enough to take anything the Germans offered them in the way of ersatz Paris styles." The bizarre incident highlighted the lengths to which Nazi propagandists were willing to stoop. It also proved that America's homegrown fashion industry, of which Dorothy was a leading proponent, had become influential enough to be weaponized by the enemy.

Since the birth of haute couture in the mid-nineteenth century, the city of Paris was the sun around which all else revolved, and the couturier was its gravitational pull. The term "haute couture," or "high dressmaking," referred to the exorbitantly expensive, custom-made clothes that were created for wealthy, private clients in an atelier, or workshop, by teams of seamstresses poring over every thread and seam. The first great haute couturier was Charles Frederick Worth. Born in England, Worth moved to Paris in 1845 and quickly gained a following as a dressmaker. In 1858, he opened the House of Worth, and his elaborate creations, made from exotic materials like peacock feathers, earned him worldwide fame and a royal clientele. One devoted fan was the empress Eugénie of France, whose notable House of Worth pieces included a skirt handcrafted from Alençon lace, a prohibitively expensive textile that reportedly took eleven years to create.

It was the Chambre Syndicale de la Couture, created in 1868, that supervised and regulated the hierarchical French dressmaking ecosystem. In the buzzing hive of the atelier, the couturier was queen bee, assisted by his *modéliste*, while the *première*, or fitter, cut the clothes and served as the taskmaster. The sewers, or *petites mains*, were the worker bees, artisans who trained for years, and even generations, in intricate tasks such as pleating and embroidery, painstakingly transforming the designer's vision into a physical reality.

In a city where a dress by Madeleine Vionnet was as important as an Impressionist landscape by Claude Monet, Paris hummed with anticipation as couturiers readied their seasonal showcases of designs, as handwoven textiles were cut and folded into elaborate, dramatic lines, and as socialites and nobility flocked to showrooms to watch young, thin models walk in slow circles to show off the fashions. Once customers chose the pieces they wished to purchase, a labyrinthine process began whereby they arrived for a series of fittings, carried out in minute detail, with at least five measurements taken for their backs alone. The interminable, highly individualized, and exceedingly costly process culminated months later, when the handmade gowns were finally delivered to their owners. For one young aspiring American designer living in Paris in the 1920s, the French couturier process was bewildering but inevitable. "It is medieval, it is anachronistic," said Elizabeth Hawes, "it is why all beautiful clothes are supposed to be made in France and all women are supposed to want them."

American fashion—if you could call it that—had nothing on France. Paris was a city of haute couturiers who performed their artistry in ateliers, serving an exclusive clientele. New York, on the other hand, was home to the needle trade, a stretch of midtown Manhattan known as the Garment District, where ragmen supervised grimy, cavernous warehouses filled with largely Jewish immigrants, who bent their backs for hours over sewing machines churning out identical, cheap, anonymously designed clothes for the masses. America's apparel industry began in the mid-nineteenth century as a collection of wholesale dealers, largely German Jews, and centered on the Lower East Side. Over the next several decades, the industry expanded as an influx of immigrants from southern and eastern Europe, some Jewish and some not, provided cheap, skilled labor and as rapid industrialization, including the invention of the sewing machine, increased productivity and profits.

By 1880, there were more than twenty-five thousand workers toiling in the city's sweatshops, producing ready-to-wear clothing for a broad swath of America's public. By 1900, that figure had swelled to nearly eighty-four thousand workers who labored in crowded, deplorable conditions, suffering under exploitative practices, such as covering clocks and locking doors to prevent early exits. In 1911, the devastating Triangle Shirtwaist Factory fire, which killed 146 people, the vast majority young women and girls, bolstered the power of the nascent labor movement and helped usher in shorter workdays, higher pay, and improved safety measures.

Manufacturers began abandoning the cramped, poorly constructed tenements of the Lower East Side, seeking out affordable commercial lofts that could accommodate their growing factory floors. By 1920, the rag trade had begun settling in a west side neighborhood known as the Tenderloin, its residents, mostly African Americans and Irish immigrants, increasingly displaced to make way for the new industry. By 1926, the Tenderloin was gone, and the area bounded by Thirty-Fourth and Forty-Second Streets, between Ninth Avenue and Broadway, had been renamed the Garment District. Over the ensuing decades, the industry grew exponentially, and by the middle of the twentieth century, the Garment District produced 100 million wardrobe pieces a year, or 72 percent of all of America's domestically manufactured clothing.

A key turning point for the industry was in the early 1920s, when the country became captivated by capital-F fashion. Having grown wealthy from the inflated stock market, Americans began touring Europe in greater numbers, and there they became acquainted, and quickly enamored, with Parisian style. Women crowded into Coco Chanel's small boutique near the Place Vendôme, eager to ditch their restrictive Edwardian corsets for her loose-fitting jersey fabrics and to dab their necks with her Chanel No. 5 perfume. They flooded Jeanne Lanvin's shop to ogle her evening gowns in bold colors with dropped waists and full skirts, and they flocked to Jean Patou's for his daring sleeveless tennis dresses, his sweaters featuring Cubist images, and the famously tanned designer's Chaldee oil, an early suntan lotion. "Fashion had gone democratic, but still it paid golden tithes to Paris," wrote Morris De Camp Crawford, a longtime fashion editor at *Women's Wear Daily*. "Ocean liners were crowded with new customers. Paris hotels and restaurants were filled. There was a seemingly endless succession of American millionaires literally wallowing in the franc-dollar exchange." Dorothy, too, had watched this shift, noting how customers were ever more "spellbound by the phrase 'a Paris original,'" adding, "The great names of the Parisian haute couture, overnight it seemed, were on the lips of women from the tip of Cape Cod to the Golden Gate."

With the public so attuned to Parisian fashions, Garment District manufacturers were forced to pay attention to new styles from abroad, rather than simply recycle the previous seasons' clothes. A new system was created whereby New York's needle trade began importing—and copying—French designs. Manufacturers and wholesalers, as well as buyers from the country's large department stores, specialty stores, and even small regional chains, sent representatives to France to attend the couture shows. There they would buy select Paris "models," as haute couture outfits were known, and take them back to Seventh Avenue, where they were brazenly copied and reinterpreted for the American mass market. Within this highly mechanized production system, clothing designers were anonymous, salaried employees working in garment warehouses, their sole task to translate original Parisian couture designs for the American consumer. As a result, by the close of the 1920s and into the 1930s, American department stores were inundated with cheap, dumbed-down copies of Parisian originals. "In New York in 1928, you could meet one lady in a Chanel she'd bought on the rue Cambon for $200," Hawes, the American designer in Paris, wrote. "She could meet a lady who'd bought the same dress at Hattie Carnegie for $250. That lady could meet another lady who'd bought the same Chanel at Lord & Taylor for $59.50. And there were other ladies who also bought the same Chanel, well, maybe not the same material, but the same design, for $19.75 or $10.50."

The market devolved into confusion, with both designers and consumers increasingly baffled. A select few fashion industry leaders began reconsidering the entire arrangement. Some, most notably Dorothy, began to recognize that French couturiers were designing for a minuscule audience almost entirely made up of wealthy socialites. The old system, Dorothy realized, had little relevance for most American women who spent their days working in offices as secretaries, or chasing toddlers around kitchens, or attending weekend football games. Copying French designs not only created chaos in pricing and the quality of clothes but also overlooked an entire sector of the vast domestic market. "We began to realize that the life of the American woman and young girl differs quite radically from that of the Frenchwoman," Dorothy said. Buyers just back from Paris complained, "This stuff is no good for us. Why don't they make some good afternoon dresses? Why don't they design more sport clothes?" A backlash against Paris began to take hold. "We whose work it is to keep our fingers on the pulse of fashion and to watch for the first faint signs of a turn in public demand, began to find here and there an American woman who wanted 'something different,'" Dorothy said. "She was still under the influence of the great Parisian names. She wanted a Paris copy, but wasn't there 'something different'?"

The 1929 crash hastened this paradigm shift. Now suffering from the Depression, Americans stopped traveling to Paris and kept close watch on their spending. High import duties were placed on foreign goods, and Parisian fashions became particularly costly. As was her talent, Dorothy saw this as a prime opportunity for change. If one of the goals of her 1928 Art Deco exposition had been to inspire American creators by exposing them to the best of French high design, her new goal was to supplant French design altogether and create space for uniquely American fashion. The biggest obstacles, however, were the long-standing cultural dominance of France and the conventional wisdom that America lacked style. "America had no designers to speak of at all," Dorothy said. "Yet I knew that America was full of talented young people who needed only encouragement and an opportunity to develop. But how to overcome the snob appeal of Paris? How to convince the American fashion magazines and the American public of the designing talent all around us?"

While Dorothy was questioning Paris's dominance, American designers who had been toiling anonymously for the large manufacturers began asking themselves the same thing. Like the department store buyers and the garment manufacturers, American clothing designers had traveled to Paris in the boom years before the 1929 crash, attending couture shows and visiting the fashion ateliers. Some had been

inspired and were already breaking away from the system. Hattie
Carnegie, for instance, was selling original creations, including
her "little Carnegie suit," which
featured a fitted jacket and a skirt
with rounded hips. Born Henrietta Kanengeiser in the 1880s,
she was a Jewish immigrant from
Vienna who had begun her career
in fashion as a thirteen-year-old
messenger for Macy's and by the
1920s had built a multimillion-
dollar business out of her clothing
shop on East Forty-Ninth Street.
But Hattie's success was unusual.

The designer Hattie Carnegie in 1947.

There was an underground scene of other young designers, but most
remained unknown. Dorothy, however, had a unique front-row seat
to their abilities. Following the success of her 1928 Art Deco expo,
Dorothy continued to rise through the ranks and in 1931 was made a
vice president. As a senior executive at Lord & Taylor, she decided to
use her platform to bring these domestic fashion designers to the fore.

In the spring of 1932, Dorothy launched a new campaign, which
would be dubbed "the American Look," meant to promote unheralded
American fashion designers. "We still doff our hats to Paris," Dorothy
said. "Paris gave us our inspiration, and still does. But we believe that
there must be clothes which are intrinsically American, and that only
the American designer can create them." She touted the new direction in *The New York Times*, running an advertisement that declared,
"Lord & Taylor recognizes a new trend toward clothes of, by and for
the American Woman," continuing, "Lord & Taylor, ever eager to
sponsor a new idea, recognized in the work of three young designers
a new expression in clothes created for the American woman. Clothes
that understand American life, as she lives it." Beneath this ad copy
there were pencil drawings of three women in different outfits. The first
was a checkered day dress with a dark cape and matching hat, dubbed

LORD & TAYLOR

recognizes a new trend
toward clothes of, by
and for the American
Woman, as created by
Three Young American Designers

Lord & Taylor, ever eager to sponsor a new idea, recognized in the work of
three young designers a new expression in clothes created for the American
woman. Clothes that understand American life, as she lives it. We worked
closely with these designers, and tomorrow present collections from each:

Elizabeth   Annette   Edith Marie
HAWES   SIMPSON   REUSS

These young women began designing clothes for their acquaintances, typical
American girls. One designs fabrics only — prints — because she knows that
prints are essentially an American fashion. Each of them has gathered a clientele
so large that she has become a HOUSE. In presenting these collections we
believe that you will discover a new satisfaction in buying, and wearing, clothes
that understand you. See them in our Fifth Avenue windows, and in the

WOMEN'S AND MISSES' DRESS SHOPS, THIRD FLOOR
THE YOUNG NEW YORKERS' SHOP, FIFTH FLOOR
SILKS BY THE YARD, STREET FLOOR

LORD & TAYLOR, FIFTH AVENUE

Lord & Taylor was among the first
to publicize the names of American
designers in an advertising campaign in
The New York Times, from April 1932.

the "City Child." It was designed by Elizabeth Hawes, who had returned from Paris by then and had opened her own shop, similar to Hattie Carnegie's. The second outfit, called "Casino Night," was by the designer Annette Simpson, with the illustration featuring a woman leaning back in a slinky gown, festooned with an enormous corsage, while the third was of a woman in a frock covered with a floral print by Edith Marie Reuss. "In presenting these collections we believe that you will discover a new satisfaction in buying, and wearing, clothes that *understand* you," the ad declared.

While it was not the first time that a department store had prominently publicized American designers by name—Best & Co. had attempted something similar several years earlier—it was the first time it gained considerable traction. "Women came into the store, advertisements in hand, asking for specific models by name," Dorothy said. "We sold 50 of one number and 150 of another in just a few days. We were convinced we had planned correctly."

As part of the promotion, Lord & Taylor also created a series of window displays focusing on American fashion, featuring placards with brief, breezy introductions to the clothing, as well as photographs of the designers, most smiling, staring directly into the camera and looking approachable. The window displays were relatively unfussy, with few of the flourishes associated with high fashion, save for life-sized sewing needles, spools of thread, and other tools of the trade to enliven the tableaux. For the fashion designer Clare Potter, for instance, the windows featured a number of mannequins outfitted in her telltale sportswear and included a dash of glamour with an image from *Vogue* of the actress Katharine Hepburn, leaning back casually, dressed in one of Potter's white linen duster coats.

But while Lord & Taylor customers were receptive to Dorothy's American Look, the American Look designers themselves faced an uphill battle for recognition. "For the next few years there was a game which you could start in any group of fashion people," Hawes joked. "You just said, 'Who are the American designers?' Then you watched everyone scurry around looking in corners to try and find them." The reasons were twofold: While Lord & Taylor promoted individual designers, even displaying their photos in store windows, other merchants held firm to the belief that designers should remain nameless. These retailers believed that keeping designers anonymous elevated the importance of their own store name and lent them an air of exclusivity.

A second, and perhaps even greater, hurdle for American designers was the refusal of many newspapers and magazines to publicize their names. These young designers, who, like Hawes, were still establishing themselves, often agreed to exclusive agreements with department stores to carry their merchandise. Publications feared that if they mentioned one designer by name, it would infuriate stores whose designers were not mentioned, and they would pull their advertising. Some publications did include a small box with information where readers could write in and discover where to buy the designs. But most just ran generic headlines like "American Designed Clothes" and "Our Own American Designs." It enraged Hawes. " 'Our own American designs.' By whom? Why, by Americans," she vented. "Who are they? What are their names? Never mind that, these are 'Clothes designed in America,' whoopee—by perfectly nameless people, by robots maybe."

In 1940, nearly a decade after Dorothy's initial push to promote American designers, France fell to the Nazis, and the fashion equation changed. Parisian design houses were cut off from the outside world, and New York was left adrift from its continental connection. With curfews, rations, and a swastika flag flying from the Arc de Triomphe, many French designers shuttered their businesses while others went into exile or chose to collaborate with the occupiers. "Paris is a city of brooding and bitter silence," Morris De Camp Crawford wrote. "A few ghostly survivors of the couture drag out a miserable existence; most of the houses are closed, and most of the artists who reigned before June 1940 have left Paris, perhaps forever." Stanley Marcus, whose family founded the department store Neiman Marcus, noted how, "for decades, our garment industry has depended for inspiration on a handful of Paris designers." The SS *Normandie*, the era's fastest passenger ship, "shuttled so many American buyers back and forth between Paris and New York that she was familiarly known as the Seventh Avenue Express. Now she lies at anchor at the North River and the American garment industry is left to its own devices. How will it get along?"

For Dorothy, who in 1937 was once more promoted—this time to first vice president in charge of advertising, display, and publicity—the occupation of Paris lent greater urgency to her efforts to advance the American Look and deepen the well of domestic fashion designers. Months into the French occupation, Lord & Taylor opened the Designer's Shop, a boutique within the store that sold solely American designers, the clothing featuring their names prominently sewn into the labels. It copyrighted the phrase "the American Look" and offered an annual award, the Lord & Taylor American Design Award, giving $1,000 to four lucky recipients. The store also expanded the roster of American designers it promoted, including Clare Potter, who created sundresses and trousers and who helped popularize the two-piece swimsuit, and Claire McCardell, whose functional designs included bicycle shorts and menswear-inspired clothing, such as an evening shirtdress made from men's cotton ticking.

Dorothy was not alone in her interest in American designers. Several peers and competitors began their own initiatives, largely through the Fashion Group, a powerful industry organization that Dorothy helped start in the early 1930s with other prominent women, including Edna Woolman Chase, editor of *Vogue*, and Eleanor Lambert, the powerful fashion publicist. They, too, took up the mantle, with *Vogue* publishing glossy pages featuring the gowns of Norman Norell and the weekend wardrobes of Vera Maxwell, while Eleanor spearheaded programs such as New York Fashion Week, which was called Press Week when it debuted in 1943. Even Eleanor Roosevelt, also a Fashion Group member and the first lady of New York State at the time, was involved, throwing her support and name behind numerous campaigns.

In addition to helping establish the American fashion industry, Dorothy was actively engaged in the official war effort. In 1942, the quartermaster general hired her as a merchandising consultant, and while Dorothy kept her day job at Lord & Taylor, she began frequently commuting to Washington, D.C. Among her responsibilities was to help spearhead a project to redesign the uniforms of army nurses. This had become a critical mission following the Battle of Bataan, a brutal campaign against the Japanese that had taken place in the jungles of the Philippines. The nurses were caught up in the fighting and quickly realized to their horror that their uniforms—starched white skirts and shirts with numerous buttons, white stockings, and low white oxford shoes—were utterly impractical. The white color made them obvious targets for Japanese fighter pilots who were diving and shooting from the air, while the oxfords left their ankles easy prey for swarms of mosquitoes that covered them with bites and caused their legs to swell. Less critical but equally true: it was impossible to keep their white clothing clean and ironed, never mind starched. The nurses were forced to swap out their uniforms for those worn by the GIs, donning khaki slacks and shirts borrowed from the smallest soldiers in the ranks and exchanging their oxfords for military boots, even if they were mostly too large.

Dorothy was asked to advise on the design of uniforms that made sense for nurses on the front, and after months of research and review she approved several inventive, and far more practical, designs. The new uniforms consisted of shirts and slacks made from khaki herringbone twill that acted as camouflage, as well as steel helmets and field boots. Nurses were given laced canvas leggings that could fit over the slacks to protect them in mosquito-infested areas and buttonless wraparound dresses in brown-and-white-striped seersucker. These outfits required neither starching nor ironing and had other useful details, like pockets. Some even boasted multiple uses, such as the wind- and water-repellent trench coat, which came with a wool lining that could be removed and

Advance field uniform is olive drab twill shirt and trousers, field shoes, canvas leggings, combat helmet.

Dress uniform is olive drab wool jacket and skirt, khaki shirt and tie, soft cap with visor, Corps insignia.

America's Best-Dressed Woman

The Army Nurse gets a new and necessary wardrobe

African mud and fox-holes in the South Pacific region have taught America more than one bitter lesson. We learned, with

Corps, the new government issue (G.I.) clothes are practical. Most noticeable changes in the uniform of the Army Nurse are

An article published in 1943, reviewing the new army nurse uniforms that Dorothy spearheaded.

used as a bathrobe. "A lot of people seem to think that the Army uniform will bring on duller women's fashions because it is severe," said Dorothy. "What they fail to realize is that a military uniform, properly fitted, is glamorous and no woman is going to be out-glamoured by a man, be he a sailor, soldier or marine."

Most embraced the redesign. "Fur-edged parkas, reversible for greater utility, and numerous other ingenious ideas save packing space and assure comfort for our Army nurses in every climate," said one paper in a review. But of course, there were also controversies, namely that the new uniform featured pants. (No matter the dangers of traipsing around the jungle in a skirt.) "The Army Nurses Corps threw 40 years of tradition overboard yesterday and put its second lieutenants in long pants," bemoaned the *New York World-Telegram*. Dorothy tried to make light of it, reassuring critics that while nurses on the battlefield may wear pants, it had no bearing on their outfits at home. "If anybody thinks that a woman will stick to slacks, he has to ignore every theory of human nature displayed since Eve plucked the first fig leaf. Slacks? Don't make me laugh. Most of us wouldn't be found dead in them."

While Dorothy helped women at war, she also focused on those who were battling on the home front, running households, and raising kids single-handedly. "In a tribute to the largest women's army in the world, Lord & Taylor this week devotes its entire group of Fifth Avenue windows to the WIVES," declared *Women's Wear Daily*, "the soldiers with broomsticks, who, with homes to tend and children to care for, are silently doing their share to preserve the heart of the family and home that their men are fighting for." Each of the oversized Fifth Avenue windows featured a different scene, with mannequins cleaning, mending clothes, salvaging materials, and preserving food. Dorothy had come up with the idea while attending a lunch where she sat next to a mother of three small children who had told her that she was so overwhelmed caring for her family while her husband was away fighting that she hadn't found time to carry out any official war work.

Just as happened during World War I, World War II changed the trajectory of women in the workforce. Once again, men were being drafted and leaving for the war front, creating vacancies that enabled women to enter positions that had previously been closed to them. Between 1940 and 1945, the male labor force declined by nearly nine million, while the female labor force surged, increasing by more than seven million. This was the decade of Rosie the Riveter, famous for her red bandanna and her flexed bicep, when the War Manpower Commission recruited female workers to munitions factories and the federal government lowered the age limit for employment to sixteen from eighteen. Many women took jobs in manufacturing, and college-educated women started white-collar jobs in offices or as teachers, nurses, and social workers. Patriotic narratives blared on the radio and were endlessly repeated in newspaper columns of how female workers were critical to stopping Hitler; warned that should he win, American women risked being forced back into the kitchen or, in the more salacious propaganda tales, used as "sex slaves."

Many department stores entered these years in a precarious position, having suffered through the Great Depression and now the challenges of a wartime economy. Stores cut staff, shuttered expensive tearooms and replaced them with lunch counters, and offered increased credit to cash-strapped shoppers to improve sales. There was even a campaign to have President Roosevelt officially declare the fourth Thursday of November as the Thanksgiving holiday, to permanently extend the lucrative Christmas shopping season. The effort began after 1939, when Thanksgiving fell late, giving retailers fewer days of shopping until Christmas. The president acquiesced, paving the way for today's Black Friday shopping blowouts. And while department stores were making staff cuts, when they did have openings, it was difficult to find suitable applicants because women were being lured away by larger salaries offered in the ballooning defense industries.

The twin factors of the draft and the proliferation of higher pay offered at wartime factories created vacancies that proved an opportunity for some African American job seekers. Most large department stores relegated their Black employees to lower-paying positions stocking merchandise in warehouses or doing janitorial work. There were a small number of Black-owned department stores, such as the short-lived St. Luke Emporium in Richmond, Virginia, and some white-owned stores that hired Black employees in senior posts, most notably the South Center Department Store in Chicago. Owned by two Jewish brothers, South Center catered to a largely Black customer base, and in 1928 it hired Richard Lee Jones as its general superintendent. The only African American to fill such a senior position at a large department store, in 1939, Jones was appointed to South Center's board of directors. There was also a "Don't Buy Where You Can't Work" movement, iterations of which began as early as 1919 and accelerated during the 1920s and the Depression as customers were urged to shun stores with racist hiring policies.

But in the 1940s, when stores could find neither white men nor white women to fill their ranks, some of the country's major department stores began hiring African Americans in more visible roles. In New York, Lord & Taylor was one of the first, recruiting four Black saleswomen in 1942. One of these saleswomen was Ruby Harris, who was stationed on the main selling floor in the umbrella accessories department. "When I saw this girl, I was almost struck dumb with amazement," wrote Richard Dier, a reporter at *The Afro-American*. "She's an exact double of the glamorous screen actress and singer, Lena Horne. She is young, pretty, and has the most beautiful smile, and I can easily see why she's so well liked."

By 1947, fourteen major New York department stores had Black women on their sales staff. Yet, relatively speaking, the numbers remained small. In 1944, for instance, Lord & Taylor had 3,000 employees, just 135 of whom were Black. And the store maintained hiring quotas, even if they were unofficial. "It seems to me that it is only fair that the person with the best qualifications should be hired, regardless of color . . . with limitations, of course," one Lord & Taylor executive told *The Afro-American*. "It is only natural that we don't want to flood our place with colored people, even if they all had the best qualifications."

As World War II ground on, department stores and the fashion press increasingly embraced Dorothy's American Look. Through the 1940s, driven by patriotism in a time of war, as well as the economic advantage of producing and buying clothes domestically, American fashion designers became ever more entrenched. In May 1945, *Life* magazine ran a multipage photo essay titled "What Is the American Look?" The story included an interview with Dorothy, who described the Look as "that certain kind of American figure—long-legged, broad-shouldered, slim-waisted, high-bosomed." But the real focus was undoubtedly a series of photos that ran alongside the interview and ostensibly epitomized the aesthetic, with models who were athletic and natural, casually posed riding a bicycle in short shorts, or looking secretarial, wearing glasses, and holding a dictation pad.

The platoons stationed in far-flung locales from the Pacific theater to Czechoslovakia were hungry for just such all-American fodder, and Dorothy was inundated with letters from soldiers desperate to contact the models. "How's about doing a favor for one of your *gallant, courageous* countrymen in uniform?!!" one Welby C. Wood of the U.S. Marines pleaded, the object of his desire a wholesome twentysomething

A woman modeling a sporty design in "The American Look" photo essay in *Life*.

An outfit designed for busy
mothers in *Life*.

Dorothy talking with the artist Dorothy
Hood while models look on, in a still
from *Life*.

in a jaunty hat and big grin. "Even if it has to be a little off the record. Give me her name and address so I can look her up when I come back." He was one of scores of homesick GIs who wrote Dorothy fan mail following the *Life* article. An ensign in the naval reserve pined for the same woman, writing, "We have seen our share of 'Pin-up' girls, and I for one, am tired of them." Lawrence M. Demarest wanted a girl who was grounded, and this one "seems like the girls you spent that last beach party with, your date at the gone, but never-to-be-forgotten college prom, or the one you spent that leave with skiing and skating." While it isn't clear if Dorothy ever responded to the soldiers' entreaties, their adoration clearly meant something to her. The fan mail was collected and codified in a leather-bound book, *The American Look*, that is archived at the Smithsonian.

Fashion Is Spinach

In the summer of 1925, Elizabeth Hawes had just completed her studies at Vassar and was newly arrived in Paris. This was years before Dorothy would choose Hawes as one of the first designers to be featured in Lord & Taylor's American Look campaign. Hawes was still completely green and eager to absorb all she could about the world of French fashion. That morning, she had arrived on rue du Faubourg St. Honoré to start work at a typical Parisian copy house. In these years, even as copying designs was rampant on Seventh Avenue, it was also a scourge in Paris, where the city's cobblestoned side streets were filled with small dressmaking establishments where customers could purchase less expensive versions of haute couture dresses. The particular copy house where Hawes reported for work was run by the diminutive

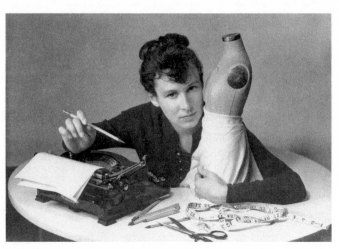

The designer Elizabeth Hawes in 1942.

Madame Doret, a savvy businesswoman whose main claim to fame was that she never copied a dress unless the original was in her possession. Hawes pulled open the heavy stone-rimmed door and walked through a dark, untidy hall and up a winding stair until she reached a large brass nameplate with the word "DORET" imprinted in block letters. The door to the copy house was usually open, although there was a gong attached, and if ever there was suspicion of an approaching police raid—copying was illegal—it was locked. Only customers who were properly vetted, those vouched for by other trusted sources, could purchase copies from Madame Doret. If an unknown person appeared at the door, they were shown a few simple, original dresses that the copy house had dashed off, and that served as its front, and sent on their way. If they passed muster, the customers were ushered into a small salon, where they were presented with several copies of couture outfits, a Lanvin Breton suit, maybe, or a handkerchief dress by Vionnet. Most were partially finished, in the process of being sewn for other customers, and it was from these incomplete outfits and a handful of sketches that shoppers placed their orders.

Madame Doret's copies were nearly perfectly executed—made with the exact material, color, and embroidery as the originals. By working at the copy shop for a few months, Hawes discovered how this was accomplished. "I became sufficiently trusted to become embroiled in the business of stealing," she wrote in her memoir, Fashion Is Spinach: How to Beat the Fashion Racket. (The book's title was taken from a popular 1928 New Yorker cartoon that featured a child staring unhappily at a plate of spinach. "It's broccoli, dear," the mother says, imploringly. "I say it's spinach," the child responds. "And I say, the hell with it!")

Some of Madame Doret's originals were legitimately purchased, with Hawes and others posing as customers and placing orders at the important couturiers. Others came from trusted customers, whose wardrobes consisted of both originals and bootlegged copies and who would share their originals in exchange for discounts on the copies. Mistresses were another source. Madame Doret's best mistress source was the kept lover of a famous designer; with an unending supply of originals, she ran a side hustle renting the outfits out to various copy houses.

Buyers were the final source for copies. When American manufacturers and department stores sent their buyers to France, the buyers had to rely on their Paris-based counterparts, who worked in what was known as resident buying offices, to arrange for fashion show tickets, access to various fashion events, and assistance shipping their purchases home. One day, Madame Doret enlisted Hawes in a ruse that involved a resident buyer, a beaver coat, and several stolen Chanel dresses. Madame Doret had a particularly close friendship with Madame Ellis, an American who had worked in a resident buying office in Paris for years. "She was about fifty-five, exceedingly attractive, and pretty smart. Anything she lacked in brains she had fully made up for in experience," wrote Hawes. Madame Doret requested that Hawes wear her beaver coat to meet Madame Ellis at her office one afternoon. "A fur coat in Paris is quite a rarity among the working class. Mine turned out to have a special value." Hawes found Madame Ellis alone in her office, surrounded by a large pile of boxes from Chanel. "The boxes were hastily opened, dresses pulled out and shaken from their tissue paper covers," recalled Hawes. "Put them under your coat," Madame Ellis told her urgently, "and get them back here as fast as you can."

Hawes, her coat bulging with the booty, flew downstairs, jumped into a taxi, ran up the backstairs of the copy house, and unloaded her loot onto the floor of Madame Doret's stockroom. "The workgirls had gone home. The fitters were there. They took the clothes and made accurate patterns of them, while I made accurate sketches. Madame Doret even more accurately examined every line, made notes on buttons, belts, cut bits of material from the seams, and looked over the finishing." When it was all over, "We had six or eight new Chanels to sell." Hawes then jammed the dresses back under her fur coat, jumped into another taxi, and rushed back to a waiting Madame Ellis. The resident buyer then carefully wrapped the models in their tissue paper and their Chanel boxes, "and off they went to New York on a fast boat."

Hawes's career as a knockoff artist did not end there. Following her stint at Madame Doret's copy house, she took a position as a sketcher for an American manufacturer. "The situation among American buyers in Paris during the years I worked there was very simple. As a buyer of expensive French models for American mass production, you stole what you could and bought what you had to," she wrote. "Almost every important buyer took to the first showing of every couturier a sketcher. The sketcher was ostensibly an assistant buyer. Her real job was to remember as many of the models as possible and subsequently sketch them for the buyer to copy in New York later."

Sketching was not easy. For one thing, there was nowhere to sketch. At fashion shows, attendees were handed a program with the number and name of each dress. As the models sashayed by, buyers were meant to check the numbers on the program that interested them. Then, when they were leaving the show, they handed those numbers to a saleswoman who would make an appointment for the buyer to return and review the selected pieces, after which they would place their orders. Sketchers had only these skimpy programs on which to ply their trade, surreptitiously scribbling their marks in the hopes of going unnoticed. Evading detection was critical, for once a sketcher was no longer incognito, she could be barred from future shows, essentially ending her career. "All the houses knew perfectly well that one in every eight people at an opening was a sketcher. The sketchers were all young," Hawes wrote, and "not particularly well dressed. A sketcher has a special photographic way of looking at a dress, engraving its image on her mind, marking her program a little too freely." Some small houses begrudgingly allowed sketchers to work, but the important couturiers ruthlessly enforced the rules.

The last challenge to being a sketcher was the issue of memory. At one of Hawes's first shows in her new job, held at the couture house Premet, she was planted between two buyers who worked for her boss, the American garment manufacturer. "Every time one of them wanted a dress sketched, she'd poke me in the ribs with her elbow. I'd settle my eyes on the dress and leave them there until the mannequin who wore it had made her last turn, her final flip of the fanny. . . . After that I would very carefully not look at anything else until I got another poke in the ribs." Hawes made shorthand notes on her program as each requested dress passed, and as soon as the show ended, her mind swimming with images, she ran outside and dove into the first taxi she found. Back at her apartment, gulping down a glass of milk for lunch, Hawes drew up her notes. "Then, into another taxi and so to Lanvin at 2:30. After Lanvin, 5:00 back to Premet to look over the clothes while the buyers bought one or two. By seven, I'd be home again, correcting the Premet sketches and making drawings of the notes on Lanvin. By 7:30, I must be out again with a book containing the finished sketches from the day before. If I didn't catch the buyers while they were dressing for an evening of gaiety, I never would."

In 1920s Paris, fashion shows were often elaborate affairs. At Jean Patou, for instance, "his showrooms were vast, delicately Louis something-or-other, and jammed with the united buying strength of the world," Hawes wrote.

"We sat with our backs to the long and tightly closed windows. The Place Vendôme lay peacefully without. Within, the haze of cigarette smoke became thicker and thicker as Patou poured out his new elegance, his new colors, his champagne." Chanel, meanwhile, "the battle cry of the world of fashion for nearly a decade," was the most exclusive. With only two small salons and a limited number of tickets, only the biggest buyers could gain access. "We got in, our hats over one ear, our coats half pulled off our backs," Hawes recalled. "We drove our way through a mob of screaming men and women who filled the rue Cambon with their wailing. They were wailing because they didn't have any tickets and Chanel was in a position to be firm." While at shows like Patou, champagne flowed freely as attendees socialized, at Chanel there were no drinks and no friendly chatter. "Nothing but very tall saleswomen posted in every corner, overlooking the crowd, fixing their icy stares on every little sketcher and every mink-coated buyer alike. No long program to write on. Just a small slip of paper. No long looks at the models. They simply flew in and out." The Chanel show was, Hawes wrote, a "violent mental exercise. If you made any more moves with your pencil than enough to write the equivalent of a number, someone suddenly leaned over your shoulder and grabbed your paper out of your hand."

After the Chanel show, the buyers headed straight for the tall, chilly saleswomen, crowding around, elbowing one another, pleading for the first appointment to the showroom. Once they made it to the Chanel showroom, they were greeted with a madhouse. "Clothes were lying in tired piles on every chair. Harassed salespeople were dashing about, telling their assistants for the love of heaven to find No. 234. The minute anyone heard someone else asking for No. 234, every buyer in the place asked for it too." Hawes's two buyers directed her to a fitting room, and one remained stationed outside the door, while the other went foraging for outfits. Every few minutes, Hawes, comfortably ensconced in the room, isolated from the surrounding chaos, was handed a dress to sketch, which she quickly executed before handing it back to the buyer stationed outside. "We got away with practically the whole collection. Then, carried away by their success, one of the buyers began stuffing bunches of samples into her mink pockets. The other one tore fringe off all the fringed dresses so she could have it copied in New York. Finally, one of them stole a belt off a dress." Shortly thereafter, Chanel prohibited any belts from being carried into the fitting rooms.

Hawes's career as a sketcher, and her time in Paris, came to an end when her subterfuge was discovered. "One day, during my third and last season of sketching, the summer of 1926, I had an appointment to meet my buyers at Miller Soeurs," she wrote. Miller Soeurs had once been a copy house, but it had lately begun creating original designs. Hawes arrived at the show early. "When I got there, they just took one look at me," she recalled. " 'We're sorry, but we won't let you in.' I said, 'You're perfectly right,' and left, feeling much better." After a bicycle tour in the French countryside and a holiday in Italy, Hawes left sketching behind forever, decamping for New York.

—◆—

Chapter 7

Geraldine at *Glamour*

Geraldine Stutz stood with her slim, five-foot-six frame ram-rod straight, her large brown eyes staring at the floor, her thick hair pressed into a sophisticated wave, waiting nervously.

"My dear, you are too young," Elizabeth Penrose Howkins, the editor in chief of *Glamour*, told the twenty-three-year-old before her. "And you do not have enough experience."

The pair were in Howkins's office on the nineteenth floor of a Lexington Avenue skyscraper, the Condé Nast headquarters, down the hall from *Vogue*. It was 1947, and Geraldine had been working steadily for two years, since graduating from college, in junior editing jobs at movie magazines. This was fashion, though. A position at *Glamour* was everything.

While inexperienced, Geraldine had preternatural confidence for her age and obvious flair. "I shall hire you anyway," Howkins suddenly concluded with a nod, "because you have style, and that's the only thing we can't teach you."

Geraldine could not believe her good fortune. "I didn't know beans about the fashion business," she said. "The only way I could get around New York was to think of the East River as Chicago's Lake Michigan." A girl from north of Chicago, the product of years of strict Catholic schooling, Geraldine quickly found an apartment in the West Village with several roommates and took to city life, and her job, with vigor. As associate fashion editor, Geraldine was responsible for sourcing accessories, especially shoes, that were featured in the magazine's style stories. Her first months in New York were spent venturing out on what she dubbed "safaris," wandering Manhattan's avenues and side streets, peeking through store windows, stopping into shops, ferreting out "just what the Girl-with-a-Job has been hankering for . . . and can afford."

Started in 1939, *Glamour* used the tagline "For the girl with a job," and its pages reflected readers who, like Geraldine, were young, educated, mostly white, and enthusiastically entering the workforce. The pendulum of female wage earners had swung again, from the opportunities of the 1920s, to the strictures of the Great Depression, and now back, as the World War II draft created a vacuum increasingly being filled by women workers. In addition, advances in information technologies spurred demand for office and clerical work, and as more women graduated from high schools and colleges, they had the relevant skills to fill these positions. Meanwhile, household appliances such as washing machines became more readily available, easing the path for women to have a job and also maintain a home. *Glamour* was filled with advice columns on how to conduct yourself in an interview, decorating tips for living on your own, and dinner recipes that could be thrown together after a long day at the office. Under Howkins's direction, the magazine published essays on balancing relationships and work, travelogues on where to spend your two-week holidays, and pages upon pages of colorful photographs illustrating everything from budget-friendly office wardrobes to fashionable yet functional hairstyles.

As the postwar years continued, and the ethos of the 1950s took hold, *Glamour* became ground zero for discussions on women's work outside the home. There were special "Career Issues," and articles like "Who Is Indispensable to the Boss?" that profiled female assistants to male luminaries like the journalist Edward R. Murrow and the composer Hoagy Carmichael. In one *Glamour* article, "Who Works Harder: The Wife Who Goes to the Office or the Mother of Two Who Stays Home?," there were side-by-side schedules of two women, as well as an accompanying photo essay, illustrating them busily completing their days. The magazine even housed a special conference room in its Manhattan offices, where readers were invited to come and peruse the library of career pamphlets and fact sheets on women's employment. If you couldn't make it in person, you were welcome to write in for advice.

"A job has become more than a weekly paycheck—it's our guarantee of confidence in ourselves," wrote Howkins. "We know that jobs are no longer 'amusing,' nor a stopgap until marriage, nor a tiresome way to piece out the budget. They're something a girl needs to know just as she knows her way home in the dark."

Geraldine excelled at *Glamour*. She instinctively understood the reader, since she herself was one, and she had a fashion editor's deft eye. As part of her job, Geraldine found and collaborated with illustrators, whose work accompanied her fashion features. The most famous was Andy Warhol, who was of a similar age and was newly graduated from art school when he was hired by *Glamour* to draw his first shoe illustrations. It was in 1949, for a piece Geraldine edited, titled "On the Way Up: The Walking Pump." Warhol's drawing was a wash of warm brown, with various shoe styles hanging from ladders that crisscrossed the page at steep angles. Next to the fashion feature were twin essays, "Success Is a Job in New York" and "Success Is a Career at Home," and Warhol drew the same spindly ladders in brown, but with smartly dressed young women perched on the rungs, rather than shoes, the ladders rising above sketches of the New York skyline. Warhol was "straight from the hinterlands with his portfolio under his arm," Geraldine said of the moment they met. "In so many ways, Andy came from nothing. That's the wonder of it." When Geraldine eventually left *Glamour*, she hired Warhol at her next job as well, only stopping when he grew too famous to limit himself to shoes.

At *Glamour*, Geraldine wrote occasional pieces and used her nickname Jerry for a byline. It was a habit she later broke, after being inundated with letters addressed to "Mr. Jerry Stutz," including numerous invitations to clubby men's groups. Geraldine frequently penned columns on the importance of accessories, such as how a bold scarf or a leather belt could elevate an old, tired outfit. The best accessories are not "extraneous, spur-of-the-moment purchases," she wrote, "but adaptable wearable pieces, each one right in character and color for her clothes and the life she leads." Being able to choose the correct accessory was a "sixth sense possessed by every really chic woman," Geraldine maintained. It was those women "about whom a best friend or beau says, 'You look wonderful' . . . not, 'That's a wonderful suit.'"

It was a statement that could very well have been made about Geraldine herself. In fact, her sixth sense would propel Geraldine's career, and she eventually settled on her own trademark accessories: a turban wrapped around her head, loud bangles running the length of her wrists that jangled as she gesticulated, and a dramatic diction that sounded, inexplicably, English.

Growing up with her younger sister and her mother in Evanston, a middle-class suburb on the shore of Lake Michigan, Geraldine did not have an upbringing that screamed high fashion. Her father, Alexander Hamilton "Bearcat" Stutz, was a roofer who abandoned the family when she was a teenager, and Geraldine's mother, Estelle, rarely spoke of him. Estelle, who was a devout Catholic, had worked at DuPont before her marriage. "I know she had 12 people reporting to her, but that's all I know," Geraldine later said. "I feel bad that I never discussed my mother's life and times as a career woman with her." When she married Geraldine's father, Estelle quit DuPont. But when he left and she was forced to raise her daughters single-handedly, Estelle went back to work, getting a job at a local doctor's office answering the telephones. Estelle was always exceedingly proper, a trait that Geraldine herself would adopt, with impeccable manners and grooming. Her nails were always manicured, her hair perfectly set, and every morning for work Estelle wore a suit. "She held herself like she had a two-by-four tied to her back," said Mathew Hopkins, Geraldine's nephew. "Oh, my grandmother was perfection," added his sister, Martha Hopkins, "and she was definitely overdressed for her job."

Estelle worked hard to send Geraldine and her sister, Carol, who was four years younger, to St. Scholastica, a convent school not far from their home. In high school, Geraldine was an achiever, constantly seeking recognition. She was active in a variety of clubs and "always wanted to be president of everything," one schoolmate recalled. In 1941, in her senior year, she was editor of the yearbook, and next to her class photo classmates wrote "vital personality marks her as a leader" and "'41's diplomat." Upon graduation, Geraldine won a scholarship to nearby Mundelein College, another all-girls Catholic school, where

Geraldine with her mother, Estelle, and her sister, Carol.

she planned to major in drama, with dreams of coming to New York and performing on Broadway. But after being cast in only a handful of minor roles, Geraldine, ever a realist, switched her major to journalism. If Broadway wasn't in her future, then writing would get her to Manhattan, she rationalized. Geraldine was similar to her mother in many ways, including Estelle's penchant for dressing and her emphasis on propriety, but her social conservatism was not one of them. Embracing acting, and writing, Geraldine espoused a more liberal ethos, rejecting her Catholic upbringing and what she came to regard as its repressive, damaging dogma.

It was in 1945, as a college senior, that Geraldine had her first taste of the fashion industry. She was president of Mundelein's student activities council, and it was her responsibility to produce the annual fashion show fundraiser. Geraldine booked a hotel ballroom for the runway and managed to persuade the department store Marshall Field's to donate the wardrobe for the show. The students were the models, and Geraldine was not only walking but also opening the show. The rehearsal went without a hitch, all the models, including Geraldine, prancing down the length of the room in their stylish clothes. But hours before showtime, the hotel staff waxed the floors to make the runway shine. This had the unintended consequence of rendering it dangerously slippery, and taking her first steps in front of the crowd, Geraldine skidded

ONI GILMAN | GERALDINE STUTZ | MERCEDES McCAMBRIDGE

Geraldine at a college alumnae event in 1963.

and landed flat on her behind. "I quite literally fell into it," she said of her first experience of fashion. "I looked around at the audience of 500 horrified women and made the right choice—I could either have burst into tears or laughed. I chose to laugh." Her stumble notwithstanding, Geraldine became a regular fixture at Marshall Field's, walking as a college model in the store's fashion shows to earn extra money.

Geraldine graduated from Mundelein cum laude, and bitten by the fashion bug, she joined thousands of other young fashion journalism hopefuls and applied for *Vogue*'s Prix de Paris. It was a highly competitive essay-writing contest, and its winners, who were awarded coveted *Vogue* internships, included a young Jacqueline Lee Bouvier. While Geraldine didn't win, she did draw the attention of Mary Campbell, who had been the personal secretary to the publisher, Condé Nast, and now supervised the company's personnel department. Mary told Geraldine to keep in touch. After graduating, Geraldine found a job with a movie library that booked films as entertainment at dinner parties. For one of her first selections, for a stuffy gala, Geraldine picked the movie *Nothing Sacred*, a 1937 black comedy featuring Carole Lombard, about a madcap heroine who feigns her own death. The host wasn't amused, and Geraldine was fired. But she was able to use the position to get a job in New York, working as a fashion editor for a group of movie magazines. After several weeks in Manhattan, Geraldine reached out to her Condé

Nast contact, and now here she was, with a job at *Glamour*, inhabiting the cosmopolitan lifestyle that she had longed for.

W hile at *Glamour*, Geraldine met the man who in many ways would become her father figure. Maxey Jarman was the chairman of Genesco, a large shoe conglomerate that he had grown from a small company he had inherited from his father. With reddish hair and a friendly grin, Maxey was a Southern Baptist deacon, an unapologetic Republican, and a teetotaler. He was sorely out of place among both the Seventh Avenue needle trade and the Madison Avenue fashion set. Based in Nashville, Maxey liked to begin his stockholders' meetings with a prayer and peppered his annual reports with mentions of the Almighty. Geraldine, in her work as the shoe and accessories editor at *Glamour*, had frequent interactions with Maxey. While she was a lapsed Catholic who drank socially, smoked enthusiastically, and was an avowed liberal, Geraldine liked Maxey. And even though their personal interests diverged, when it came to retailing, they nearly always found common ground.

Geraldine had been working as a fashion editor at *Glamour* for seven years, commanding increasing influence in the industry, when Maxey surprised her with a proposal. He had acquired I. Miller, a shoe manufacturer, and he wanted Geraldine to leave Condé Nast and become the fashion coordinator of its wholesale branch. Geraldine demurred, arguing that she had no experience as a merchant. Maxey pushed, assuring her that the skills she had honed at *Glamour* were all that she needed to succeed. Maxey had an instinct for spotting people's strengths, often before they recognized these characteristics in themselves. "Don't try to strengthen people in their weaknesses; it's less productive than utilizing their strengths," he liked to say. He zeroed in on Geraldine's natural leadership skills, forcing her to see it his way: How many times had she been president of her class? (Several.) Editor of the school yearbook? (Check.) Prefect of the sodality? (Affirmative.) Geraldine hadn't made such a connection before. "It just never dawned on me that this was any kind of preparation for the business world," she said. Geraldine had always been a rule follower, not an "ideas" person. "Like most young women of my background and education, I always performed on demand and never anything else."

Over time, and with his cajoling, Geraldine warmed up to the notion of quitting *Glamour* to work for Maxey. But she wanted money—a lot of it. Not long before, she had experienced a harrowing medical scare that had shaken her deeply. Geraldine was diagnosed with uterine cancer and underwent a hysterectomy that left her unable to have children. Only in her late twenties, it was a difficult blow to absorb. "That was a very tough thing that I could not have a child," she later recalled, one of her few public references to this period of her life. Grieving the loss, Geraldine sought help from Freudian analysis. "At one point, I felt I couldn't cope—it took me longer and longer to decide how to arrange a scarf around my neck. I was scared to death," she said. Therapy was expensive, and Geraldine was earning only a fashion magazine editor's salary, which was notoriously low. "I had just embarked on psychoanalysis with a borrowed $1,000 and I needed money," she recalled. "So, I demanded triple my salary, a staff, the works. And they kept saying yes." Maxey agreed to pay Geraldine $40,000 a year, or more than $400,000 in today's dollars, making her one of retail manufacturing's highest-paid women—although admittedly there wasn't much competition. "Miss Stutz' salary is a favorite luncheon topic among her friends," wrote *The New York Times*. Geraldine merely blushed and told the paper, "I'm paid awfully, awfully well."

In 1954, when Geraldine joined I. Miller, she threw herself into her new job, welcoming the distraction. She was the fashion coordinator, and as the austerity of World War II gave way to 1950s prosperity, shoe fads proliferated. Hollywood glamour became an inspiration, with pointed-toe stilettos all the rage, and new materials, like patent leather. The rise of the teenager in this decade also ushered in the popularity of saddle shoes and penny loafers. Geraldine, with her editor's eye, proved an ideal choice for the job. "Fashion rather than comfort sells women's shoes," Maxey told her, giving her free rein and a large budget. She was so successful running the wholesale business that within a year Maxey promoted Geraldine to vice president in charge of I. Miller's seventeen retail shoe stores. She oversaw a staff of two hundred, mostly men. "They took a little winning at the beginning," she said of her male underlings, "but they're a practical lot. If business gets better, they like you better." She piloted new ideas, like broadening the array of merchandise that I. Miller stores offered customers, including complementary accessories such as belts and gloves, and under Geraldine sales at the chain increased by 20 percent.

During the postwar years, there had been a consolidation of businesses across the board, and the same pattern was under way in the retail industry. Maxey had steered Genesco into becoming a major player, gobbling up dozens of shoe companies. It became so large, in fact, that the Department of Justice determined it was a monopoly and its size was damaging industry competition. Forced to switch strategies, Maxey started investing in department stores. By 1957, Genesco was valued at $230 million, or $2.4 billion in today's dollars, with stakes in businesses from Bonwit Teller to Tiffany. That year, Maxey made another purchase, acquiring a struggling, old-fashioned department store, Henri Bendel.

Henri Bendel had once been New York's most fashionable retailer, a rarefied space where film stars shopped for gowns for their New York premieres and debutantes with surnames like Whitney and Vanderbilt were outfitted for their coming-out balls. Henri Bendel, the eponymous founder, was born in a French-speaking part of Louisiana some 150 miles south of New Orleans, where his father ran a general store. After graduating from a Jesuit college in nearby St. Landry Parish, Mr. Bendel traveled to New York. He arrived on the cusp of the twentieth century, just as the city was transforming into a major metropolis. In 1897, Mr. Bendel opened a small millinery shop on East Ninth Street, selling a mix of elegant custom-made and imported hats, and eventually expanded into evening gowns and other luxury apparel. He made frequent buying trips to Paris, and with his French-tinged accent and impeccable taste he gained a devoted following among the city's most discerning society women.

"There is nothing too expensive, nothing too rare or too difficult to get, for me to bring to New York for the American woman to use to adorn her person," Mr. Bendel told *Women's Wear* in 1914. With dark hair parted in the middle and black, expressive eyes, he was a sharp and clever assessor of the female form. *Harper's Bazaar* recruited him to write columns on topics ranging from the impracticalities of the hoopskirt to the need for older women to consider their body types before dressing in the latest fads. He also wrote syndicated newspaper columns, informing readers which fur was most in vogue that season and the best hat for traveling by carriage.

With his name splashed across magazines and newspapers, Mr. Bendel became a nationally known arbiter of style. By 1907, his firm had outgrown its storefront on East Ninth Street, and it relocated to fashionable Fifth Avenue, before moving for a third and final time in 1912, to 10 West Fifty-Seventh Street. Henri Bendel was a pioneer in moving that far uptown. At the time, the area was largely residential, home to New York's richest citizens, as well as the newly opened Plaza Hotel. While Mr. Bendel became one of the first merchants to realize the area's potential, over the next several years other high-end retailers followed suit. Eventually, the block on Fifty-Seventh Street between Fifth and Sixth Avenues had so many shops that it was dubbed New York's rue de la Paix, after the Parisian shopping street. Henri Bendel, meanwhile, was known as the largest, most exclusive retailer for gowns and hats in New York City, employing eleven hundred men and women "and carrying the accounts of some of the wealthiest and smartest dressed people in the city," according to *Women's Wear*.

Mr. Bendel's store was a technological marvel, with workrooms that featured light fixtures specifically designed to be bright without casting a shadow and a fur vault lined on all four walls with cooling pipes that kept the air a steady eighteen degrees Celsius, the ideal chill for preservation. Henri Bendel sold only the most opulent and extravagant items, accompanied by equally rarefied price tags. With such expensive merchandise, the store began holding wildly popular semiannual clearance sales. Like the famed Barneys Warehouse sale decades later, when Mr. Bendel held his massive sales, throngs of shoppers arrived to pick through racks of couture items at deep discounts. It became such a to-do that traffic along Fifty-Seventh Street gridlocked and Mr. Bendel was forced to open his doors at 7:00 a.m. to satisfy demand.

Mr. Bendel was known for spending all day at his store, walking the selling floors, working closely with sales staff, and personally handling important clients. Concerned about his store's longevity, and wanting to ensure that it would outlast him, in 1923 he made the unusual decision of distributing 45 percent of Henri Bendel stock, valued at $1.8 million, or $30 million in today's dollars, to his employees. Long-serving tailors, hat trimmers, and saleswomen received equity, one getting a windfall worth $25,000, more than $400,000 in today's dollars. "My purpose," Mr. Bendel said at the time, "is to perpetuate the house, as well as reward its employees for faithful services which have made possible its upbuilding." He had no plans to retire, he said. "Many firms enjoy their heyday and go to smash. I hope that the division of stock will keep up the interest of employees, making the business perpetual."

It was a prescient move, for a little more than a decade later, in 1936, Mr. Bendel died of a heart attack at his home on Park Avenue. The sixty-nine-year-old widower, whose Parisian wife died decades earlier, lived with Abraham Beekman Bastedo. Bastedo was a Bendel employee of more than thirty years and the store's vice president and treasurer. In his will, Mr. Bendel called him a "faithful employee" and bequeathed Bastedo $200,000, or $4.2 million in today's dollars, as well as the use of his estate in Stamford, Connecticut, and half of his stock in the store. Bastedo also took over the running of the business, but he wasn't the visionary leader that Mr. Bendel had been. The store began to fall out of favor, and several years after his death *The New York Times* called Henri Bendel's an "old and conservative house," its fashions promoting "distinction rather than so-called 'high style.'"

In 1953, Bastedo died and was buried next to Mr. Bendel in Valhalla, New York. The store's future was murky, and rumors circulated that the famed department store would be sold. In 1955, the store changed hands for the first time in its history. Then, two years later, it flipped again, this time to Maxey Jarman. The businessman was confident that he could reverse the store's fortunes, returning Henri Bendel to its former position as leader of New York's beau monde. And he knew exactly who could accomplish such a feat—the young former fashion editor who spun straw into gold.

Chapter 8

>—<

Hortense Has a Rival

In the spring of 1939, Salvador Dalí, the Surrealist artist, stayed up all night decorating the windows of Bonwit Teller. He found an old wax dummy that he outfitted in a negligee made from several strategically placed green coque feathers, a long blond wig that was crawling with beetles, and tears of blood running down her face. He posed her as if she were about to step into a claw-foot, aluminum bathtub, which he had covered in Persian lamb wool and half filled with dirty water. Emerging from within the grimy depths were one hundred wax arms holding in their hands small mirrors that reflected back the mannequin's face. Dalí called his window "Day," and it was intended to illustrate the parable of Narcissus, the Greek myth detailing the affliction of excessive vanity. For Dalí's second window, which ran beside the first, and which he had dubbed "Night," a mannequin stretched across a bed, her figure covered with a black satin sheet. The bed's headboard was in the shape of a water buffalo, or, in Dalí's words, "the decapitated head and the savage hoofs of a great somnambulist buffalo extenuated by a thousand years of sleep," while the mattress was made to look as if it were burning, or, the "smoldering coals of desire."

After some twelve hours of laboring over the Surrealist images, the artist went back to his suite at the St. Moritz and fell fast asleep. Meanwhile, Bonwit Teller opened and, unveiling its new windows, began receiving a litany of complaints from customers and passersby who found the work disturbing and obscene. By 2:00 p.m., the store had fielded so much criticism that it ordered the scantily clad wax figure in the Day window be replaced with a traditional mannequin dressed in a tailored suit. At 4:00 p.m., Dalí awoke from his nap and strolled a few blocks to the store to appreciate his creation. When he arrived and discovered that it had been altered, however, the temperamental artist was enraged. He marched up to the eleventh floor of the department store and burst into the office of Sara Pennoyer, the director of publicity and the author of *Polly Tucker*. There, in a mixture of French and Spanish, Dalí roared how he was "hired to do a work of art" and refused to be "associated with typical window dressing." Hortense, who wasn't there at the time, later acknowledged the artist's "unquestionable genius," but noted that "these particular examples were perhaps a bit on the extreme side and slightly too macabre for Fifth Avenue shop windows."

A store lawyer who was meeting with Sara Pennoyer when Dalí interrupted happened to speak Spanish, and he tried to mediate. But before he could succeed, the artist stormed out and rushed back downstairs, brushing past stunned employees, and stepped through the side entrance of the Day window. Letting out a loud "Caramba!" Dalí gave the Persian-wool-lined tub a powerful shove. The heavy object was hurled through the oversized window, where it dangled above Fifth Avenue, caught on jagged shards of glass. Dalí was heaved through the window along with his tub, but stood up unharmed on the side- walk, gamely brushing glass from his pants. "I really have tremendous sympathy with what must have been his first stunned reaction," said Hortense, but "it was quite a dramatic exit."

The disturbance drew the notice of two policemen who happened to be passing by. They arrested Dalí, and several hours later the much- chastised Catalan Surrealist sat on a hard wood bench at night court in lower Manhattan, eating canned pears and drinking milk, his lawyer and his wife beside him. The sullen Dalí pleaded guilty to malicious mischief and was fined $500, the exact price of his commission. "These are some of the privileges that an artist with temperament seems to enjoy," the judge noted dryly.

Since the very inception of the department store, windows were critically important to their success, nearly as significant as the qual- ity of the store's designer dresses or the variety of its merchandise. If at their worst they caused drama, at their best window displays lured

The hole in Bonwit Teller's Fifth Avenue window after
Salvador Dalí crashed through the pane in a fit of rage.

customers who might otherwise pass by without a glance. The modern
window display was born when the dry goods emporiums gave way to
the department store, and small windows showcasing careless, hap-
hazard piles of wares were replaced with plate glass and dazzling, ingenious tableaux. In the early years, as merchants realized the importance
of windows and window-shopping became a new pastime, some even
hired professional "window gazers" to draw crowds to their spectacles.
Windows were the perfect selling medium, teasing potential customers by offering enticing visuals but closing off senses such as smell and
touch. This drew them inside, where they could satisfy their curiosity,
smelling and touching at will. By the 1940s, there was a retail rule of
thumb that one-third of all sales could be credited to impulse purchases
resulting from window displays.

A noteworthy pioneer of the display window was L. Frank Baum, the
author of *The Wonderful Wizard of Oz*. Baum was an actor and show-
man who held a variety of jobs to support his theater work, including
intermittent stints as a traveling salesman. He eventually settled with
his wife's family in South Dakota and throughout the late 1880s and
early 1890s watched as the small general stores and dry goods empori-

ums around his town began experimenting with the display techniques that were just then taking form. When Baum and his family relocated to Chicago, the home of Marshall Field's, he became fascinated by the new display strategies he saw all around him. Even as he was writing the children's stories that would make him famous, in 1897, Baum launched *The Show Window*, a monthly journal that featured articles advising merchants on how to use windows to attract consumers' attention. Drawing on his experience in the theater and as a traveling salesman, Baum recommended proper lighting techniques, advised on the depths and dimensions of windows, and urged the use of mechanical displays. The following year, Baum founded the National Association of Window Trimmers, which soon boasted two hundred members. But the wild success of *The Wonderful Wizard of Oz*, published in 1900— the famous movie wouldn't come for another thirty-nine years—caused Baum to leave retail behind.

By the time Baum published his blockbuster book, window displays were catching on, and the art form was developing. In addition to advertising merchandise, windows were being used to draw attention to current affairs, such as when, in 1916, the Chicago department store Carson Pirie Scott used its windows to support women's suffrage in anticipation of the National Women's Party convention; or when Bloomingdale's set aside a "neighborhood window," donating the space to highlight various local charities. During World War I, windows were used to promote the sale of war bonds and were deemed so important that men who designed and installed the displays were exempted from military service. By the time that Bonwit Teller featured Salvador Dalí's controversial windows, these displays had become finely tuned, a celebrated, weekly spectacle, with crowds lining up in anticipation as the curtain rose on some extravagant new offering. Even as they were increasingly common, window displays did not lose their ability to entertain, shock, or, most important, draw a crowd.

Like Bonwit Teller, Lord & Taylor was famous for its store windows, such as one display with mannequins in swimsuits frolicking in actual sand and beach grass and a perfume exhibit that used giant atomizers to spray scent onto crowds outside. During an unseasonably warm winter, with November temperatures soaring to seventy-eight degrees, Lord &

Taylor had been bemoaning the lackluster sales of winter coats when the display director thought to fill the windows with a faux snowstorm. Snowflakes were created from Epsom salts and cornflakes that were spray-painted white, and leaf blowers were hidden behind the display to make the flakes appear as if they were gusting. The sound of howling wind bolstered the effect, with record players placed on the balcony, the noise blasting over loudspeakers onto the sidewalk below. Instead of coats, a sign was placed amid the storm that read "It's Coming," followed by a scrawled inscription, "Sooner or Later," which looked as if it had been made by a child's finger. Over the next twenty-four hours, the sales of winter coats doubled, and for days after cars stopped in front of the store as awestruck children got out to gape. But while the windows were often extravagant, Lord & Taylor also employed restraint, occasionally pulling back to create pared-down, yet equally arresting, images. In 1938, with the country still struggling through the Great Depression, at the height of the Christmas season, rather than lure shoppers with the typical festive merchandise, it emphasized the holiday's spirit over its commercial appeal, keeping its Fifth Avenue display bare except for a series of large gold Christmas bells that chimed peacefully, against a simple velvet backdrop.

A Lord & Taylor window display in 1955.

❧·❦

While Hortense was managing the egos of Surrealist artists, her all-male board of directors, and the many hundreds of employees she supervised (not to mention motherhood and a failing marriage), Jackie Cochran was enjoying a whirlwind romance with Hortense's husband. Jackie was a decade and a half younger than her rival, and she eschewed the traditional values that Hortense aspired to, embracing instead a life of adventure and thrill.

Jackie's origin story was rife with vivid, unusual details—and numerous fabrications. Among her claims was that she grew up in poverty in Florida's sawmill camps and cotton fields (true), that she was an orphan (false), and that her childhood was wild and itinerant (mostly true). Jackie, who was born Bessie Pittman, claimed that she had her first job at age eight, pushing a cart filled with spools of bobbins in a cotton mill, and that she used her first paycheck to buy her first pair of shoes—red high-heeled pumps. With only two years of formal schooling, Jackie said that she learned her ABCs by watching boxcars passing on the railroad tracks behind her house and subsisted on a meager diet of wild plants and fish from the local river. By the time Jackie was ten, she claimed, she was living on her own in Georgia, working fourteen to sixteen hours a day at a beauty shop. Charismatic, with a good figure, blond hair, and big brown eyes, Jackie had "the most beautiful skin I've ever seen," said a friend. "It was like the loveliest whipped cream." By the time she was fourteen, she was pregnant. Jackie married the father, a salesman, Robert Cochran, five years older than her, and three months later gave birth to their son, Robert Cochran Jr.

The relationship soon broke up, and Jackie left her child with her parents in Florida and headed to Montgomery, Alabama. There, she worked odd jobs, often at beauty salons, eventually saving up to buy a car. She purchased the Model T Ford that she had told Floyd about at their first meeting at the Surf Club, and she used the car to get a job as a traveling saleswoman. When the car's engine broke down, which it often did, Jackie fixed it herself, without the help of the car's manual, since her reading skills were too rudimentary to decipher it. Jackie also claimed to have trained as a nurse and boasted that her most interesting surgery was a Cesarean section, which she performed on a little person, a member of a traveling circus wintering in Montgomery.

Jackie's young life carried on as a series of fantastical journeys until 1925, when, at age nineteen, tragedy struck. Jackie's toddler son had been playing with matches in his grandparents' outhouse, when he accidentally set the structure on fire. He survived long enough to explain what had occurred, before succumbing to his burns. Jackie was devastated, immediately returning to her parents' home for the funeral. But after a few weeks, she had little money and nothing else to keep her there, so Jackie continued on. She journeyed to Mobile, Pensacola, Biloxi, and Philadelphia, working as a beautician and a traveling saleswoman and dating several navy pilots along the way. In 1929, just as Floyd was minting his fortune, she took the train to New York City. Stepping off the platform, Bessie Pittman rechristened herself Jacqueline Cochran. She made her way to Antoine's, the salon at Saks Fifth Avenue, where she charmed her way into a job as a manicurist.

Floyd was a shrewd observer of people, delivering his few, choice remarks in a wry deadpan. Jackie's working-girl persona and brash behavior possessed for him a singular mystique. In Forest Hills, Floyd had socialized with sheltered women who spent their days playing cards and gossiping, and he took inordinate pleasure watching his girlfriend's colorful antics enliven even the staidest dinner parties. Floyd called Jackie "the most interesting person I have ever met." She always claimed that it was Floyd's brain, and not his money, that drew her to him. "He could have been a small-town lawyer on a winter vacation in Miami for all I cared," Jackie said. "Every orphan dreams of marrying a millionaire, but I had no idea at first that Floyd Odlum was worth so much money."

After meeting Floyd in Miami in the winter of 1932, Jackie returned to New York and to her job as a manicurist. While waiting for Floyd to call her, she thought back on their conversation at the Surf Club and how she had told him she wanted to go on the road again, to be a traveling saleswoman hawking cosmetics. Floyd had responded that given the Depression, she would have to fly to cover enough distance to earn sufficient money. It wasn't the first time that Jackie had considered getting her pilot's license, "but this time it made sense, practical sense," Jackie said. After they started regularly seeing each other, Jackie took a vacation from Antoine's and began flying lessons at nearby Roosevelt Field on Long Island. She had a clear talent for engines and machinery, and in a matter of weeks Jackie earned her wings. With Floyd's financial backing, she quit her job to pursue her new passion.

When Jackie earned her license, in the summer of 1933, female aviators were still rare, and as she racked up transcontinental speed and altitude records, she began distinguishing herself. Over the next three decades, Jackie petitioned Eleanor Roosevelt to create a women's division of the U.S. Army Air Forces; she became the first woman to fly a bomber across the Atlantic, the first woman to break the sound barrier, the first woman to break the altitude record, and the first to break the women's world speed record.

Her accomplishments were heady, and she proved stiff competition for Hortense. They were still married, and Floyd asked his girlfriend to keep their relationship quiet. "He didn't want me to talk about him," Jackie said. "With the money he had amassed and the notoriety neither of us needed I saw no reason to put our relationship before the public's eye." According to Jackie, by the time they started dating, Floyd's marriage "was over except on paper." Yet they would continue the affair for nearly four more years. It wasn't until the fall of 1935, almost exactly one year to the day that Hortense had been appointed Bonwit's president, that she traveled to Reno, Nevada, and obtained a divorce. Hortense cited "extreme cruelty" as the reason for the marriage's dissolution. For the rest of her life, anytime Jackie was mentioned, Hortense dismissed her as "nothing but a manicurist" and "déclassé."

Stanley and Bruce did not take their father's years-long indiscretion well. Shortly after Hortense filed for divorce from Floyd, twenty-year-old Stanley was thrown out of Dartmouth for drinking. Several months later, in May 1936, Floyd and Jackie picked the date of her thirtieth birthday for their wedding, the same date that Floyd had made his fateful call to her at Antoine's. But two days before their ceremony, Stanley acted out and eloped, marrying a girl a few years older than him whom he knew from Forest Hills. While Bruce didn't do anything quite so rash, like his mother, he felt nothing but disdain for his stepmother.

When Jackie opined, as she frequently did, that she hoped to be the first woman on the moon, Bruce would quip that he hoped it was "a one-way trip."

Stanley and his new wife remained in New York near Hortense, while Bruce chose to attend the University of Southern California, moving closer to where his father was based. Floyd and Jackie had purchased a sprawling, seven-hundred-acre ranch near Indio, in the Coachella Valley, with citrus tree groves, a golf course, horse stables, a skeet range, and a staff of servants. The ranch also employed telephone operators, secretaries, and bookkeepers so that Floyd could run his business from there. He had begun suffering from painful bouts of rheumatoid arthritis, and the ranch also boasted an Olympic-sized heated swimming pool, where Floyd would spend hours, even conducting work meetings while soaking in the shallow end.

At the ranch, Jackie, now a famous aviator, and Floyd, a millionaire businessman, entertained a constant stream of celebrity guests. There was the dashing, eccentric business magnate Howard Hughes, also a pilot, who once arrived for a formal dinner at the ranch dressed in sneakers and enormous pants that he'd belted with a rope, proudly

Amelia Earhart (left) and Jackie Cochran (right)
in 1936.

announcing he had purchased three pairs of the unflattering trousers for just $1. President Dwight D. Eisenhower was also a friend, and he frequently used the ranch as his office, later staying in a guesthouse on the property to write his memoir. Jackie was close with several famous fliers, including Chuck Yeager, who wrote the foreword to her autobiography *The Stars at Noon*, and the trailblazing Amelia Earhart, who also often stayed at the ranch. She usually arrived without her husband, the publisher George P. Putnam, whom Jackie did not like, and stayed there even when Jackie wasn't home, sleeping in her friend's bedroom. Amelia also occasionally took part in Floyd and Jackie's growing interest in psychic phenomena and their unusual hobby of extrasensory perception. The couple liked to practice "automatic writing," covering their eyes and, putting pencil to paper, uncontrollably writing messages that they believed stemmed from the subconscious. Jackie believed that her psychic abilities saved her life several times while in the air and that they enabled Floyd to pull off his financial feats. She also claimed to have a psychic connection with Amelia and wrote of being plagued with "hunches" before Amelia took off for her final, ill-fated flight. When Amelia disappeared, Jackie claimed that she told George Putnam where to find his wife, but to no avail. "If my strange ability was worth anything it should have saved Amelia," Jackie later wrote.

Hortense was foremost a creature of her generation. Unlike Jackie, who reveled in attention, Hortense emphasized the quiet dignity of traditional female roles and downplayed her numerous achievements at Bonwit Teller. When Hortense filed for divorce from Floyd, she was making regular appearances on the radio, was a frequent speaker at women's clubs, and was the subject of a plethora of adulatory newspaper profiles. She was a national household name, with *Woman's Day* placing her between Florence Nightingale and Marie Curie in a feature that queried readers on which woman they admired most. Yet in interviews and in her personal writings, Hortense often seemed uncomfortable with her career, preferring instead to focus on her identity as a wife and mother. Her demeanor reflected the overwhelming ethos of the time and echoed in the broader culture, such as in the popular 1942 film

Woman of the Year. The movie starred Katharine Hepburn as a globe-trotting reporter and Spencer Tracy as her aggrieved sportswriter husband, and revolved around Tracy's character's frustration with his wife's insistence on prioritizing her career ambitions above their relationship. In the final scene, Hepburn's character realizes her mistake and, ruing her choices, goes to the kitchen to cook her husband breakfast, vowing from then on to be the perfect wife. While played for laughs, the message that underpinned the perfect Hollywood ending was clear.

But it was too late for Hortense to reverse her storyline. Her marriage was over, and her career successes could not make up for her loneliness. Stanley and Bruce were no longer living with her, and after a long day at the store Hortense's chauffeur would drive her black Packard the twenty-five minutes to her castle-like home in Forest Hills, where she retreated to the den with a sandwich, eating her cold dinner and reviewing the day's receipts. "I am alone now," she said in an interview with *Women's Wear Daily* as she sat in her office at Bonwit Teller. "Last night I went down the freight elevator after seven o'clock and I expect that will be my schedule for some little time." Eventually, the large, empty house became too much, and Hortense traded it in for a series of rooms at the stylish Drake Hotel on Park Avenue in midtown Manhattan. The expansive floor-through apartment, with its shelves of leather-bound books and its large dining room with mirrored walls, could not compare with the affection she felt for the home where she had once happily raised her sons. "It still breaks my heart to think of it. Now I have no home," she said. "This is just a place where I eat and sleep."

Despite her circumstances, Hortense clung to the notion that she was just like the women with whom she used to socialize in Forest Hills—a gracious, elegant, sophisticated wife who hosted dinner parties, cared for her children, and prioritized her home. She carefully maintained her appearance, still having her hair done with the other wealthy wives at Antoine's and remaining youthful and trim by eating a strict breakfast of two raw egg yolks in a glass of orange juice, smoking endless cigarettes, and smothering her face with pricey, age-defying creams. She also tried, as quickly as possible, to shed her status as a single woman. In fact, it barely stuck for five months.

In need of a change of pace, several weeks after the divorce was finalized, Hortense joined Bonwit Teller buyers attending the season's couture fashion shows, sailing with them to Paris. While there, she rushed from Chanel to Elsa Schiaparelli to Madeleine Vionnet, watching models sashay by in lace and tulle. In the midst of her frenetic schedule, Hortense met a man. Porfirio Dominici was a Dominican-born doctor and diplomat, the chargé d'affaires of the Dominican Republic legation to France, Belgium, and Italy. Dark-haired and handsome, with a seductive charm, Porfirio swept the new divorcée off her feet. She was so carried away by the excitement and thrill that only weeks into their courtship Porfirio proposed, and Hortense agreed to marry for the third time. The wedding was in Montmartre, at the town hall, with a reception following at the Ritz. The newlyweds sailed back to New York, where Porfirio began practicing medicine and "Mrs. Dominici" relished her regained status as a wife. But the romance was short-lived, and in 1938 Hortense found herself, yet again, dissolving her marriage. In the separation papers, she alleged that Porfirio had "misrepresented his financial and social status." Mrs. Dominici went back to being Mrs. Odlum.

Many years would pass before Hortense got a last stab at love. But, like her three previous marriages, the fourth was similarly ill-fated. Nearly two decades after her whirlwind Parisian love affair, Hortense married Angel Kouyoumdjisky, a mercurial Bulgarian-born financier who spied for the Americans during World War II. They wed in an intimate ceremony in New York, with only Stanley and his wife there to serve as witnesses. However, like her starter marriage to Floyd Manges, the Los Angeles car salesman, and her last union, with Porfirio, the relationship with Kouyoumdjisky was brief, a mere footnote. In the end, despite her many attempts, Floyd Odlum, the man with whom she had shared a two-decade-long marriage, children, and a business, was the one person whom Hortense could not shake, front and center even as she struggled to move on, a relationship that haunted her until her death.

⋟⋞

As Jackie and Floyd's adventurous life continued apace, Hortense grew increasingly isolated and unhappy. She moved to Los Angeles, to be nearer to Bruce and his family, but she stayed only briefly, before returning to New York. "I know it was Tenny's interest in Bruce and his children that prompted her to move to Los Angeles," Floyd wrote to his brother-in-law, but "it was the lack of interest on Bruce's part in his Mother that prompted her to leave." Floyd was writing to Hortense's brother so that he could pick up her things; Hortense had fled back to New York in such a hurry that she had left everything behind.

The more sour Hortense became in her personal life, the more bitterly she spoke about women's careers. In 1937, three years into her Bonwit presidency, she was giving interviews and saying things like "Women executives in the field of retailing are receiving more and more recognition, a recognition to which they are entitled on their own merits." But by 1938, she was adopting a more circumspect tone. A "hard boiled" businesswoman "scares me to death," she said. Her advice to women aspiring to fashion careers included "Don't be tough, don't wear the pants," and "The greatest asset of the businesswoman is feminine charm and feminine clothes." In 1939, Hortense was more strident. "I never had the least desire to be a businesswoman—never in all the world—and I don't like business any more now than when I came to it," she told *Women's Wear Daily*. "My home always has come first, and the biggest satisfaction I get is to urge someone else on to success." Hortense insisted that despite what readers might think, being president of a department store was not a job or—heaven forbid—a career. "It embarrasses me to tears when people tell me what a marvelous work I have done here, for whatever I have done has not really been in a business capacity."

In 1940, after six years at the helm of Bonwit Teller, Hortense quit. During her tenure, she had transformed a department store that was on the brink of bankruptcy into one of the most successful retail operations in the country, leading it to record-breaking profits and a nearly 200 percent surge in sales. "When I came to Bonwit Teller, it was nip and tuck whether we'd be able to keep the store open from day to day," she said, in her retirement speech to her employees. "I have always told you I am not a businesswoman," she added. "I never wanted to be one, and I'm not going to be one now that I can look at the store with a clear conscience and see that it's ready to carry on by itself." She concluded the talk by saying, "As you all know, I tackled this job because there was no one else to do it at the time. I never planned to make it my life's work."

Hortense's longtime lieutenant, William Holmes, was named as her replacement. In a filing with the Securities and Exchange Commission six months after her retirement, Hortense's salary was listed at $18,978, or $377,000 in today's dollars. Holmes was only a vice president, but he was paid more than twice as much, with a salary of $42,184, or $838,000 in today's dollars. When Holmes was elected president, his salary rose to $50,000, or more than $1 million today.

Hortense's sudden retirement came as a surprise to her colleagues. She had informed Bonwit Teller's board of directors that she wanted to step down, but they had assumed it would not be for some time. Instead, at the next board meeting only a few months later, Hortense not only reiterated her desire to quit but told them she was doing so immediately—within the week. She was forty-nine years old, with no children at home and no partner. It isn't clear why she had a sudden compulsion to depart, but Hortense did agree to remain on as chairwoman of the board.

She used her extra time to campaign for Wendell L. Willkie in his bid to upset President Roosevelt's third term. She "loathed" Eleanor Roosevelt, she said, and in the buildup to the election Hortense went on radio shows and wrote newspaper columns praising Mrs. Willkie. "We all know that in back of every great man, somewhere along the line, was a great woman whose love and inspiration was his guiding star," Hortense said. "Mrs. Willkie is all that to her husband—modest and simple—great, too, because she is courageous, loyal, understanding, tolerant and kind and asks no reward." After Willkie lost, Hortense threw herself into war work, leading bond drives, giving interviews where she urged women not to hoard items, and peeling eggs and making turkey sandwiches for the canteen at the Merchant Seamen's Club.

During these years, Stanley, who remained in New York, became increasingly troubled. Married, with two young children, he had held a number of positions at Atlas, working for his father. But the jobs were mostly for show, with nominal responsibilities. Bruce, who had married and lived on Floyd's ranch, also worked for his father. While Floyd was careful with his health, never eating red meat or drinking coffee or tea and totally abstaining from alcohol, Stanley was the opposite of his father, wild and a heavy drinker. As the firstborn son of an immensely successful Wall Street financier, Stanley was constantly struggling to find his purpose and to escape Floyd's long, imposing shadow.

Stanley's alcoholism had been a problem since he was a teenager. When he was seventeen, just four days after his high school graduation, Stanley was driving not far from his home in Forest Hills when he rammed into a vehicle. While the other driver escaped relatively unharmed, his passenger, a sixty-one-year-old former transit worker from Brooklyn, was hurled through the windshield and thrown onto the pavement, where he died. Stanley was driving without a license and was likely drunk. He was arrested and charged with homicide, and called his father from the police station. Floyd furiously contacted his extensive list of politically connected friends, and within the week Stanley was exonerated. But the accident marked only the beginning of Stanley's troubles, and over the years Floyd's son continued to have alcohol-infused run-ins with the police.

In 1943, Stanley enlisted with the U.S. Army Air Forces, serving as a bombardier. He flew B-17s on nearly two dozen missions, until September 1944, when he was shot down over enemy lines in Austria. Stanley was captured and sent to a prisoner of war camp, one of some nine thousand Allied fliers who were interned in the far north of Germany. Hortense had only just been told of her son's fate when she gave an especially raw interview to the newspaper PM. "I feel completely lost because nobody needs me," she told the interviewer. "A woman must be needed by someone. That is her role in life." Blaming work for taking away precious time that she could have spent mothering, and for causing much of her personal disappointments, Hortense voiced a deep regret. "The only career I ever wanted was in the home," she said. "I was forced to take the job. I worked like a Trojan. . . . The whole thing leaves me cold."

The Real Rachel Menken

Beatrice Fox Auerbach at her desk at G. Fox.

Among the long list of Don Draper's romantic conquests in the television series *Mad Men*, Rachel Menken, the savvy, beautiful president of Menken's department store, stood out. Driven and ambitious, she charmed Don with her intelligence and witty banter, even as she commanded a conference room full of ego-driven admen in designer suits. Rachel, who broke it off with the infamously desirable Casanova, is often cited as "the one who got away," and even earned her own thread on Reddit, "Don Draper's True Love?"

Rachel's real-life inspiration was Beatrice Fox Auerbach, an even more impressive woman when it came to running the country's largest family-owned department store, albeit, perhaps, without the same movie star looks.

Like Rachel, Beatrice was Jewish and single when she took over the store from her father, following his death in 1938. (Unlike Rachel, Beatrice was widowed with two children, and many surmised that, while not exactly dating Don Draper types, Beatrice did have a romantic relationship with her lawyer.)

Menken's department store was a stand-in for G. Fox, a staple of Connecticut life for more than a century. G. Fox was founded by Beatrice's grandfather Gershon in 1848, but it was his granddaughter who transformed it into one of America's most successful stores. When not walking the aisles wearing white gloves, swiping the underside of counters, and running her finger along shelves to check for dust, Beatrice sat on a raised stool in her office, placing low chairs for guests, to obscure the fact that she stood barely five feet tall. Fastidious and tough, "Mrs. Auerbach brooks no opposition," wrote the publisher Bennett Cerf, "she doesn't even recognize it. When she sails through her domain, even the steel girders tremble slightly."

Beatrice claimed a number of firsts. During the Great Depression, when companies regularly fired married women employees, Beatrice not only hired them but also frequently promoted them. In fact, G. Fox did not let go of a single worker during the entire period of economic depression. In 1942, she again broke with precedent by employing African Americans in sales positions and management roles. "G. Fox is one of the few department stores in the United States where a Negro employee may say with quiet confidence, 'I'm working hard for the next step up,'" wrote Marjorie Greene in the magazine *Opportunity* in 1948. That year, G. Fox had 2,500 employees, 250 of whom were Black, working in sales, as telephone dispatchers, clerks, gift wrappers, seamstresses, floor stock handlers, and elevator operators. Lester Holmes was an African American former GI who was hired to handle warehouse stock and was eventually promoted to head of the department that sold sheets and blankets. Anaretha Shaw, a Black mother of six, was a personnel counselor, responsible for recruiting and hiring G. Fox employees. When she resigned, Sarah Murphy, a Black major in the Women's Army Corps and a graduate of New York University's personnel administration program, replaced her. While Sarah was trained in personnel work, she wasn't familiar with retail selling, so as part of her introduction to the store G. Fox made her a saleswoman in the lingerie department. That was particularly notable, because lingerie departments rarely hired Black sales staff, on the assumption that white customers would object to Black employees handling their intimates. The

National Urban League recognized Beatrice's efforts, and the NAACP gave her a lifetime membership.

"She was a tiny little thing. Very petite and thin, almost fragile," said Janet Cramer, who worked at G. Fox while in high school in the early 1960s. Her jobs were in the swimsuit department (it was awful telling women they looked good when they didn't), jewelry (she was relocated after making a billing mistake), and the Russell Stover chocolate counter (her favorite). Janet was the recipient of a scholarship from Beatrice to attend the University of Connecticut's pediatric nursing program, and she visited her boss's office for the first and only time to thank her. "She was proud that she could help a nice Jewish girl like me become a nurse," Janet recalled of the conversation. A few years after Janet left for nursing school, Beatrice decided to sell G. Fox to the May department store chain for $41 million, or more than $380 million in today's dollars. When news of the sale broke, Beatrice said she would give most of the money away. "One thing you can be certain of is that I won't be spending it on yachts and horses," she quipped.

The Jewish community had a long, storied history in the retail industry. Numerous Jewish immigrants from Germany, eastern Europe, and elsewhere arrived in America at the turn of the nineteenth century, presiding over stores that became household names. In New York, there was Isidor Straus and his brother Nathan, Joseph Bloomingdale and his brother Lyman, and Horace Saks and his cousin Bernard Gimbel. From F&R Lazarus, to Kaufmann's, to Neiman Marcus, Jewish merchants became well known throughout the country. Jewish women were also merchants, many of whom worked at these early stores and carved out careers in sales and advertising, and some, like Beatrice, either inherited leadership roles or founded stores themselves.

Mary Ann Cohen was the Dutch-born daughter of a rabbi. She married the Englishman Isaac Magnin at age fifteen, and the couple had eight children. Mary Ann and her brood immigrated to America in the early 1870s and headed straight for San Francisco. There, Isaac got a job at Gump's, a department store, and Mary Ann opened her own small shop out of the family's home, where she used her sewing skills to create lingerie for the wealthy ladies of Nob Hill. Mary Ann's offerings became so popular that she soon expanded to bridal gowns and baby clothes, ordering lace and linen from

Europe. Although her merchandise was expensive, she did a brisk business with the help of the city's carriage trade, and by 1880, Mary Ann had her own store in downtown San Francisco. She named it I. Magnin, after her husband.

When the 1906 earthquake destroyed the city, I. Magnin was leveled along with the rest of downtown, but a large loan enabled the family to rebuild, and by 1912 the store was doing so well that it expanded into its first branch location. I. Magnin specialized in high-end goods, from $500 day dresses to $5,000 evening gowns. One customer placed a $25,000 order for dresses every year—over the phone. Another flew to San Francisco to have her measurements taken, then asked that every Norman Norell–designed gown with sequins be sent to her by mail. For the first three years, the I. Magnin buyer sent her dresses and in return received effusive thank-you notes. But then, suddenly, the customer stopped writing. The buyer continued to send the sequined gowns and continued to receive checks for the dresses, but there was no comment as to whether the customer liked the buyer's selections. Several years later, the buyer finally discovered the reason. He was in the customer's hometown when he bumped into her at a dinner party. She had put on weight since they had first met, and decided it was easier to pay thousands of dollars for the dresses every year than to write back and admit she was now two sizes larger.

By the turn of the century, Mary Ann's sons, but not her daughters, joined her in business. Still, the aging matriarch had no intention of retiring. Mary Ann continued working at the store, arriving each afternoon at 3:00 for her daily inspection, even after she was confined to a wheelchair, until she died at age ninety-four, in 1943. One son, Joseph, did break away from the family after falling in love with a millinery worker at the store, refusing to abide by his mother's rule that family members not fraternize with the staff. Joseph married her, then opened a competing store nearby, the Joseph Magnin Company, which became famous for handling the 1967 trousseau of the presidential daughter Lynda Bird Johnson.

Another Jewish female merchant of renown was Lena Himmelstein, the creator of Lane Bryant. Lena did not have very auspicious beginnings: her parents died in a pogrom in their Lithuanian village just days after she was born, in 1879. Her grandparents raised Lena before shipping her off to America at age sixteen. She was booked on a passage accompanied by distant relatives, but no one informed her that she was making the transatlantic journey for the express purpose of marrying the family's homely son upon landing in New York. Lena refused to go along with the scheme and instead joined her sister, who was already living in New York, and got a job as a seamstress in a sweatshop for $1 a week. At age twenty, in 1899, Lena finally chose to marry, but her husband, David Bryant, a Brooklyn jeweler, died of tuberculosis soon after their first child was born. All of the couple's money had been spent on her husband's illness, and the only thing left of value was a pair of diamond earrings that he had given Lena as a wedding gift. With little choice, Lena pawned the diamond earrings to make a down payment on a sewing machine and began to sew negligees and tea gowns to support herself and her infant son. She earned a loyal following of customers, and she was successful enough that in 1904 she opened a store on upper Fifth Avenue in Harlem, the sign on the door reading "Bridle Shop." The error was thanks to an illiterate sign painter—the store specialized in bridal gowns, not headgear for horses.

While Lena had racked up misfortunes, some of her trials turned fortuitous. Another spelling mistake would ignite her career. While she was running her small store, in 1907, a customer requested an outfit she could wear while pregnant, and Lena fashioned one of her tea gowns with an accordion-pleated skirt to camouflage her belly. Instead of a belt, she attached the skirt to the bodice with an elastic band. The dress caught on, and Lena was soon inundated with orders. Excited by her success in originating what would become the maternity wear market, Lena was quickly scribbling a deposit slip at the bank one day, when she transposed two of the letters of her name into "Lane." At first, she was too embarrassed to correct the misspelling, but then she realized how much she liked it. When her success with maternity wear enabled her to move to larger quarters on West Thirty-Eighth Street, the sign she hung above the door read "Lane Bryant."

While Lena's company was booming with its maternity line, the new market was not without its challenges. Most significantly, newspapers held to prudish rules that forbade advertisements for maternity wear, deeming it unseemly. In 1911, *The New York Herald* finally broke with precedent, and after advertising, Lena saw her sales double within the year. "It is no longer the fashion nor the practice for expectant mothers to stay in seclusion," read an early Lane Bryant advertisement. "Doctors, nurses and psychologists agree that at this time a woman should think and live as normally as possible. . . . Lane Bryant has originated maternity apparel in which the expectant mother may feel as other women feel because she looks as other women look."

By then, Lena had married for a second time, to a mechanical engineer, Albert Malsin. He began managing his wife's business and persuaded the manufacturers along Seventh Avenue to mass-produce her designs. Albert also started an enormously successful Lane Bryant mail-order catalog and helped pioneer ready-to-wear clothing for "women of larger proportions." As an engineer, Albert had a knack for numbers, and he and Lena studied insurance company reports and used a special yardstick that Albert had invented, and that conformed to the angles of the body, to examine more than forty-five hundred of Lane Bryant's customers' figures. Lane Bryant began creating inclusive sizes, and by 1923 the company had reached $5 million in sales in those sizes alone, or $85 million in today's dollars. In 1915, it opened its first branch retail store in Chicago. In 1947, Lane Bryant announced the opening of a flagship store at Fifth Avenue and Fortieth Street. "It's a miracle, and yet I suppose it's a typical American success story, too," said Lena.

Chapter 9

❖

President Dorothy

Over her two decades at Lord & Taylor, Dorothy's abilities and ingenuity were undeniable, and in December 1945, she finally took the helm, becoming the store's first female president. As she settled into her new role, Dorothy arrived at the store every morning at 9:30, stepping from a black limousine into the side entrance on Thirty-Ninth Street. "As she sweeps across the main floor, a tall, handsomely dressed woman of indeterminate age, it is 'Good morning, Miss Shaver,' from the salesgirls, the service managers and the elevator starter," wrote Jeanne Perkins in a profile in *Life* magazine. Dorothy's office, adjacent to the lamp department and with two secretaries stationed outside, was sparsely decorated, with stark white walls, chrome accents, and several cactus plants. There, the "lady president" spent her days reviewing dress orders with manufacturers, debating with stylists, and receiving financial reports from accountants. Now fully in command, Dorothy began transforming Lord & Taylor. She removed the traditional staid, mahogany furnishings that typified the store's interior, and installed instead a modern, pastel-colored palette. The long-stemmed red rose, an icon of American beauty that she had chosen as the store's symbol, was painted on wall murals and awnings and even featured on the store's matchbooks.

Dorothy's management style was a combination of New York tough, an attitude that she had fine-tuned after so many years in her adopted home, and the southern gentility of her Arkansas roots. Like many women at the time, Dorothy never gave out her age, leaving it vague when interviewers were bold enough to ask, and her speech was inflected with a slight drawl. She was known for peppering her sentences with quirky phrases, like "dits and dats," such as when admonishing her communications staff, "Don't give me dits and dats, give me four big public relations ideas a year, and you can relax the rest of the time." Dorothy's highest praise was to call an idea "tops, tops, tops," and her deepest criticism was to deem something old-fashioned. "Who cares about the past?" was a frequent refrain.

Dorothy was a master at the art of persuasion, cajoling others to her side of a debate before they even realized that they were following her lead. "Of course, I don't have to sell this idea to *you*," Dorothy would say to a male vice president—except for the advertising and publicity director, all her lieutenants were men—cornering him into agreement. "The best way to sell an idea is to make the other person think he thought of it first," Dorothy said. "I will never give an ultimatum—ideas must be sold to be effective." After everyone was convinced of the correctness of her side of an argument, Dorothy would then innocently exclaim, "Darned if I know whether we ought to do that or not," giving her underlings the sense that it had been their idea all along. To further this approach, "I always knock on wood at directors' meetings," she said, noting that it had the effect of making her success seem more a matter of chance than ability. "It makes the men feel superior—and that's how they love to feel," she said. "Her friends say she is a diplomat; her enemies say she is a Southern soft-soaper, playing the clinging vine," wrote *Vogue*.

At the time Dorothy ascended to the presidency, Lord & Taylor was worth $40 million, or nearly $600 million in today's dollars. Under Dorothy's reign, the retailer would expand exponentially, its value soaring as it came to employ a staff of five thousand and boast a string of branch stores. In its profile, *Life* magazine called Dorothy America's "No. 1 Career Woman," a reference to her eye-popping salary of $110,000 a year, the equivalent of more than $1.5 million in today's dollars, the highest published salary ever for a female executive at that time. Still, Dorothy was paid "only a quarter of the sum paid to her friend, Thomas J. Watson of International Business Machines," Perkins helpfully pointed out in *Life*. "It would not occur to Miss Shaver to make an issue of the obvious example of sex discrimination in a system which confers upon the male business executive rewards four times greater than those fixed for the senior lady business executive," Perkins wrote. "But as the general leveling between the sexes proceeds, inequities of this sort will clearly come in for drastic correction. For in any case, Miss Shaver's day, in most executive respects, is indistinguishable from a man's."

While Dorothy gave *Life* magazine relatively unfettered access, she typically shied away from doing interviews. "I refused to talk about myself. I knew exactly what the interviewers would write," Dorothy said. "They would tell what I wore, how much make-up I used." It can be hard to prove a negative—sexism, racism, and other prejudices can be unspoken while still pervasive—but Dorothy had no interest in giving oxygen to silly minutiae when she had a business to run. Throughout her career, there was rarely a story on her that didn't include such details as "She often does her own hair. . . . However, she does have her nails done by a manicurist," or comments like "Miss Dorothy Shaver, whose personality and grace belie all the preconceived notions of what a great store's executive should look like," and "first and foremost [she's] a charming picture of a gracious woman." As the columnist Alice Hughes wrote the year that Dorothy became president, "Success is a pitfall for woman. The very qualities which in a man's rise to the top are so attractive are the undoing of a woman as—a woman." Even Perkins made a point of emphasizing Dorothy's displays of femininity. "The typical career woman encountered nowadays," she wrote in *Life*, "on the whole is very difficult to get along with. Miss Shaver, in contrast, belongs to the Little Woman school. She makes a feminine fuss over thunderstorms, crossing the street and lighting a cigaret."

It seems highly unlikely that Dorothy feared thunderstorms. Or crossing a street. But this emphasis on her femininity was likely an attempt to render her business successes more palatable to a broad audience. Still, Dorothy herself had little interest in playing along. "I am tired of hearing about career women," she said. "After all, women are people and should be judged as individuals without regard to their sex." Sometimes, however, she had little choice. In an interview with Tex McCrary and Jinx Falkenburg, hosts of the popular *Tex and Jinx* radio show, for instance, Dorothy was speaking of the importance of executives such as herself taking on leadership roles in the country and the world, when she used the generic term "businessmen."

"You said 'American businessmen know how to make things work,'" noted Jinx. "Don't forget, you are president of Lord & Taylor, and you're a woman . . . ."

"Well . . . ," replied Dorothy.

"So, you've got to say businessmen and women."

"Oh my—yes—I must not forget that, Jinx," Dorothy said, charming the host. "But there are so many wonderful men in this country doing such outstanding jobs, and I just feel so comfortable when I think of the brains and ability we have, that I keep on talking about American businessmen."

Dorothy was a strategic thinker, and she steered Lord & Taylor through choppy industry waters, until it commanded a lucrative piece of the consumer market. While competitors like Macy's and Gimbels zeroed in on budget-focused shoppers, and Henri Bendel and Bergdorf Goodman appealed to high-fashion clientele, under Dorothy, Lord & Taylor had "carefully and painstakingly separated a specific kind of customer—the wives and daughters of successful men, the upper-middle-class women who fancy good style rather than high style," wrote Perkins in *Life*. She was so successful, in part, because as broadly as she thought, Dorothy was also a detail-oriented tactician, involving herself in even the smallest decisions. For customers who arrived before the store opened for the day, for instance, Dorothy thought to serve warm coffee and fresh juice, and even placed folding chairs in the vestibule so they could sit comfortably. She ordered red-felt cushions for the glove counter so that customers could easily rest their elbows while trying gloves on, and she handed out tiny hearts encrusted with pearls free to every prospective bride, as well as pink or blue rattles to every purchaser of a baby layette.

As part of "the Shaver Touch," as some in the press dubbed it, Dorothy opened several new departments at Lord & Taylor, including one of the first College Shops, catering to young women who wanted stylish yet affordable clothes, as well as one for petite customers under five feet four. She ordered staff to study how shoppers were navigating the main floor and narrowed entryways and installed directional lighting to stop them from congregating around the entrance, draw-ing them farther inside. She painted the aging stairwells with colorful murals, hid ungainly fire equipment behind a display of angels creatively made of gauze, and decorated the children's department with fanci-ful papier-mâché cows. Dorothy opened New York's first department store lunch counter, called the Bird Cage, a minuscule tearoom that was always jam-packed, its entrance in the shape of a golden birdcage, where customers chose a variety of finger sandwiches served from roll-ing carts and free cigarettes. Dorothy also opened the Milk Bar, where mothers could drop off their children with a nurse while they shopped and where the little tykes could enjoy a room filled with toys and a menu full of ice cream sundaes. For men, she created the Soup Bar, complete with "a wise-cracking counterman" who served Scotch broth and apple cobbler.

Dorothy also overhauled the store's advertising, employing her trade-mark originality and creativity. Department store advertising typically followed a pattern, with small white boxes that were filled with type, informing readers of the latest merchandise on display and advertising sizes, fabrics, and colors. Stores did not want to waste expensive adver-tising space, so every inch was covered with text, few images were used, and style and layout were an afterthought, if considered at all. Dorothy bucked this trend. She realized that department store advertising was more about creating want than fulfilling a need, and she relied on art-istry and humor to intrigue and seduce. "How many women who are customers of Lord & Taylor really need another dress?" she said. "They purchase in order to be in fashion or to satisfy an emotional desire, which, by the way, is the most important reason for buying anything above bare necessities. . . . We believe that sledgehammer tactics are not nearly as effective as tempting the customer if we are to satisfy the emotional urge of the customer to buy."

Dorothy hired the artist Dorothy Hood to create black-and-white wash drawings, the overlay of paint and pen atmospheric and ideal for newspaper print. With Ms. Hood's signature included on the ads as if they were real paintings, the images were unusual and instantly recog-nizable. Dorothy also dispatched an art director at the store to create a new logo using freestyle lettering rather than typeface, rendering the

Harper's Bazaar, March 1955

15

Watch
the new importance of
the straight-as-a-die
town dress;
black linen-weave silk,
slimness emphasized with a wide flat band.
79.95 in the designer collections.
Lord & Taylor—New York, Manhasset, Westchester, Millburn, West Hartford, Bala-Cynwyd

Hood

Lord & Taylor advertisements
featuring wash drawings by the artist
Dorothy Hood were iconic.

Lord & Taylor signature utterly unique. These new advertisements
were clutter-free, with large white spaces and minimal text. Dorothy
didn't see any rationale for listing an item's price or the sizes or colors
that were available. "We're selling style, not specifics," she said. "The
only place for a woman to buy a dress or coat is in the fitting room."
The ads typically featured a single item or concept—"Why sell one
pair of slippers against another pair?" she noted. They were also clever
and topical. When Paris was liberated, for instance, Lord & Taylor ran
a full-page ad with the Empire State Building leaning toward the Eiffel
Tower, the caption reading, "My, it's good to see you again." When
the store had a sale on Early American furniture, with prices half off,
an advertisement featured the image of a Puritan, who was being sawed
in two. Under Dorothy's direction, Lord & Taylor's advertising became
so identifiable that it occasionally didn't even include the store's name,
a cheeky "You Know Who" sufficing.

※•※

At 5:20 each evening, Dorothy's chauffeur would begin circling the block around the store, navigating traffic and waiting for her to appear at the side entrance for the short drive home to the duplex penthouse on East Fifty-Second Street, where she lived with Elsie and their dog, a Scottie named Brandy. The apartment boasted unimpeded views overlooking the East River and Roosevelt Island, with a drawing room featuring polished black linoleum floors, two walls painted white, the other two a pale terra-cotta, and furnishings that included Louis XV chairs in chartreuse satin and two curved sofas in gray. A winding staircase led to the dining room downstairs, outfitted in colorful Directoire furniture upholstered in pink, chartreuse, and green, and walls that had been hand painted by Elsie with clouds and nosegays, as well as a tulle bow that she painted on the wall to frame a rococo mirror. Downstairs, too, were the bedrooms, Elsie's in shades of green and Dorothy's in vibrant rose and blue. Elsie's bathroom had three white plaster doves that she had created and that were permanently perched

Dorothy and Elsie's penthouse in New York featured Elsie's artwork and whimsical touches, as well as a few items chosen by Dorothy, including the tiger-skin rug.

Elsie at the New York penthouse
that she shared with Dorothy.

on the shower-curtain rod. While Elsie supervised most of the decor, Dorothy's aesthetic, which was less whimsical, was also visible, including a tiger-skin rug by the fireplace and two bronze-doré andirons that Dorothy bought for $3,500, or $45,000 in current dollars—one night's winnings in Monte Carlo.

The press, notorious for its dogged inquisitiveness, was largely quiet when it came to Dorothy and Elsie's dating life. The two sisters lived together most of their lives, from their childhood in Mena, to their short stay in Chicago, and throughout their time in New York. And while prominent unmarried women in the public eye during these years sometimes asked a male friend, or even hired a male escort, to accompany them to public events, Dorothy usually went by herself or brought Elsie. "An earlier generation would have called them spinsters; today they are career women," wrote Perkins in *Life*, the only reference that she made to the sisters' status as single women without children.

Dorothy had once had a fiancé, decades before she was a public figure.

It was after she had dropped out of the University of Arkansas following her sophomore year and was home in Mena teaching at a local middle school. The relationship, as well as Dorothy's brief teaching career, ended as soon as she joined Elsie in Chicago. The press occasionally referenced this long-ago broken engagement, but other than that there was no talk of a beau. Elsie insisted that her sister enjoyed men's company, although she never broached the topic of romance. "Being completely feminine she liked men," Elsie wrote in her unpublished recollections, "Didi and Me," "and most of her life she was surrounded by them. In her work, in her play. It went back to her earliest childhood when she used to spin tops and shoot marbles with the boys and take most of their agates too." Elsie's only mention of her own romantic inclinations was when she was a girl and "in love with a little boy in knickers who for the first time in my life made me conscious of how I looked."

Dorothy brushed the topic aside when pesky interviewers asked, and the Shaver family narrative held that there were potential romantic partners over the years but that each time, the other sister, feeling their twosome threatened, put a stop to it. As one became interested, "the other would apparently talk her out of it," according to their sister-in-law, Agnes Shaver, who maintained that Dorothy didn't want a partner who earned less than her, severely limiting her dating pool. There also might have been relationships that went unreported, a gentleman's agreement of sorts. Considering the Shavers' numerous journalist friends, it might have been an industry secret so well kept that there remain no existing records. But more likely, Dorothy and Elsie were part of a rich historical record and literary tradition of unmarried sisters who became each other's lifelong companions, from the author Jane Austen and her sister Cassandra, who wrote to each other nearly daily when they were not together, to Emily Dickinson and her sister, who shared a room and a bed into their twenties. And considering that at that time there were hardly any examples of women who were successfully navigating both a career as demanding as Dorothy's and a marriage and children, it is not much of a surprise that she chose not to compromise her ambition. "I have always maintained—and the universities bear me out—that brains have no sex," Dorothy said. "When you consider how relatively few women are free to devote all their time and

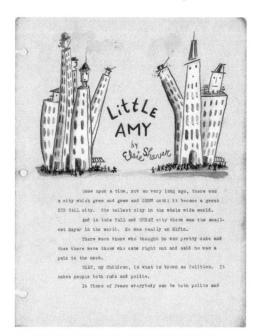

Elsie wrote dozens of unpublished short stories, including "Little Amy," which featured her hand-drawn illustrations.

energy to a career outside the home the way a man does, I think women have made remarkable strides."

While Dorothy was at the department store, Elsie spent her days painting, as well as writing and illustrating children's tales. These were often parables, with veiled political references, such as her story "Little Amy," a book-length work written during the wartime reign of the lilliputian New York City mayor Fiorello La Guardia. "Once upon a time, not so very long ago, there was a city which grew and grew and GREW until it became a great BIG TALL city. The tallest city in the whole wide world. And in this TALL and GREAT city there was the smallest Mayor in the world. He was really an Elfin. There were those who thought he was pretty cute and then there were those who came right out and said he was a pain in the neck. THAT, my Children, is what is known as Politics." The story was accompanied by a series of drawings in black ink of skyscrapers, of Eleanor Roosevelt, and of the Women's Army Corps marching like ducks.

Elsie's books were never published, but she did occasionally exhibit her art. In 1942, a year in which she was particularly prolific, Elsie had a solo show at the Wildenstein Galleries where she exhibited large cotton dolls that were reminiscent of her Little Shavers of twenty years earlier, as well as paintings in oil and watercolor. Later that year, Dorothy featured Elsie's cotton dolls in a Valentine's Day display for Lord & Taylor's Fifth Avenue windows, and Elsie was commissioned to paint a twelve-foot mural depicting a line of dancing girls with parasols for the entryway of the Tobé-Coburn School for Fashion Careers.

Elsie creating one of her doll sculptures.

Dorothy and Elsie filled their nonworking hours with numerous intellectual and physical pursuits. Most Monday evenings, Dorothy played badminton with her sister and Eleanor Lambert, the famous fashion publicist and a close friend of the Shavers'. Dorothy always excelled at sports, playing tennis and basketball avidly as a child, and as an adult continually pushed herself to try new activities. She learned to mountain climb, and "at the risk of life and limb, I learned to ski," she said. "Once I had mastered it, I came back to New York, put my skis on the shelf and thanked heaven it was over. But I wouldn't stop until I had learned it."

Dorothy was also involved in multiple nonprofits, serving as a member of the women's committee of the United Negro College Fund, for instance, and sitting on the Board of Trustees of the Metropolitan Museum of Art. Dorothy chaired the fundraising committee that facilitated the merger of the Costume Institute with the Metropolitan Museum of Art, helping to validate the notion that American fashion and its designers were artistically and culturally significant. It was Eleanor Lambert, her badminton partner, who conceived of "the Party of the Year," the Costume Institute's annual fundraising ball. But without Dorothy, the world's most exclusive fashion gathering, overseen by *Vogue*'s editor, Anna Wintour, since 1995 and now known simply as the Met Gala, might not have come to be.

Dorothy frequently visited Paris with Elsie in tow, and the Shaver sisters traveled extensively through Europe. They even took a rickety plane—three years before Jackie Cochran took her first flying lesson—to Stalinist Russia. "If you want the most complete mental bath you have ever had—go to Russia," Dorothy wrote to her old boss and distant relative, Reyburn, from her hotel in Paris in July 1930. She had just returned from the U.S.S.R., which was in upheaval over the mass collectivization of farmland, rapid industrialization, the imprisonment of so-called enemies of the people, and a clampdown on organized religion. "Never have I been so taken out of myself," she wrote of the illuminating experience. The country was "upside down," the very air charged with a palpable intensity. "It is not difficult to see the suffering, feel the fear and note the iron hand of the Soviets' regime everywhere," she wrote. The sisters spent their days exploring Moscow and Leningrad, and their evenings locked in conversation with expat intellectuals, dining at the home of the *New York Times* Moscow bureau chief, Walter Duranty, and talking Russian politics deep into the night with the writer Maurice Hindus. "One moment one finds oneself overcome with admiration for the brains that have conceived and are putting over this idea on such a huge scale," she wrote. "The next moment you find yourself in a rage at the outrageous unfairness of the whole thing."

Dorothy (left) and Elsie (right) embarking on one of their many travels.

Current affairs and politics were exceedingly important to Dorothy, and in the postwar era, as the civil rights movement took hold and paranoia over a looming cold war began to grow, Dorothy leveraged her position as the president of Lord & Taylor to engage with the issues. "I believe so deeply in getting involved," she told Edward R. Murrow on his radio show, *This I Believe*. "In fact, I believe that whatever spiritual growth, whatever small success I have achieved is because I have become involved: involved in extra work, in extracurricular activities, in the ideas, the problems, the joys of other people." Quoting Edgar Lee Masters, the poet who wrote about small-town America, she said, "The branches of a tree spread no wider than its roots. And how shall the soul of man be larger than the life he has lived?"

Back in 1937, Dorothy had conceived of the Lord & Taylor American Design Award to support nascent American designers. In these early years, figures like Nettie Rosenstein and Clare Potter stopped by the store to pick up $1,000 checks to help support their burgeoning businesses. But Dorothy realized the potential that the design awards could have in highlighting the day's issues, and her ambitions grew. She began using the awards to honor a vast array of luminaries, from the inventor of a semiautomatic rifle, to the dancer Agnes de Mille, to Albert Einstein. She held grand luncheons at the Waldorf Astoria, where fifteen hundred guests gathered, the recipients' acceptance speeches broadcast over national radio. Dorothy herself spoke out against totalitarianism and racism, giving speeches that praised the abolitionist John Brown, widely quoted Abraham Lincoln, and touted the Nineteenth Amendment.

At the height of the Red Scare, when Senator Joseph McCarthy was enjoying the peak of his power crusading against alleged communist infiltration in American life, Dorothy gave an expansive speech to the National Conference of Christians and Jews. In it, she rebuked the "spreading passion for conformity," arguing how "conformist thinking has the potential power to destroy all the qualities which have made our country great." *The Hartford Courant* took up her point in an editorial, writing, "She spoke of the paradox of this nation, born of nonconformity, nurtured by nonconformists, and grown great by its diversity of minds and talents, now becoming infected by fear of nonconformity." It continued, "As Miss Shaver observed, if carried to its terrible conclusion, this fetish of conformity will destroy all the qualities that made us great." Under Dorothy, the department store evolved from a commercial, profit-maximizing endeavor to one with cultural and geopolitical significance and influence. But progress comes in many forms, and there were changes on the horizon that would soon threaten Dorothy's impressive legacy.

Chapter 10

❖

Geraldine's Street of Shops

When Maxey Jarman bought Henri Bendel, the department store was in steep decline. Half a century ago, its location was the epitome of chic, Fifty-Seventh Street considered New York's rue de la Paix. But over the intervening years, prevailing views changed, and a location sandwiched in the middle of a crosstown street was seen as less prestigious than one squarely situated on Fifth Avenue. Meanwhile, the building was smaller than its rivals and in poor shape. "Even the stockroom roof was leaking," said Geraldine, drumming a finger on her desk to mimic the sound of falling rain. It was "a beautiful old name slightly tarnished, a bad locale that was left over from the carriage trade, old time clientele, and skilled personnel, but it was out of fashion," wrote *The Milwaukee Journal*. "Financially speaking, [it] was falling flat on its elegant face," wrote *Cosmopolitan*. "The Duke and Duchess of Windsor, it is true, were continuing to store her furs and his kilts there (Teddy Roosevelt had done the same with his African hunting gear and Franklin Roosevelt with his auto robes), but the store's proprietors were discovering, to their dismay, that they had more dignity than dollars."

Maxey wanted his protégée to leave her post at I. Miller and revamp the department store. But Geraldine refused. "I knew—and he knew I knew—that Maxey Jarman had already asked every good merchant from here to California. No one would tackle a dowdy white elephant of a store doing $3 million annually—and losing $1 million." Maxey had a plan, however, that he hoped would convince her.

While searching for a permanent candidate, Maxey ran Henri Bendel himself and every Friday went to see Geraldine and update her on his progress. As Maxey outlined his bungled ideas for improvements, Geraldine couldn't help telling him they were "all so wrong!" She grew increasingly frustrated at Maxey's ineptitude, but she wouldn't budge on her decision not to take over. After five months of this ruse failing to entice Geraldine, Maxey changed tactics. He gave Geraldine a list of successors he was considering, all of whom were women. "And when I vetoed the last one, I found myself saying, 'Look, do you really want me to run the store?'" recalled Geraldine. "That's what I was waiting for!" Maxey crowed. But just as she had done before agreeing to leave *Glamour* for I. Miller, Geraldine made several demands. "I want five years to pull the store into shape," she told him. "And I want full financial backing and no quarterbacking." Maxey was only too happy to agree. In recalling the incident, Geraldine noted that among her mentor's many talents was his slightly annoying knack for being "a clever psychologist."

Arriving at Bendel's in November 1957, Geraldine, who was decades younger than many of her employees, did not receive a warm reception from the staff. "I had just been installed as a 33-year-old whiz kid most people had never heard of," she recalled. "Most of the existing store people wouldn't talk to me. So, for the first few months, rather than make the drastic changes everyone expected, I just sat on my hands. . . . I mean that literally. In this old building, even the temperature was cold."

After sitting on her hands for a while, Geraldine finally decided to go shopping—at her rivals. She ventured to Bergdorf Goodman around the corner, Lord & Taylor to her south, and Bloomingdale's a few blocks east. "I had the advantage only a woman could have," she said. "I wear the clothes. A man in my place at that point might have fallen on his face." What she discovered on these jaunts was "there was no longer a small specialty shop, one that's warm, personal, dedicated to the single customer. All of the old specialty shops had either grown so big they'd lost their personalness, or they had become hopelessly outdated." Geraldine had discovered a path forward: she would remake Henri Bendel by doubling down on its smallness, with an unabashed focus on exclusivity.

Geraldine decided she would begin right at the store's entrance. H. McKim Glazebrook was the display director with whom she had worked at I. Miller. A patrician, sensitive man, he possessed a uniquely imaginative eye, exactly the type of contrarian, canny, often humorous creativity that Geraldine most admired. If she was going to attempt a completely new Bendel's, starting by reconceiving its entryway and ground floor, Glaze, as she called him, was the person to do it. Geraldine and Glaze wandered through the space brainstorming how best to overcome the store's numerous structural issues. In addition to being on the side street, rather than the main avenue, Bendel's had small windows that were difficult for passersby to see from the sidewalk. Even worse, the main floor was long, narrow, and small. "Every other department store had a whole bowling alley, and we had only half," complained Geraldine. The ceiling also soared upward, reaching 110 feet, compared with the room's width of just barely 25 feet. "It was like a cathedral," said Geraldine, "the proportions were all wrong." The pair looked and talked and fiddled. "What we want is something intimate and small and broken up," Geraldine told Glaze. But how to do it? He went away and returned a month later to present his concept to the new store president. It was a maquette for a pedestrian retail street inspired by his childhood in Palm Beach, Florida. "I almost died; I thought it was so wonderful," said Geraldine. Without hesitation she told him, "You bet."

According to Glaze's vision, Bendel's main floor would be a "Street of Shops," a single road, paved in off-white marble laid out in a herringbone pattern. It would be a concept that would shape a generation of department stores, a new merchandising strategy that would come to redefine how the industry approached its all-important main floors. Using the pedestrian mall Via Mizner in Palm Beach, as well as the Faubourg St. Honoré in Paris, as his starting point, Glaze placed a small piazza at the top of the street made from gray stucco. It featured three niches tiled in lapis lazuli mosaic and a burbling fountain surrounded by velvet-cushioned benches and leafy, exotic plants, creating a garden-like ambience. Along the street, the shops were individual spaces, each with its own architectural style and offering a curated selection of items, many one of a kind. There was the Bag Shop, with a gray-and-white facade of Corinthian columns, which sold an assortment of travel bags in alligator and lizard skin and satin clutches that could be dyed to match a customer's gown. The Glove Shop was finished in Directoire style, with a chamois-and-charcoal interior, and featured unique items such as silk-lined leather gloves from France. The Bagatelle was a Baroque space in light tones of aubergine and offered a selection of scarves and stoles, while the Bijoutier featured a multi-arched roof supported by tapering columns of malachite, between which counters for displaying jewelry were suspended. Gold metal tassels swung from the ceiling, producing flashes of light. The Gift Shop was circular, decorated in the style of Louis XVI, and offered stationery adorned with real pressed flowers. The Street ended at the Milliner, a two-story space of Palladian influence, carpeted and furnished in shades of beige and white, selling hats that were custom-made in the store's workrooms, as well as chic capulets and pillbox styles imported from modistes in France and Italy.

"I was struck dumb because I thought the idea was so extraordinary and wonderful," said Geraldine. "The consensus at that minute in retailing countrywide, and perhaps internationally, was that the best kind of main floor was one in which you had lots of counters, everything exposed," the merchandise highly visible, with glass counter displays set up in long rows. "The theory was that if you didn't snag the customer in one place, you'd trip them up in another, that their attention would be caught along the way." The Street of Shops was something entirely different, with the merchandise hidden within small, jewel-like stores, each one its own tiny creation. "It was very brave to have this kind of concept; nobody had ever seen anything like this before," Geraldine said.

Work began immediately on Glaze's vision, and the entire main floor of Bendel's was shrouded in scaffolding and mystery. "Until two days before we were to open, we had no idea what it was going to look like," said Geraldine. "Some terrible side show maybe, or a series of little cardboard boxes." Despite her trepidation, Geraldine bet her retailing future on Bendel's revamped main floor. "We invited every store president and every major bigwig involved with retailing and merchandising in New

York," she said. She had already been president for eighteen months and had implemented several changes, but all without any fanfare. "We had been doing lots of things, but we'd done it quietly and purposefully, and without making a big noise," Geraldine said. Now she wanted to make a fuss. "This was to be, in theatrical terms, our talking dog. You know how, in a carnival, you have a talking dog outside the tent to get people inside? This was it."

In September 1959, Nikita Khrushchev became the first Soviet leader to visit the United States, Vince Lombardi made his NFL debut as head coach, and merchants of all stripes arrived at Henri Bendel to witness what one of America's youngest and highest-profile department store presidents had been up to since taking over. The anticipation was palpable, and Geraldine nervously stationed herself at Bendel's front door, beneath its famed awning, greeting each person as they arrived for the unveiling. Only a few of the nearly all-male crowd looked her in the eye. Most gave her a quick nod as they brushed past, eager to cast their judgment.

It was an unseasonably hot day in early September, and after the viewing, guests began congregating in groups outside the store and along the sidewalk, gossiping among themselves and reviewing what they had seen. "They stood in little queues," Geraldine ruefully recalled, "and laughed, ho-ho-ho." One older male executive told her, "Well, you've got guts," as he walked past, while Andrew Goodman, president of Bergdorf Goodman, started referring to it as "the Street of Flops" behind her back. Others dubbed it "Jerry's Folly."

In the years ahead, industry gossip pages would sometimes run blind items critiquing her. *Women's Wear Daily* called Geraldine a "nice girl," before adding that while she had admirers, she also had legions of critics, quoting one who described her as "a snippy, snarky little girl who can't stand not to get her own way." Geraldine disliked confrontation and dealt with the naysayers by keeping her head down and getting on with her job. "Many men did expect that I would not be able to produce, but I didn't work doubly hard to prove them wrong—I just did what I knew how to do and learned what I didn't know," she later said. "If men regarded me suspiciously, I dealt with it by not dealing with it." And while some of her male competitors were dismissive of her vision,

A shopper perusing Henri Bendel's Street of Shops.

Geraldine managed to largely charm the press. "Although many stores have 'prettified' their physical plants through the years, there have been too few new approaches to store design and layout," one newspaper wrote, calling the Street of Shops "a humdinger." It was easier to shop in these small areas, reviewers agreed, and the merchandise looked much better in such intimate settings.

The white paved road lent the Street of Shops a luxurious solidity, grounding it in the high-ceilinged space, while the many different shops, each beautifully appointed with unique detailing, provided shoppers with a sense of adventure and exploration. It was a visual treat, but it was also a sensory experience, with the water falling from the fountain, a soundtrack of popular music piped through speakers, and an atomizer that released a fresh, citrusy aroma into the air every fifteen seconds. "Won't you come in and wander down the new street of shops on our entrance floor?" read an advertisement in *The New York Times*, calling it a "serene and beautiful world." It was the type of atmosphere where celebrities and the general public comfortably mingled, where in later years the model Christie Brinkley shopped with her mother and the actress Mary Tyler Moore freely wandered without fear of harassment.

Geraldine did not only change Bendel's entry floor. Upstairs, she created a Shop for Brides on the fifth floor, made up of five salons, each individually decorated and resembling a period room in a stately mansion. The salons fanned out from a central rotunda, where a receptionist was stationed, assigning customers their own salons and individual "bridal consultants." A children's department, Growing Up, boasted a centerpiece of an enormous hot air balloon, with mannequins that stood in the basket showing off the latest children's designs, and was complemented by a pink-and-white layette area with ice cream parlor chairs and a lollipop tree. The small fitting rooms that had once been a mainstay throughout the store were replaced with large areas replete with sofas, and some even with writing desks, where customers could relax as saleswomen brought them clothes to try on. It was all about intimacy and friendliness, a tranquil shopping atmosphere that offered customers personal service and unique merchandise.

Geraldine continued to tweak the Street of Shops, adding new entrants as she thought of them. A year after first unveiling Bendel's main floor, Geraldine opened the Gilded Cage to sell cosmetics. Inspired by an eighteenth-century birdcage, its entryway was made of delicate brass bars taken from antique birdcages, its floor was lined with amethyst-colored rugs, and its walls were entirely mirrored and veiled in shirred pink chiffon. Chandeliers hung from the ceilings, and the counters were in the shape of antique sewing tables. The overall effect "is like being inside a fabulous pink pearl," wrote *Women's Wear Daily*, noting the store offered an astounding 160 shades of lipstick and 90 types of eye-shadows. The saleswomen at the Gilded Cage were "soft-spoken, wise in the ways of what make-up can accomplish and refreshingly pretty in specially designed pink cotton smocks," marveled *The New York Times*.

The Gilded Cage was the purview of Helen Van Slyke, a slender blonde who was a beauty editor at *Glamour* before joining Bendel's. Helen would go on to have a notable career, promoted to advertising and promotional director at Bendel before joining an advertising agency. Eventually, Maxey Jarman appointed her to run the House of Fragrance, making her the second female executive, alongside Geraldine, to oversee one of his subsidiaries. Maxey would cement his reputation as a mentor of professional women when, two years after appointing Helen to the

House of Fragrance, he brought on Mildred Custin to run his recently purchased Bonwit Teller, years after Hortense retired from the store. "Women who are interested in a career and have a feminine viewpoint," Maxey said, "usually have intuitiveness as well as good promotion and advertising sense."

The relationship between Maxey and Geraldine, as well as those between Maxey and his other female executives, fascinated many. In "Maxey and the Girls," the *New York Herald Tribune*'s fashion writer, Eugenia Sheppard, wrote, "Maxey Jarman is famous as a Southern Baptist, a rock-ribbed Republican, and a high-powered commuter across the country. . . . He has another asset, though, that an average man may envy almost more than any other. Maxey Jarman understands women. He likes them and knows how to work with them." Geraldine, interviewed in the piece, said that her mentor believed "if women are any good, it's because they are women, not in spite of it." Maxey, said Geraldine, "is one man who really understands that a woman's hair appointment is sacred."

Geraldine and Helen were friends for decades, sharing their experiences as editors at *Glamour*, later working together at Bendel, and then both running Genesco subsidiaries. When Helen eventually quit her job as a beauty executive to write romance novels, she mined the relationship between Geraldine and Maxey for source material. The result was *The Rich and the Righteous*, a dishy roman à clef published in 1971 that centered on Bridget Manning, "the high-powered career woman who never mixed business with pleasure—until she found herself drawn to the man who was her most dangerous rival," according to the book's back flap. Geraldine was clearly the model for Helen's heroine, and far from being offended, the Bendel president threw Helen a book party. In the book, Bridget works for Joe Haylow, a fashion tycoon who, like Maxey, eschews alcohol and tobacco and embraces religion. "You can't help soaking up personality traits of people when you work with them," Helen said, when asked about her inspiration for the novel. Joe is a paternal figure, and just like Maxey his connection to Bridget was purely platonic. (Bridget's romantic interest was Joe's son, a storyline that was not taken from real life.). Of her connection to Joe, Bridget says, in the book, "It's easier and more fun to assume that an attachment between a man and a woman has got to be physical. The real truth is too dull . . . or too simple."

Like Bridget and Joe, "Jerry charmed Maxey," recalled Karol Kempster, who ran the Gilded Cage after Helen. "Jerry could get anything she wanted from him, she knew how to handle him," and "he understood her," Karol said. In another section of *The Rich and the Righteous*, Helen wrote of Bridget words that could easily have been transposed onto Geraldine. "Bridget wore her success simply, naturally, and becomingly. She was not given to the unreasonable tantrums, the petty vindictiveness, or the unpredictable behavior of which most women executives were accused. She took her setbacks as calmly and unemotionally as she accepted her victories. Like Joe Haylow, she was firm but fair."

While Geraldine continued to refine her vision for Bendel's, she kept some remnants of the old carriage trade. The most important was Buster the doorman. Born James Jarrett Jr., Buster had arrived at Bendel in 1906 as a teenager, and there he had remained, stationed beneath the store's front awning, ever since. "When I came to Bendel, it was a faded little white elephant with a vivid past—a charming carriage trade shop in the teens, a chic, small store with international cachet in the twenties and thirties, the cynosure of dowagers and debutantes in the forties and fifties," Geraldine wrote in an essay for *New York* magazine. "By 1960, only two vestiges of those earlier days of grace and glory were visible. One was Bendel's own soap, made to a formula that dated from the long-gone days when the original Henri was a boy. The other was James Jarrett Jr.," whom Geraldine described as "diminutive and dapper in his brass-buttoned uniform and the Buster Brown hatbox hat that gave him his nickname."

Buster had been at Bendel for so long that he'd witnessed horse-drawn carriages replaced by taxicabs, and single-name monikers like Astor and Carnegie swapped with Cher and Barbra. "He trots out to the curb and opens the Cadillac doors just as briskly as he handed ladies down from their carriages," wrote *The New York Times*. "Over the years, his role became somewhat analogous to that of a maître d'hôtel at a good restaurant who treats everyone politely, only some more so." Buster was such an institution that the *Tobé Report*, a fashion trade publication, wrote about his hat, calling it "bell-boy chic" and noting that it had spurred a new fad. "Young fashion trendsetters have been having their fun with uniform dressing," it wrote, and "we think caps with the look of Buster's wonderful little cap will have broad appeal this fall and winter."

Geraldine immortalized the doorman with a fifteen-inch toy doll that was dressed in his uniform and famous hat and was sold on the Street of Shops. "He carried his celebrity lightly—pleased but scarcely surprised when a doll made in his image met with runaway success," Geraldine wrote in her essay in *New York* magazine. "But then, pride of place was Buster's strong suit. The very set of his shoulders implied that he was, after all, Buster of Bendel's." As Buster aged, Geraldine sent taxis to his home to bring him back and forth to work. Sometimes, she sent her driver, her green Jaguar pulling up in front of his house in Astoria, Queens, much to the neighbors' surprise. Buster worked at Bendel until 1980, resigning after more than seventy years of service. He died of a stroke just before his ninety-first birthday.

Even as Geraldine was overhauling the store's interiors, she was also changing the type of customer she was targeting. "From the beginning, I felt that if we were going to survive, we should not try to compete with the bigger, more established shops," Geraldine said. "We should be an individualistic shop. Fill a special need, for the special customer." The larger stores like Lord & Taylor and Bonwit Teller could offer a variety of styles and price points to a broad swath of customers. But because Bendel's was physically smaller, with less space to display merchandise, it had to be more strategic. Like the store's founder, Henri Bendel, Geraldine aimed for what she said was "a serene atmosphere, gracious personal service, the finest merchandise for the woman of taste who is interested in beautiful things—regardless of cost." This woman aspired to what soon became known as the Bendel Look. "Our customer is big-city aware, contemporary, anywhere from about 18 to 60—and has a terrific, small figure. She wants individual clothes that are totally today but not gaggy, avant-garde but not kooky," said Geraldine. The Bendel Look was "elegant, chic, but not the last gasp. It is, rather, a contemporary, current look—one that plays up the woman herself rather than what she is wearing." The Bendel Look was not an exact science, but Geraldine, and the women (and a few men) whom she gathered around her to execute her vision, implicitly understood it. "As the originator of the look, and the philosophy behind it, Geraldine Stutz has become the personal symbol of Bendel," wrote *Cosmopolitan* in 1960. " 'The Bendel Look,' they agree, 'is the Stutz Look.' "

One signifier of the Bendel Look was how a customer pronounced the store's name. "Correctly pronouncing the name is the test of a true aficionado," Geraldine said. "The reason most people get it wrong is visual—the 'i' in Henri makes everyone pronounce it as French. But Bendel was an American from New Orleans," and the proper way to say it was just plain-old Henry. Another indication that a customer had achieved the Look was size—a small one. Geraldine rigorously enforced a strict regime at the store that weeded out customers who weren't thin. When she first arrived, 75 percent of the clothing that Bendel sold was sized 16 to 20, or the equivalent of sizes 10 to 14 today. "The dresses were mostly less than svelte," she said, "that gives you an idea of the customers." In the 1940s, standardized sizes were established, and the smallest size offered typically was an 8. At Bendel, within four years of Geraldine's taking the helm, 83 percent of the clothing the store sold was sized 6 to 12, or sizes 0 to 6 today. Its most popular size—which also happened to be Geraldine's—was a size 8, or a contemporary size 2. It was " 'dog whistle' fashion," Geraldine memorably dubbed it, "clothes with a pitch so high and special that only the thinnest and most sophisticated women would hear their call." Geraldine even doubled down on her size prejudice, creating the Smaller Than Small Shop, which offered everything—buttons, belts, even prints—scaled down for the tiny figure.

While the Bendel Look was very specific, there were enough rich women who fit the bill. Among some of Bendel's most avid adherents were Princess Grace of Monaco, Patricia Kennedy Lawford, and Lee Radziwill. "Their drivers would drop them off, Buster would open the door for them, and they would just come in and shop," said Ellen Hopkins, Geraldine's niece, who worked at Bendel's in the late 1970s and early 1980s while pursuing a career in acting. Geraldine hired employees who instinctively understood the Bendel Look and who were as stylish and attractive as their boss. Geraldine had no specific hiring criteria; she just knew it when she saw it. "At Bendel's there is no special training program for beginners," she said. "The kind of girl I would want to work for Bendel is a girl who would love my store and want to work there." Geraldine adhered to the same strategy as her mentor Maxey when it came to discovering and fostering young talent. "The talented should be given everything they need— patience, equipment and confidence," she said, "then expect miracles from them and you will probably get them."

Miriam Marshall at Port of Call.

Miriam Marshall exemplified the Bendel saleswoman. Born on a fishing boat outside what was then Palestine, to Jewish refugees from Poland who were fleeing the Holocaust, Miriam led a migratory life, spending her childhood in Palestine and Australia, and her early twenties in Hong Kong. She had a flair for the unusual and was well traveled, which helped her secure a job dealing in Asian artifacts. Her employer boasted a clientele of prominent, wealthy buyers, including Stanley Marcus, the scion of the Dallas-based department store chain Neiman Marcus. He was in Hong Kong to source eye-catching items for the store, and Miriam was assigned to help him. Miriam was young yet confident, filled with original ideas, and Stanley was taken with her. "When he was getting ready to leave, Stanley asked me if I wanted to come to Texas and work for him," Miriam recalled. "I said, 'No, no way. I want to go to New York.'"

When Stanley returned stateside, he spoke to Geraldine and urged her to meet Miriam, going so far as to arrange her visa to New York. "My flight landed at 6:00 a.m., and my appointment with Geraldine was for 10:30 a.m.," Miriam recalled. She was harried and exhausted from jet lag. "But after about twenty minutes of talking, Geraldine turned and said to me, 'Do you want to have your own department, kiddo?'" Miriam was shocked, but Geraldine was acting on instinct, and soon they had a new concept for the Street of Shops. Port of Call was shaped like an open, Bedouin-style canvas tent and sold unusual items hailing from far-flung locales, like a mobile of colorful, hand-painted fish from Thailand, ivory horses studded with semiprecious stones from Hong Kong, and aboriginal bark paintings from Australia.

This was 1962, and Miriam, who was in her mid-twenties, had no experience running her own department. Nonetheless, she soon found herself zooming around Burma in a rickshaw, sourcing hand-made objects from village artisans that would prove appealing to the aristocratic sensibilities of Manhattan's elite. One of Miriam's earliest successes were tiny animal boxes, made from beaten silver and studded with semiprecious stones, which she had discovered in Cambodia. They soon became de rigueur among a certain set of women, who carried them as evening purses. The trend even spurred a feature in the *New York Times* style pages, with a photo of the Duchess of Windsor carrying an egg-shaped box so small it fit in the palm of her hand. In another instance, Miriam found herself in a wobbly canoe in the middle of a lake in Kashmir, while an agent of an Indian maharaja sidled up next to her in a second boat. "He opened up this blanket and there was the most incredible treasures," Miriam said. "The best was a 24-karat golden horse bridle with green enamel made from crushed emeralds, with a ruby in the middle. I made it into a belt that we sold for $22,000."

Geraldine had made a deal with Maxey that she would reverse Bendel's fortune in five years. She accomplished her goal, and to celebrate, she held a catered, sit-down dinner at the store, inviting every employee, from the janitorial staff to the head of merchandising. "Bendel's has just gone from red ink to a more fashionable shade of black," wrote *The Saturday Evening Post.* "It has developed a fashion impact out of all proportion to its size by capturing hundreds of editorial mentions in the fashion magazines. It has won the obeisance of women who make a lifetime career of looking well dressed." But while Bendel's was outperforming all expectations and disproving the industry naysayers who called her vision Jerry's Folly, Geraldine created something so unique and specific that it was impossible to scale. And while Lord & Taylor and a multitude of other department store competitors were duplicating themselves, opening branches and expanding their reach into the sprawling suburbs, Bendel's took a completely different tack, a decision that would come to haunt Geraldine.

July 29, 1980

Jill Krementz

Geraldine Stutz, photographed by Jill Krementz
on July 29, 1980, in front of Henri Bendel.

Part 3

What's wrong with a woman wanting power? It's a natural human drive.

—*Geraldine Stutz*

‹›—‹

Chapter 11

Dorothy Branches Out

In the winter of 1955, bells tolled and spotlights flooded the crowd as forty thousand people swept through the wide, two-story Lord & Taylor Bala Cynwyd, as the department store's fifth, and grandest, suburban branch was called. Designed by the famed architect Raymond Loewy, the store, just outside Philadelphia, was made of gleaming Pennsylvania fieldstone and whitewashed brick, punctuated by a ninety-four-foot picture window. In the sprawling parking lot, every spot was filled, and a line of cars stretched back toward the avenue, the heaviest traffic jam in Main Line history, according to the overwhelmed police. To celebrate the grand opening, seventy-five thousand dogwood blossoms, crafted from heavy rice paper imported from Japan, were twisted onto hundreds of tree branches, the flowers dipped in a solution to appear as if covered in ice, creating the illusion of a springtime thaw in the February cold. At each of the store's four entrances, giant pink-velvet hearts looked as if they were palpitating, the feat of hidden motors, while gallons of Guerlain's Shalimar perfume—selling at the equivalent of $220 an ounce—were sprayed over the crowd. On the roof, the colorful flags of sixty area schools and universities flapped in the wind.

Under Dorothy's strategy of suburban expansion, planning was already under way for the sixth branch, to be located in the Long Island suburb of Garden City, and with more to follow. Bala Cynwyd was the largest so far, boasting ninety thousand square feet of selling space. Inside, there were numerous wall murals, which took ten artists three weeks to paint, celebrating local history, with maps of the City of Brotherly Love, images of the Liberty Bell, and portraits of famous citizens including Ben Franklin and Betsy Ross. There was the Bird Cage restaurant that had made a splash when it first opened at the Fifth Avenue store and was now a fixture at every branch, featuring a real birdcage with a dozen parakeets noisily chirping. And interspersed throughout the store were images of Lord & Taylor's famous long-stemmed rose.

The Philadelphia outpost also boasted several firsts, including the first escalator in Lord & Taylor history and, at eight thousand square feet, the largest menswear department in any of the branch stores. It was the only store, except for its Fifth Avenue flagship, to have a 54 Shop, for women five feet four and under; a Hermès leather goods store; a maternity shop that included a private suite of fitting rooms; and an interior decorating service. For the staff of more than three hundred, there was an employee restaurant, a lounge, a hospital, and a training room. To feed some thousand people a day, the kitchen included a peeler that peeled fifty pounds of potatoes and an electric mixer that mixed a hundred quarts of mashed potatoes. The stove prepared three hundred chickens at one time, and a seven-shelf baking oven baked a hundred cakes. The steam kettle could heat fifty gallons of soup, and the vegetable steamer cooked 150 pounds at once.

Ever masterful at creating drama, in the afternoon before the opening, Dorothy hosted a special ribbon-cutting ceremony for hundreds of area officials, including women's club presidents and local philanthropic groups, as well as the press. Another six hundred manufacturers and fashion designers arrived from New York City via a specially chartered Pennsylvania Railroad train. "Lord & Taylor moved in on staid Philadelphia this week with all the whistle and whee of a Hollywood premier," wrote Time.

The first branch stores dated back to the late 1850s, when the grocer the Great Atlantic and Pacific Tea Company, known by its acronym A&P, expanded nationally. By the early twentieth century, retailers such as Woolworth and J. C. Penney had multiple branches, and retail conglomerates included the May Department Stores, incorporated in 1910, and the Federated Department Stores, in 1929. These were the exception, however, not the rule. For most of their history, American department stores were single-location retailers, owned and operated by private families or small partnerships. But in the late 1940s and the 1950s, the country—and the department store industry—underwent profound change.

Wartime production finally pulled the economy out of the Great Depression. In the postwar era jobs were plentiful, wages were rising, and after years of rationing, Americans were starved for goods. Couples were marrying at unprecedented rates, there was a baby boom, and new and expanded federal programs, like the GI Bill, spurred a wave of home buying by offering low-interest loans to returning veterans. To participate in what marketers dubbed the good life, Americans embarked on a nationwide spending spree, much as they had during the stock market heyday of the 1920s. This time, they were purchasing new cars to fill their new two-car garages, new television sets and sofas for their new sunken living rooms, and new refrigerators, vacuums, radios, and more, in unprecedented numbers. In 1945, the country had twenty-five million registered vehicles, and by 1959 that number had jumped to fifty-nine million. Sprawling new neighborhoods altered the geographic landscape, as suburban populations grew seven times faster than those of major cities.

America's increasing dependency on cars, and the proliferation of the suburbs, forced department stores to rethink their strategies. Downtown locations lost significance as retailers turned their attention to the sudden fervor for suburban shopping centers. These low-slung retail destinations, with their homogeneous designs and matching signage, offered middle-class white customers a safe, controlled environment where they could easily drive and park, shop and socialize. At the end of World War II, there were only a few hundred shopping centers across the country, but by 1963 there were more than seven thousand. With shopping centers came branch stores. Between 1954 and 1963, the number of American department stores jumped 54 percent, to more than 4,250, and by 1966, more than half of department store sales in America were made in branch stores. New York was ground zero for suburban sprawl. Between 1940 and 1947, New York City's population grew a paltry 4.6 percent, while the New York–Connecticut suburbs grew by nearly 13 percent, and the New Jersey suburbs by nearly 15 percent.

Lord & Taylor was one of the first to embrace the branch store. In 1941, the year that the United States entered the war, Dorothy, who was a vice president, proposed opening the store's first suburban location, in Manhasset, on Long Island. In 1945, when Dorothy became president, she expanded the program, making branch stores a key part of Lord & Taylor's growth strategy. Using the Manhasset store as a model, Lord & Taylor opened in Scarsdale, New York, in 1948; Millburn, New Jersey, in 1949; West Hartford, Connecticut, in 1953; and Bala Cynwyd. The expansion would continue with Garden City, followed by Washington, D.C., before Dorothy's tenure as president was over.

An unintended consequence of this rush to open branch stores was the siphoning away of customers from retailers' flagship locations. Lord & Taylor and its competitors assumed that their main stores would be unharmed, that these flagships were critical to their identities, and that suburban branches would only reinforce this branding. But as retailers established suburban locales, there were fewer reasons for suburban families to venture into the city and deal with its many hassles, like parking. As such, downtown stores were increasingly neglected. Lord & Taylor, for instance, had long-standing plans to relocate its main Fifth Avenue store farther uptown, to a new, renovated building between Fifty-Second and Fifty-Third Streets, bringing it closer to competitors such as Bonwit Teller and Henri Bendel. In 1952, however, in the midst of Lord & Taylor's suburban expansion, Dorothy announced that she was postponing the move. She cited the "abnormally high cost of building and equipping a large store in the Manhattan area," and said she would await "more favorable conditions." In the end, conditions were never quite right, and Lord & Taylor never proceeded with the relocation.

It wasn't only the advent of branches that transformed traditional department stores. In the mid-1950s, a new type of retailer, the discounter, upended the landscape. Given America's seemingly insatiable demand for new goods, several entrepreneurial merchants set out to deliver what their fellow citizens wanted—at lower prices. Lord &

Taylor and other traditional department stores based their business models on providing customers with superior service, a variety of fashionable clothing, and luxury amenities, such as in-store restaurants and personal shoppers. Discounters, on the other hand, capitalized on the self-service trend that supermarkets had modeled, paring their service and decor down to a minimum and relying instead on low overhead, high sales volumes, quick turnover, and very little style, to make a profit.

Discount chains leased cheap sites on the outskirts of the new suburbs, furnished them with basic fixtures and equipment, and operated mostly on a cash-only model. Like the old dry goods stores of the pre-department-store era, discounters piled cameras, gardening tools, television sets, sporting goods, and a random assortment of other merchandise on bare-bones displays, with prices that were significantly below manufacturers' suggested prices. With minimal sales staff, shoppers were largely left on their own to comb through the jumble of goods, pile their items into grocery-store-style carts, and push them to the front of the store, where cashiers waited to check them out. The model was ideal for the changing times. "Not having their money tied up in huge and costly property, the discounters moved out to where the housewives and buyers were, catered to the car-borne family trade by providing huge parking lots, kept night hours, and sold on Sundays," reported *Time* magazine. (Most department stores were still closed on Sundays.) "The typical discount center became part supermarket, part department store, part carnival."

The idea of discounting an item to promote its sale was nothing new; department stores as far back as the late nineteenth century "marked down" prices as part of their promotions. Some stores, like Macy's, relied on low prices as a key means of distinguishing themselves from competitors. But these new discounters, including Walmart, Kmart, and Target—all of which happened to be founded in the same year, 1962—took price-cutting to unprecedented lows. In addition to severely curtailing expenditures, discounters benefited from the fact that by the early 1960s the pent-up demand for goods that had characterized the postwar years was somewhat satiated. This meant that U.S. manufacturers, eager to keep up their production lines, were more willing to look the other way if discounters sold their products significantly below their suggested prices.

Meanwhile, department stores did not help their own cause. The amenities they offered, like a wider selection of merchandise or conveniences like home delivery, didn't hold as much appeal for the new suburbanites, many of whom were young do-it-yourself families. Department store brands were also being diluted, their branch stores making it harder to differentiate between them, while the decentralized control left room for indifferent sales staff and ineffectual managers.

Most discounters started out as small mom-and-pop stores. But as their popularity grew, discounters expanded—exponentially. Walmart, for instance, opened a hundred stores in its first three and a half years. In 1958, discounters made up just 6 percent of general merchandise sales, but by 1965 their sales volume overtook that of conventional department stores, and in 1967 almost 40 percent of the merchandising trade was the purview of discount chains.

At first, department stores barely raised a well-plucked eyebrow at these discount competitors, although they soon came to realize the threat they posed. Department stores had a stark choice: lower their own prices, potentially hurting their bottom line, and risk a race to the bottom, or discontinue certain product lines, giving them up to the discount chains. Some smaller, family-owned department stores advocated for federal regulations, such as price protections, but the effort didn't gain much traction. Instead, traditional department stores joined the fray, forced into price wars that severely diminished their profits. Over time, many had to unshackle themselves from the very things that had once endeared them to their customers: they were forced to trade in their trained staff for harried, part-time employees; swap carefully curated merchandise for cheaper selections; and forgo the elaborate window displays and cultural events that they were known for.

It wasn't only the customer experience that suffered. As department stores engaged in price wars with discounters, employee salaries were also affected. In the twentieth century, retail was one of the most important industries for career advancement for white women. While it was rare to reach the highest executive positions at department stores, female workers could aspire to become buyers, sales managers, and the heads of departments. With the rise of the discount chains, however, this equation was irreversibly altered. Some 80 percent of workers at the discount stores were part time, earning minimal wages and receiving few benefits. Department stores, faced with shrinking margins and looking for cuts, began reviewing their own pay scales and eyeing their well-trained and typically well-compensated staff. As the battle between department stores and discounters intensified, department store salary rolls were among the first expenses to be targeted, and a precipitous, industry-wide downward slide in retail pay began.

The rise of the discounters also ushered in a pronounced cultural shift. Department stores had a long history of employing women, but the atmosphere at many discount chains was sometimes chauvinist and, at its worst, overtly sexist. In the 1950s and 1960s, E. J. Korvette was one of the earliest and most successful of the discount chains. It was founded by Eugene Ferkauf, a mercurial Brooklyn-born merchant and former GI, who was famous for having neither an office nor a secretary and for wearing sweatshirts in an era when suits were de rigueur. Ferkauf, whose name means "sell" in Yiddish, opened his first store on Forty-Sixth Street off Fifth Avenue in 1948. In 1951, E. J. Korvette had three locations, and a decade later it had more than a dozen, with more on the way. In 1962, the year that Walmart, Kmart, and Target were founded, *Time* magazine put Ferkauf on its cover, noting he was worth $40 million, or $387 million in today's dollars, and calling him "the founder, controlling stockholder and audacious boss of E. J. Korvette Inc., the nation's most successful and most unusual chain of discount department stores." In 1965, the chain announced that it was taking over the former Saks Fifth Avenue space at Herald Square for its flagship store. The Beaux Arts building, which Ferkauf covered in a new, brutalist facade, positioned the upstart discounter directly between two retail giants, Macy's on one side and Gimbels on the other.

The son of Romanian immigrants, Ferkauf spoke in a Yiddish-inflected Brooklynese, with phrases like "Cy, please, so why is it so schmootzig [dirty] around the soft-drink machine? I told you that should never happen. Cy, do me a favor. Clean it up." And, "Irving, so why doesn't someone pick up this shirt? It looks like a schmuttie [rag]." His top lieutenants were picked from among his rank of high school chums and former army buddies. With nicknames like Doodie and Schmultzie, Ferkauf called this all-male brain trust "the Boys." (E. J. Korvette did have one female executive, Eve Nelson, who oversaw the company's cosmetics line.) In 1968, the forty-seven-year-old Ferkauf retired after two decades running the retailer. During the fiscal challenges of the 1970s, the chain suffered major losses, and in 1980 it filed for bankruptcy. E. J. Korvette's flagship in Herald Square was later converted into a shopping mall.

While Ferkauf was establishing E. J. Korvette in New York, Sam Walton was founding Walmart in Rogers, Arkansas. Walton—who met with Ferkauf before he opened his first store—became a folksy billionaire, famous for driving a Ford pickup truck with hunting rifle on the seat beside him and his dog Ol' Roy in the back. Despite his humble trappings, in the 1980s Walton was America's wealthiest person; in 1990, Walmart was America's largest retailer, and in 1999 the discount chain was the country's largest private-sector employer. Despite its unmatched success, Walmart earned a notorious reputation for its male-dominated culture, with store policies that made it difficult for women to advance within its ranks. There was a directive, for instance, that required workers who were promoted to managers to relocate to a new store, which could mean moving hundreds of miles away, an impossibility for many women who had children, and often their husbands' jobs, to consider. The store was also known for overtly sexist messaging. In one example, in 1975 a banner was hung at an executive trainee session that read "Welcome Assistant Managers and Wives." Accusations against the discount chain culminated in what was the largest gender discrimination lawsuit in history, *Wal-Mart v. Dukes*. In 2011, the Supreme Court ruled 5–4 in Walmart's favor, arguing that the 1.5 million female plaintiffs did not have enough in common to file a class-action suit.

In the 1950s, the proliferation of branch locations and of discounters set the stage for department stores' slow decline. Dorothy had been at Lord & Taylor from its heyday in the 1920s, helping shepherd it through a depression and a world war. Like the store she ran, Dorothy was a powerhouse, an innovator who constantly broke new ground.

But in these years, her health began to falter. In December 1958, she was attending a fundraising luncheon at the 21 Club, when she collapsed. The press reported that Dorothy had suffered a fainting spell and was experiencing "complete fatigue," although it might have been a ministroke, and Dorothy took a leave from the store to recuperate. She continued experiencing health issues and in June 1959 left for an extended summer break at the country house that she shared with Elsie in Tannersville, New York. Some ten days after arriving, however, Dorothy suffered another stroke. Elsie rushed her to the hospital, but on June 28, just one month shy of her sixty-sixth birthday, Dorothy died.

"I was shocked this morning to read of Dorothy's death," the *New York Times* publisher, Arthur Hays Sulzberger, wrote to Elsie. "Terribly distressed to hear of your great loss," Governor Nelson A. Rockefeller wired. The former U.S. president Herbert Hoover, the former postmaster general James A. Farley, and even Vice President Richard Nixon wrote. Nixon called Dorothy "remarkable" and told Elsie, "The lifetime of service and achievement which Dorothy Shaver leaves behind is a greater tribute than any words that could now be spoken." The Fashion Group, later the Fashion Group International, the powerful women's organization that Dorothy helped found, wrote of her death in its newsletter. "Although we knew she had been ill for months, it was impossible to believe that she would not return to her prismatic, wide-embracing life," it said. "When one realizes that it was she who broke the barrier of prejudice against women as top executives, and that she fought so powerfully for recognition of talent everywhere—when one thinks of all these things, they seem overwhelming, almost."

Dorothy was a pioneer for female merchants, and one member of the Fashion Group, Mildred Custin, had long admired her. Nearly a decade before Mildred was appointed president of Bonwit Teller, she had been promoted to divisional vice president at John Wanamaker in Philadelphia. Dorothy wrote to congratulate her on the new position, and Mildred wrote her back. "I prize your message more than any I have received," Mildred told her. "If there had been no Dorothy Shaver to blaze the trail, there would be no such opportunities for women in top jobs such as the one I am fortunate enough to embark on."

More than one thousand mourners gathered for Dorothy's funeral

Dorothy (standing) and Elsie at their country house in Tannersville, New York.

at St. Thomas Church on Fifth Avenue and Fifty-Third Street, including a who's who of business leaders, politicians, and intellectuals. Elsie had Dorothy buried in Arkansas, not far from Mena, and on the gravestone she did her sister a final favor. Elsie inscribed her sister's birth year as 1898, rather than 1893, obfuscating Dorothy's real age, as had long been her wont. When Elsie died, twenty-two years later, in 1981 at the age of eighty-six, she was buried next to Dorothy. And as she had done for her beloved sister, Elsie misnumbered her own grave marker, inscribing her birth year as 1896. Not only did that render Elsie a year younger than she was; it made her two years older than Dorothy.

With Dorothy gone, Elsie was forced for the first time to confront life without her older sister by her side. In the years that followed, Elsie often reflected on the strength that made her sibling such a trailblazer. "I always wanted to be like mother and Didi. They had natural poise and self-assurance," Elsie wrote. "Didi was born under the sign of Leo and was a leader from the time she came into the world." Dorothy always claimed that being a woman never hurt her career ambitions, and Elsie pondered what her sister would have thought of women's progress in the years following her death. "If she were here, what she would have thought about the women's liberation movement I do not know," Elsie wrote. "She always said it wasn't a question of sex, it was a question of ability." Dorothy herself claimed, "The fact that I happen to be a woman has not stood in my way. It has even helped me. After all, women make up the largest proportion of our shoppers and a woman is better qualified than a man to know what appeals to them."

Despite her wish to the contrary, Dorothy's achievements were largely interpreted through a gendered lens. When she was first elected president, for instance, *Life* wrote how the all-male board of directors, "in the act of voting Miss Shaver into the presidency," had "congratulated themselves on picking 'the best possible man for the job.'" And while Dorothy earned an astounding salary for a female executive when she was appointed president of Lord & Taylor, it was still $25,000 a year less, or $410,000 in today's dollars, than the man whom she replaced. Dorothy's predecessor was also a member of the executive committee of the Associated Dry Goods Corporation, the chain that owned Lord & Taylor, while Dorothy never was. And when she died, after having made such an indelible mark on the American fashion industry, her salary was just $5,000 more, or $50,000 in today's dollars, than the man whom she replaced some fourteen years earlier.

Even today, Dorothy's achievements at Lord & Taylor, and her role mentoring some of America's earliest fashion designers, are largely obscured. Yet despite this general lack of recognition, it is hard to consider hers anything but a complete life. Dorothy lived fully, with few of the restraints that so many other women of her generation were forced to contend with. She had a passion for beauty and art, seeing her job as translating the ephemeral into the widely appreciated and tangible. "I am not an artist, but I can see with artists' eyes and speak their language," Dorothy once said. "And, on the other hand, I am a merchant. I listen constantly to what women want, I follow trends and guess what they are going to ask for next." In the end, she never voiced regret of any kind, relishing the excitement and adventure that her life choices afforded her. "I wouldn't change places with anyone."

❖

Chapter 12

President Geraldine

In the summer of 1959, Jean Rosenberg, a buyer for Henri Bendel, attended her first European ready-to-wear show. It was a warm morning, and she sat at a small café table in central Paris with a coffee and a croissant, watching sinewy models as they descended from a staircase and wound past her dressed in early fashions by Chloé. "There must have been maybe 20 people there, a bit of French press, and a few buyers from Paris, and maybe a couple from Italy," said Jean, the only American in the audience.

Geraldine had sent thirty-five-year-old Jean to Europe with a broad mandate: scour the side streets of Paris, the flea markets of London, and the fabric fairs of Florence in search of untapped design talent. Across the Continent at that time, a raft of young, upstart designers were toiling in basement sewing rooms, or at their parents' kitchen tables, breaking from traditional couture hierarchy to make non-custom yet expertly tailored clothing at moderate prices. Geraldine, with her innate sense of what would be next in fashion, had dispatched Jean to investigate. What she found was the vanguard of prêt-à-porter, or French ready-to-wear, and Bendel's was on the front line. "Go to Europe, buy whatever you like. If you don't like anything, don't buy anything," Geraldine told her. "No other merchant in New York City—or anywhere in America— would have said that," Jean later recalled. "I went with no budget, and I just bought what I liked."

What Jean liked were several dresses by Chloé and "charming little bits and pieces" she discovered in London. Jean traveled to Switzerland, but bought nothing, and to Italy, where she purchased quite a lot. Geraldine introduced her to two photographer friends in Milan who escorted Jean to a small house with a studio downstairs. There she found Mariuccia Mandelli, the designer of Krizia, busy sewing "some darling dresses." Jean bought armloads, and for the next three decades Bendel's was a loyal buyer of the Italian fashion brand.

The same month that Geraldine's revolutionary Street of Shops opened to skeptical reviews, Jean's European finds were unveiled at Bendel's newly opened Limited Editions Shop, so called because of its displays of well-crafted European pieces, offered in select, limited quantities. The idea was to sell merchandise that was original and—the holy grail of retailing—exclusive. "Next to a bad cold or a fight with her best beau, the most demoralizing event in a woman's life is a party to which she wears her newest dress and finds two other women in the identical garment," wrote *The New York Times* in a review. "Now Henri Bendel, a store that is extremely perceptive about the psychological subtleties of women and fashion, is offering a kind of catastrophe insurance."

The hunt for exclusive merchandise was central to Bendel's survival strategy. With the expansion of branch stores, the rise of discounters, and increasing industry consolidation, competition among department stores in the late 1950s and early 1960s was fierce. Bendel was about one-fourth the size of Bergdorf Goodman and Bloomingdale's, and it lacked the capacity to place large orders with the established French fashion houses. As a result, Bendel was being squeezed out of the all-important European couture market as designers bypassed it to strike more lucrative exclusivity deals with the bigger stores.

At the same time, high-quality copies of French couture designs were flooding the market. Bendel sold copies of Paris originals, but Geraldine made a radical decision in 1961 to upend years of store tradition. The turning point came when Bendel buyers attended the Paris couture shows with plans to buy outfits that others overlooked, the so-called sleeper styles. But they realized, too late, that Ohrbach's, the moderately priced department store, had purchased the exact same styles. "We couldn't compete with Ohrbach's," said Geraldine. "They do [copies] so well and less expensively than we could." Since Bendel couldn't win exclusives from the Parisian haute couture houses, and it could no longer afford to sell Paris copies, Geraldine announced that its buyers would skip the French couture shows. "It is unsound for us to invest the substantial amount of money required to see the collections," Geraldine wrote in a letter to French couturiers to explain her surprising decision. "We understandably cannot expect exclusivity of models and since we do not believe that Bendel ought to do inexpensive copies, we find ourselves competing with stores offering copies of our same models at much lower prices."

Despite pressures to follow the herd, Geraldine held firm to the notion that the store had to fill a unique need, "not a need for bigger and better Seventh Avenue labels that are available in many stores, but a need for tasteful snappy clothes." To get these clothes, she said, "our buyers must be creative." Jean, who had come to Bendel from Gunther Jaeckel, an old-school furrier, was up to the task. Traipsing through Paris in the early 1960s, for instance, Jean recalled how she "stumbled across a shop with charming, charming sweaters in the window." She ventured inside to inquire about the sweaters, and the man behind the counter told her that his wife was the designer. "The man's name was Sam Rykiel, and his wife was Sonia," Jean said, of the designer who would soon become world famous for her clothes. "Sonia didn't speak English then and she was very shy. I have often said to her that no woman pursued her husband more than I." During these years, Jean also discovered Emmanuelle Khanh making clothes for Cacharel and was the first American to buy Fendi furs, "long before they were anywhere else." She was also a model for Valentino, she said. After she met the designer in Italy, "Mr. Valentino made his very first ready-to-wear collection for Henri Bendel and fitted them on me!" Jean recalled. "So, you see, I had a very good time."

Jean was roughly the same age as her boss and arrived at Bendel just a few months before Geraldine came aboard as president. The pair worked closely together for the next three decades, pushing each other and joining forces to establish Bendel's reputation for high fashion. "Jean Rosenberg, the brilliant fashion merchant who came to Bendel's six months before I did, is responsible for all our buying," said Geraldine, years later. "What I've done is to lay out the character and style of the store. Jean selects the clothes that reflect that style." Insiders

Jean Rosenberg (left) and Geraldine (right)
at Henri Bendel.

considered Jean "Bendel's fashion conscience," John the Baptist to Geraldine's Jesus. "There was a symbiotic relationship between Geraldine and Jean," said the designer Jeffrey Banks. "Inevitably, if Jean liked something Geri liked it too."

At the time that Jean was scouring unheralded designers in Europe, the prêt-à-porter market was still a Wild West. "There was no pressure to place large orders," Jean recalled. "You could sample things. You could buy six pieces of something. It was lovely, they were all just pleased to be selling." She followed her gut, buying items based on instinct. "Geraldine always said that 'we can't be a me-too. We aren't going to copy anybody,'" Jean recalled. Geraldine's frequent admonishment to buyers was, "I want our own stuff, the way that we want it," her constant mantra, "Fashion says, 'Me Too,' while style says 'Only Me.'"

Jean bought directly from small-scale designers, instructing them on how to cut to American sizes and often requesting they make slight changes to a fabric or a hem. "We went with tape measures that had centimeters and inches on them," said Pat Tennant, a buyer who started shortly after Jean and who often accompanied her on these early buying trips to Europe. Jean was small-boned and petite, a perfect size 6, or a size 0 today, and would use herself as a model, trying on the clothes to determine proper fit. And often, as in the case with Valentino, she would be the model on which the ready-to-wear clothes were sized. Jean, in fact, claimed partial responsibility for Bendel's bias toward petite women. "It was probably partly my fault that we had small customers, because I was small," she said.

While in Europe, not only were Jean and Pat given unprecedented freedom to buy what they wished, but Geraldine also demanded that they spend prodigiously. "Geraldine always insisted that we stay at the Ritz, the Hassler, the best hotels," said Pat. "She wanted us to see what people wore and how they acted—also, maybe it was a little snobby." On their days off, the young women would explore. Pat, who at the time was a buyer for Young Bendel, the department that served stylish young women at lower price points, sometimes palled around with her archrival, the buyer for Bergdorf Goodman's Miss Bergdorf department, the two going to Vienna to see the opera and the Lipizzaner horses. "It was fantastic fun," Pat recalled.

But dealing with novice European ready-to-wear designers could have its downsides. These were small businesses with little experience operating on a shoestring budget. Unlike the larger European couture houses, which had developed a systemized, symbiotic relationship with American department stores, supplying them with new designs on a seasonal basis, prêt-à-porter designers were far less organized. "Inconsistency of fit, undependable deliveries, irregularity of quality, overpricing, difficulty in reordering," were some of the complaints that American stores lobbed against them, according to *The New York Times*. But Bendel's embraced the chaos, arguing that it made the shopping experience more exciting for customers. Displays at the Limited Editions Shop could be changed at random, the inventory turned over as soon as new merchandise arrived. This meant that customers who visited the department never quite knew what they would find, and "made an adventure in shopping out of what could have been a disaster." To keep its designers exclusive, Bendel's had to maintain secrecy, even sewing its own labels onto the clothing to obscure the designers' names, to prevent other stores from poaching them. "Throughout the past eighteen months, Bendel envoys have been combing the back streets of Paris in search of boutique designers," reported *The New York Times*, but "Bendel's has locked their names in the Top-Secret file."

While the Bendel strategy initially succeeded at keeping competitors at bay, it didn't manage to do so for long. Jean had been the only American at the Chloé fashion show in the summer of 1959, but by that winter American buyers were overrunning Europe, copying Jean's every move. "We had to start to sneak around, because buyers from other stores would follow us, or ask around what we had been up to," Pat recalled. "The whole thing caught on incredibly quickly." Three months after Bendel opened the Limited Editions Shop, *The New York Times* published a list of the department stores that were sending buyers to Europe, including Bergdorf, Lord & Taylor, Macy's, Bloomingdale's, and Ohrbach's. "New York buyers bought heavily," the paper reported, in an article titled "European Ready-to-Wear Attracts New York Stores' Buyers Abroad." "Estimates range from 'the largest foreign budget in store history' to 'more than I ever placed on couture originals.'" Bloomingdale's alone bought forty styles.

By the early 1960s, prêt-à-porter was no longer a market that Bendel could claim as exclusively its own. "It's becoming almost as easy for an American buyer to shop in Europe as it is to shop Seventh Avenue," said Geraldine, wistfully. "We almost had exclusivity on European ready-to-wear, when most other stores were either concentrating on couture or inexpensive merchandise." But Geraldine still held firm to her thesis that "exclusivity is absolutely essential" and that ready-to-wear, whether sourced in Paris or Florence, Seventh Avenue or Greenwich Village, was paramount to Bendel's success.

Like the couturiers in France, Seventh Avenue garment manufacturers had little reason to offer Bendel clothing on an exclusive basis. But Geraldine came up with some clever strategies to counteract the store's small size. "Considering the dollar volume of Bendel's better ready-to-wear operation," wrote the industry trade magazine *Clothes*, "how could Geraldine persuade the better manufacturers on Seventh Avenue to give her exclusives when she didn't have the purchasing power to make it profitable for them?" Well, the magazine posited, "as a former fashion editor for *Glamour* she was not short on market contacts and, as a very pretty president with a determined mind, she was hard to turn down." Geraldine "wheedled and coaxed," the magazine said, managing to get exclusives for limited periods—sometimes for as little as a single week. "But in that week the store's windows and advertisements would trumpet the news." Geraldine was also brilliant at placing Bendel at the head of the fashion curve, and her buyers soon gained a reputation for "understand[ing] the new fashion market coming on and, in many cases, would help the manufacturer by indicating certain trends that were rising on the horizon."

In addition to prêt-à-porter, the 1960s saw the advent of the boutique. These new types of retailers were smaller than department stores and offered a hip, young clientele unique and avant-garde fashions that were frequently refreshed to reflect the latest fads. Boutiques were an outgrowth of an explosion in youth culture at the time, as the baby boomer generation entered their teen years and the teens of the 1950s aged into their twenties. There was "a new economy nourished by the bumper crop of World War II babies who came of age and found themselves enjoying the highest standard of living then known to man," wrote *Women's Wear Daily*, noting that even older women were influenced. "A new breed of woman," the paper called it, "who put the accent on youth, no matter how old she was, a woman whose appearance reflected her space-age world." Geraldine, referring to a popular 1960s diet powder, quipped, "We're in an era of Metrecal, orange juice, and exercise—there's no such thing as an older woman's dress."

In fashion, the so-called youthquake was defined by figures such as Mary Quant, owner of London's fashionable Bazaar on King's Road, who was credited with popularizing the miniskirt, and the French designer André Courrèges, whose mod fashions included low-heeled go-go boots and A-line dresses in unusual material like clear plastic. New York would follow London with boutiques of its own, including Paraphernalia on Madison Avenue, featuring designs by Betsey Johnson and Deanna Littell. Geraldine wanted to capture this younger-skewing shopper. "I'm not just talking about the woman who lives in the East 60's, lunches at Orsini's and, hopefully, comes around the corner to Bendel afterwards," Geraldine said, referencing the popular restaurant spot for "ladies who lunch." "This is the era of the great leveling—money, leisure, exposure, television, and travel have produced droves of aware, assured women all over the country—from Long Island to Laredo, from Redding to Renaissance, Oregon." This new woman would "have to be deaf, dumb, and blind not to have caught the notion that the youth kick, the youth quake, the youth take-over is a basic fact of this year of grace—and if she wants to be part of the times, she has to be with it in viewpoint."

Geraldine had a fear of Bendel's returning to its previous iteration, before she took over as president, when it was known as the place where aging dowagers came to purchase fusty wardrobes. "I'm wild about the young kids. I want them to come to Bendel—I don't want the store to grow old with me. I want it to stay young," she said. And, at least according to *Cosmopolitan*, Bendel was managing to do just that. In an article titled "The Young Goddesses," it dished on Truman Capote's "swans," and the era's most fawned-over beauties, like Slim Keith, Babe Paley, and C. Z. Guest. The piece described the scene on a typical day at Bendel: "Starting at 11 a.m. daily the store is filled with a stunning flow of tightly coated, carefully coiffed young ladies in low-heeled 'status' shoes. (This year it is the metal-clip Gucci. Last year it was the pilgrim-buckle pump.) This year the girls sent burlap bags with 'Coffee Beans from Bendel' to those on their Christmas list, or a houndstooth covered crossword dictionary."

But while Bendel maintained its status as the place to shop, Geraldine faced a constant uphill battle. To stay afloat in the sea of larger competitors, she doubled down on her intuitions. She scoured the globe for hidden talent and used Bendel's platform to highlight ready-to-wear designers, regardless of whether they were European, American, or Japanese, as long as they epitomized the Bendel Look. In fact, the less well known, the better. In an extension of her Street of Shops concept, Geraldine offered unique spaces within the store to designers in return for exclusivity. One of the first of such arrangements was with Jean Muir, a member of London's swinging 1960s scene. With her cropped Vidal Sassoon coiffure, large eyes, and button nose, Jean closely resembled the era's most popular model, Twiggy, and her easy feminine pieces, perfectly crafted and flattering, were an ideal match for the Bendel Look.

Geraldine had been following Jean since her start, attending her fashion show one evening in 1966, joining a packed house as models walked without any music, the audience perched on small, gold-colored chairs. Geraldine was so taken with the clothes that she tagged along with Jean and a dozen other photographers and models for dinner after at the Dorchester hotel to celebrate. "She's simply the best dressmaker," said Geraldine, who regularly wore the clothes herself. She offered the designer a corner of Bendel's second floor, a peach-and-white space, where Jean displayed her paisley satin trousers, embroidered caftans, and floral-printed wraparound dresses. In its ads announcing the new boutique, Bendel called Jean "non-pareil," noting, "Who else knows every nuance of cut and shape and detail that goes into great dressmaking, or handles leather as if it were liquid, or turns out soft-strong shoulders ten ways?"

Another fashion designer who was close to Geraldine and would take on an important role at the store was Donald Brooks. A former window designer for Lord & Taylor, Donald was also a noted costume designer for Broadway. Over the years, Donald became one of Geraldine's best friends and eventually her landlord and neighbor, when she moved into his town house on East Sixty-Fourth Street. Geraldine loved Donald's clothes, often wearing custom pieces he would make for her, and she conceived of a notion based on his designs, which she dubbed "contemporary custom" clothes. Bendel would offer these custom items, but not in the typical couture fashion that necessitated untold fittings and months of painstaking work. Instead, the new Donald Brooks line would be a hybrid, bridging ready-to-wear and a traditional custom-made atelier. "Let the rest of the world trek to Paris. Bendel will have its own collection, designed by an American ready-to-wear designer, and produced in the store's own famous workrooms," wrote the *New York Herald Tribune*.

The method was novel, with Bendel customers able to choose from among several of Donald Brooks's outfits, picking out the color and fabric, and then having it cut to their measurements and basted. There would be a single fitting, after which the outfit would be completed and delivered within two weeks. Geraldine called it a "tiny, shining, serene little jewel" of an idea. And as with most innovations Geraldine spearheaded, several weeks after she announced it, Bonwit Teller touted a similar concept. Although in Bonwit's case, the store was quickly "deluged with requests from larger sized women," something that Bendel customers wouldn't dare; they knew better than to even ask.

Expanding on this idea of custom clothes designed by Donald Brooks, Geraldine announced that Bendel would be breaking into the larger manufacturing business. She tapped Pat Tennant to oversee a new department, called Bendel Studio, which featured designer collections that were made exclusively for the store and manufactured by the store, in a warehouse that it leased across the street. In essence, Geraldine transformed a segment of Henri Bendel from a customer of Seventh Avenue into a competitor. Over the years, Bendel Studio produced collections from several important designers, including Karl Lagerfeld, Jean Muir, and John Kloss. It was "perhaps the first vertical ready-to-wear setup in fashion retailing" history, declared *Women's Wear Daily*.

As Geraldine's star began to rise, she remained close with her younger sister, Carol, even though their lives had taken divergent paths. While Geraldine left Chicago for a career in fashion in New York City, Carol finished school and began teaching at their former Catholic high school, St. Scholastica, before marrying and becoming a stay-at-home mother to seven children. Eventually, Carol went through a painful divorce, and like their mother, Estelle, returned to the workforce to support her children. Carol went to graduate school and became a special education teacher, resettling her family not far from where she and Geraldine had grown up. Carol was thin and taller than Geraldine, and didn't share her older sister's panache for dressing, preferring instead a basic uniform of jeans with Birkenstock sandals and striped socks. Carol usually topped her outfits with a 1970s-style fringed suede coat, although she sometimes swapped it for a Burberry poncho that Geraldine had sent her. Carol did have a closetful of enviable, expensive designer clothes that she received from her fashionista sister, and on occasion, when the mood struck, Carol arrived at the conservative Catholic school where she taught garbed in $1,000 designer pants with her sandals. Despite their differences, Geraldine was a support, providing older-sister advice and encouragement after Carol's divorce. Geraldine called her sister "an extraordinary woman," marveling at how Carol survived "a traditional Catholic marriage" to become "second in command in her department at Loyola."

With no children of her own, Geraldine often visited Carol in Chicago, arriving for whirlwind weekends to "babysit" her gaggle of nieces and nephews. She was never much of a disciplinarian, though, and as the children turned to teenagers, Geraldine was more likely to let them smoke and drink, and take them to hear music or to the theater, than admonish them to behave. Geraldine was glamorous, an over-the-top presence, and when she arrived for her visits, she brought armloads of gifts. She would also spend hours rearranging Carol's furniture, moving her sofas here or her side tables there. Then, as she was preparing to head back to New York, Geraldine would call out, "Now, honey, you can just change everything back the way it was," before rushing out the door.

Their mother, Estelle, passed away, and the sisters' relationship with their father remained estranged. Still, Alexander Hamilton "Bearcat" Stutz took pleasure watching Geraldine's success from afar and would often write fan letters to newspapers and magazines that featured her in their pages. Eventually, Geraldine and her father reconnected. Growing up, "I was totally aligned with my mother," Geraldine recalled. "But quite late in life, I got to know my father, out from under my mother's wing and on his own." She called her father "rather an attractive man."

Her relationship with Carol's children helped tether Geraldine to the era's youth movement, as did the many young buyers who worked for her at Bendel. Geraldine realized that as part of this emphasis on being young, there was a large, mostly untapped business in "beauty." She jumped on the idea, converting Bendel's entire sixth floor into the Beauty Floor. Women "used to think of fashion as something that happened from the chin down and the hem up," she said. "Today, it means, in addition, glowing good health and good looks, vitality, a disciplined cared-for body, glorious hair, skillful make-up, clear tended skin." Geraldine hired David Crespin, "the underground, swinging hairdresser," according to *The New York Times*, to oversee a new salon, and asked H. McKim Glazebrook, the originator of the Street of Shops, to design decor that was inspired by a garden gazebo, with furnishings in pale green and trelliswork, flowered chintz, and ivy. The hair salon was notable for its several private rooms. "I hate sitting in bullpens," said Geraldine. "When I am at a beauty salon, I want to be fussed over, pampered . . . in private."

In addition to the hair salon, Geraldine managed to persuade Joseph Pilates, the inventor of the exercise routine, to open a Pilates studio at the store. Like many in the fashion scene, Geraldine was a devoted Pilates student, waking up in the morning, jumping into a leotard, throwing her street clothes over her arm, and grabbing a taxi to the studio on Eighth Avenue. After finishing her routine, Geraldine would get dressed and head to the store. Now she only had to go upstairs. The Pilates studio at Bendel was the first one outside Joseph's original studio, and Geraldine ordered the equipment, including the Pilates reformers, to match the rest of the floor's decor, with lacquered white handles, white vinyl padding, and polished cherrywood trimming. Joseph taught at Bendel every morning before returning to his own Pilates studio because, as he told the *New York Herald Tribune,* "important people go into that store."

Other changes at Bendel's included a refurbished fur department. The store had a long, reputable history selling furs, which it garnered from its founder, Henri Bendel, and it still boasted an active fur workroom, where coats could be repaired and stored. But in recent years, Bendel's reputation was eclipsed by rivals'. "Considering herself unable to compete against these larger furriers, yet unwilling to give up a profitable volume," reported *Clothes,* Geraldine "arrived at the idea of steering away from the big mink market and, instead, making the store a specialist in small furs." Bendel furs were unusual—short capes made from leopard, or longer belted coats in cougar—and it was the first store to feature furs by the then-obscure Italian house Fendi, thanks to Jean Rosenberg's discovery. Bendel also opened a sportswear department, called Cachet, which sold casual clothing but not any actual sporting clothes, its purpose "to provide the apparel needs for the taxi set rather than the station wagon set," *Clothes* noted.

When in 1962, right on time, Geraldine hit the goal she had set with Maxey to turn Bendel's red ink to black, it was largely because of Charles Freeman, or Charlie, as everyone called Bendel's vice president of finance. One of the few men at the store, Charlie was a number cruncher in a sea of creatives. "The store was run by all women, all women except for Charlie," recalled Carol Brown, a Bendel buyer. "He was the best." Charlie took on a paternal role with the buyers as well as with Geraldine, who was nine years his junior. "I am the father image to all the buyers," he said, "and I am also their professor of retail mathematics. They are creative artists who bring in the customers. I convert sales into profits."

Every Wednesday afternoon, the buyers, and frequently Charlie, would gather in Geraldine's office to review their latest finds, like a silk robe sourced from a shop in Chinatown or new soaps handmade in an Italian village. They would argue about stocking displays and hash out the design for the latest Bendel makeup bags. It could take hours, with Geraldine chain-smoking and waving her hands in her characteristic fluttering style, her numerous bangles jangling, calling everyone "darling" in her theatrical tone. She would sometimes hold court upstairs in the salon, getting a pedicure, a silent manicurist carefully painting polish on her toes, as her team circled around, peppering her with questions as she gamely answered them in quick succession.

Charlie's fatherly teacher style contrasted with Geraldine's dramatic flair, and the pair often teased each other. "Everyone loved Charlie," remembered Pat. "He and Jerry had this funny rapport; they were always joking." In a feature in *Esquire* magazine titled "When the Boss Is a Woman," the journalist Marylin Bender interviewed several men with female bosses, including Charlie. At one meeting that Marylin attended, Charlie was vehemently disagreeing with Geraldine over some money matter when he blurted out, "But, Marjorie!" He had meant to say, "But, Jerry!" and had mistakenly used his wife's name instead. "You don't have to bring your personal troubles to work," Geraldine shot back, not missing a beat, the entire group dissolving into fits of laughter.

Geraldine boasted a loyal team helping her at the store, and she nailed down a strategy that seemed to be working. It was still dwarfed in size by its competitors, but Bendel had become the undisputed shopping destination for very stylish women. Geraldine's staff had "an amazing esprit de corps which is today a rarity at any retail store and must account for a large measure of the success of the operation," wrote *Clothes*. *Life* magazine featured Geraldine in its pages, albeit not in the full-profile treatment that Dorothy Shaver had enjoyed. Dorothy and Geraldine met a dozen times, but they were not personally close. While Dorothy often shrouded herself in the language and imagery of the male executive, her *Life* profile declaring her "No. 1 Career Woman," Geraldine was featured as part of a six-page layout titled the "Take-Over Generation." It listed those under age forty who had "arrived" and included the novelist Philip Roth, the musician-composer André Previn, and the Broadway producer Harold Prince.

Geraldine wasn't a female approximation of a man, a female businessman. Rather, she was a wily, fashionable, attractive woman running a business. Vivacious and dressed in her favorite Jean Muir, Geraldine was part of a new breed who didn't succumb to narrow definitions of what a career woman was. If Hortense rejected being labeled a businesswoman, and Dorothy aped a male CEO, Geraldine was breaking into something altogether modern. In 1963, Betty Friedan published her bestseller, *The Feminine Mystique*, which helped usher in recognition of the pervasiveness of sexism and provided a novel take on women's work. Geraldine embodied this fresh perspective, and Bendel, under her watch, was becoming a department store that reflected this changing narrative.

Adel's Mannequins

In the late 1950s, Adel Rootstein, a South African–born prop designer, was living in a small flat in London, making wigs and props for displays in shop-windows. At the time, mannequins, the life-sized dolls that stores owned by the handful, dressing them in the latest fashions to draw in customers, were made from plaster, with heavy awkward bodies. These were robotic figures that stood stock-still, arms by their sides, eyes staring listlessly into the middle distance as parades of pedestrians passed them by. Some were so unwieldy—even the female forms could weigh in at two hundred pounds—that they had to be sawed in half when moved, leaving behind a trail of crushed feet and hands, not to mention the occasional shattered plate glass window. These enormous, ungainly mannequins looked ridiculous as the fashions of the swinging 1960s got under way, as if someone had dressed their Victorian-era grandmother in a silver catsuit and go-go boots and stuck them in the windows of a London mod boutique.

Adel bet she could make her own mannequins that looked modern and fresh, far better suited to the day's skimpy fashions. Spotting a fifteen-year-old model in a local newspaper advertisement, her boyish body epitomizing the new aesthetic, Adel hired her to pose. She had the model run and leap and strike a series of active postures—anything but the one foot forward, one foot back of the traditional mannequin—and had her likenesses sculpted in clay. Adel then took the clay sculptures and cast them first in plaster and then in fiberglass. The results were lightweight figures that looked uncannily as if they were moving like a real human. It had taken Adel several months to create her fiberglass mannequins, and by the time they were ready, the young model whom she had hired to pose was "discovered." She was no longer an anonymous, freckle-faced teenager with gangly limbs, but Twiggy, fashion's equivalent of the Beatles. And every store in London was suddenly clamoring for Adel's mannequins.

Mannequins have a long, storied history when it comes to fashion. In the centuries before there were glossy magazines to help women determine which hemlines were most in vogue, or how to accessorize an outfit with opera gloves, it was so-called fashion dolls, or small-sized mannequins, that were used as the main means of broadcasting the styles of the day. Named for the Dutch *mannekijn*, or little man, they were used by Flemish weavers and merchants to showcase their wares. By the late Middle Ages, these doll-sized figurines, which were made of wood or porcelain, were being garbed in elaborate gowns and even high heels and shipped across oceans and between royal palaces to inform wealthy ladies of the latest styles. The first record of these mannequins dates to 1396, when Queen Isabeau of Bavaria sent several to England to show the cut of Bavarian bodices. In the 1490s, Isabella of Spain placed annual orders for life-sized versions from France. In 1645, there were published complaints of German women who spent "as much for those dolls as would serve them to emulate the fripperies of the devil," while in 1788 a matron in Calcutta reported how ladies were mistakenly wearing shawls on their heads, and it wasn't until they had received a shipment of mannequins that they realized the cloaks were actually meant to be wrapped around their shoulders.

At the turn of the twentieth century, ladies began turning to illustrations in fashion magazines to learn which color shoes they should order, or how tight to make their corsets. In addition, Bon Marché and other early department stores began using life-sized figures to show off stylish clothing in their new, oversized plate glass window displays. These early versions were usually dressmakers' forms, often a shaped torso without legs, although in 1894, at an exposition in Paris, German manufacturers introduced a humanlike figure made entirely of wax. An eerie, almost grotesque approximation of the female form, it featured human hair that was meticulously attached by hand a few strands at a time and genuine teeth that came from dentists' offices.

By the early 1920s, store mannequins were ubiquitous, many with canvas bodies and wax heads. But these versions had a mortal flaw: if the sun beat too hard on the store windows' reflective glass, the heads would droop and melt, sinking down inside the bodies and making a sticky, gluey mess. Stores struck upon the only rational solution—do away with their heads. Some of the better stores placed paper cones where heads should have gone, or poles on which they could hang a jaunty hat. "Ladylike figures, surmounted by black wooden knobs in the place of the refined heads one might have reasonably expected, stood about with a lifelike air of conscious fashion," H. G. Wells wrote of the headless shop mannequins, in his 1905 novel *Kipps: The Story of a Simple Soul.*

It was Hortense, in her role as president of Bonwit Teller, who helped resurrect the mannequin head and eventually led to the mannequins made of plaster. Several years before her dramatic run-in with the Surrealist Salvador Dalí, Hortense had another confrontation over a window display. It was supposed to show off the latest bridal dresses from Paris, but when Hortense saw how the display director had set the scene, "I could have wept," Hortense said. The store's mannequins looked "stiff and without grace," and she called them "strange affairs, resembling tailors' dummies with arms." Even worse, "there was that lovely gown draped on that stiff dummy and beside it on a chair, of all places, the wedding veil." She demanded the staff find a dummy with a head so it could at least wear the wedding veil. The display team searched the bowels of the store's basement and found an old wax one, which they washed off and dressed up. But this was only a temporary solution, and not a very good one at that. Hortense tasked her team to do better. Eventually, a fashion illustrator at Bonwit Teller, Jean Spadea, along with a young designer, Cora Scoville, came up with a new, improved version of the store mannequin, one made of plaster. Hortense ordered six.

Plaster dummies were far lighter than wax, and could be made to look more lifelike, and in the 1930s and early 1940s one display director found fame through his creations. Lester Gaba created Cynthia—nearly all mannequins have names—who became a minor toast of New York when her creator began carting her everywhere he went. As a publicity stunt, or perhaps an artistic gesture, Lester took Cynthia to the El Morocco nightclub, on TV appearances, even to the wedding of Wallis Simpson and the former king Edward VIII. "One night, escorted by four detectives, Cynthia wore the fabulous 'Star of the East' diamond valued at a million dollars to a ball," wrote Lester. "That was all she wore, for she starred as Lady Godiva in a tableau." Based on the New York socialite and model Cynthia Wells, the mannequin Cynthia

Lester Gaba sitting at the bar at the Stork Club
with his mannequin Cynthia in 1937.

weighed 120 pounds and had pale skin, a small nose, fake eyelashes, and a blond wig. She became so famous that *Life* magazine ran a feature about Lester and his plaster pals, dubbed the "Gaba girls." In 1941, *House & Garden* magazine "interviewed" Cynthia, where she detailed her typical day. "I sit at the piano and greet Lester's friends as they come in," Cynthia "said." "Everyone comes over and speaks to me, but I notice that they soon drift away to other parts of the room and become absorbed in conversation. Sometimes I wish I were a brilliant conversationalist as well as a beautiful mannequin, but one can't be everything I suppose." Lester and Cynthia finally broke up when Lester was conscripted during World War II. He tried rekindling their relationship when he returned from the front, but the couple's former magic wasn't revivable, his shtick no longer appealing to audiences. Lester dropped the act and instead took a job as a columnist for *Women's Wear Daily*, where he wrote about window displays. As for Cynthia, supposedly Lester stored her in a friend's attic in the East Village, where she may remain to this day.

While Adel made her groundbreaking Twiggy mannequin out of fiberglass, she was not, in fact, the first person to do this. The first fiberglass mannequin was created during World War II, while Lester Gaba was away fighting, and it was a by-product of the atomic bomb. A firm that had been making plastic hands for wounded servicemen was asked to make a full-sized plastic man that could hold delicate recording equipment and be dropped by parachute into the eye of the Bikini atomic-test explosion. "When the fiberglass dummy survived, we figured plastic that didn't melt in atom blasts could certainly survive hot department store windows," said a spokesman for the firm. These fiberglass mannequins were sometimes used along with the heavier plaster versions, but it wasn't until Adel brought the fiberglass Twiggy into the modern era that they became the industry norm.

Adel had an ability to sense a fad before it happened, and her mannequins often captured the zeitgeist. In 1966, Donyale Luna became the first Black model to grace the cover of British *Vogue;* it would be eight more years before American *Vogue* followed suit. When the image was published, propelling Donyale to stardom, Adel was already busy capturing a full-body mannequin version of the six-foot beauty. When the Donyale mannequin, cast in Adel's characteristic animated, crouching poses, was displayed in English store windows, it generated controversy and soon became famous in its own right. Some claim that Donyale was the first Black mannequin, although Lester Gaba boasted that he made the first when he cast a series of Black mannequins in 1938 for the department store Blumstein's, on 125th Street in New York's Harlem neighborhood.

Adel continued to revolutionize store mannequins, creating plus-sized models, painfully thin models, and anatomically correct models, although that last group was not embraced stateside. American department stores "were frightened of nipples," said Adel. "They asked us to take off the nipples—and we offered them sandpaper instead." While most stores here were more puritan, Geraldine at Bendel embraced the mannequins with nipples, discovering that they were ideal for showing off the see-through blouses popular in the 1970s. "For a long time, mannequins were really stiff—they just looked like dummies," said Robert Rufino, a head of display at Bendel, which was one of Adel's first and most loyal clients in New York. Her mannequins "were really real," he said. "Sometimes you can do a group of her mannequins and you don't need props—they just talk so much."

Adel continued spotting trends. She cast a mannequin of Joan Collins months before the television hit *Dynasty* revived the actress's flagging fame, and in 1989 she invited the voluptuous downtown club scene fixture Dianne Brill, whom Andy Warhol deemed "Queen of the Night," to model for her. The full-figured Dianne mannequin, with 40-24-39 measurements, was pro-

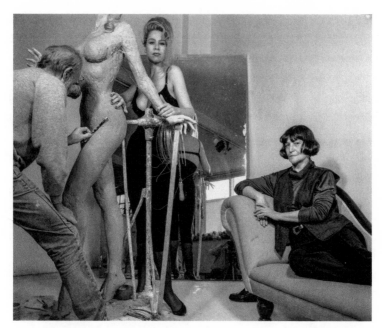

Adel Rootstein (seated) looks on as a mannequin of the model
and socialite Dianne Brill is made in London in 1989.

duced just in time for the WonderBra push-up mania, and for years the
Dianne mannequin was featured in the windows of the lingerie designer
Agent Provocateur. At the same time, Adel could also be choosy, refusing, for
instance, to make mannequins of Linda Evangelista and Kate Moss, arguing
that the supermodels were too short. One of her popular mannequins was
made following a request by Geraldine, who wanted a replica of Sara Kapp,
a model whose less-than-perfect face, with a nose that was thought too long
and slanted green eyes, made her particularly interesting.

Adel's mannequins took eighteen months of painstaking work to create.
Once a human model was chosen, they spent three weeks working with a
sculptor, who created life-sized clay models of them in various poses. After
this, plaster molds were taken, and plaster originals were cast. Blemishes that
had appeared were sandpapered away by hand in a slow, careful process, and
then, finally, fiberglass molds were made. Once the fiberglass mannequins
had been created, hair and makeup were applied in studios that the casual
observer might confuse for actual salons. While Adel's mannequins experienced excitement and glamour, it was often ephemeral. In a profile of Sara

Kapp—the mannequin—*The New York Times* wrote, "She leads a short life, but a luxurious one. Her wardrobe has dozens of designer dresses, marvelous furs and jewels, and she's at home at some of the best addresses in town. . . . Still, despite her thousands of admirers, she rarely smiles. And no wonder. Her life recently has been fraught with perils: she died of an overdose of pills in Bendel's, was found hanging at Bloomingdale's and had her nose bobbed for the San Francisco Clothing store."

Adel retired in 1990 and died in 1992. Before her death, she sold the company that she had founded to a Japanese firm. For many years, it continued to produce noteworthy mannequins under one of Adel's longtime lieutenants, Kevin Arpino, whom *The New York Times* called "brash and particular" and "a polarizing and powerful figure in the land of plastic people." Arpino eventually left, and in 2019 the family-owned Italian mannequin maker Bonaveri acquired Adel's former company. The artistry of humans creating facsimiles of humans, to sell clothing to other humans, lives on.

Chapter 13

⸻ ⟶⟵ ⸻

Hortense on Her Own

Four years after Hortense retired as president of Bonwit Teller, she gave up her seat on the board of directors and permanently stepped away from the store. By then, her views about female work had hardened, and she dismissed the notion that good could come from a woman having a job. "Careers, careers, that's all I hear," she said. In the midst of World War II, as newsreels and radio announcers touted Rosie the Riveter and extolled women wage earners, Hortense acknowledged the importance of war work, but otherwise she wanted none of it. "Women want careers because they don't want the responsibility of a home and children," she insisted. "The most beautiful career in the world is a home." She held firmly to the view that "men are leaders of the world. . . . It's biological," and, "No woman who works can take proper care of her home, her husband, and her children."

Hortense not only disavowed her time as a working woman, but she struggled to adjust to her unmarried status. Instead, she clung to her failed marriage to Floyd and to the idealized domestic version of herself that she remembered. Save for a few months when she was known as Mrs. Dominici, Hortense retained the Odlum name, even decades after her divorce, and even after a second Mrs. Odlum replaced her. For years, the press reported on "Mrs. Odlum"—Hortense—at Bonwit Teller, even as it covered "Mrs. Odlum"—Jackie—and her daring flying feats. Of course, names are fungible, and Jackie made use of her ex-husband's moniker, Cochran. Plus, divorce carried a stigma that

Hortense likely wished to avoid. Still, from the perspective of today, her pining for a former life is poignant and hard to ignore.

Hortense never publicly acknowledged her split from Floyd, and even used the phrase "my husband" years after that was no longer true. In 1935, on her one-year anniversary as president of Bonwit Teller, and just three days before she filed for her Reno divorce, Hortense gave an interview to *The New York Times*. In the story, the paper dubiously reported that "Mrs. Odlum added that her work had not interfered with her home and social life." A week after their divorce was finalized, in another interview, Hortense casually peppered her conversation with comments like "As I told my husband the other night . . ." Similarly, in her autobiography, *A Woman's Place*, Hortense keeps her personal story limited to her childhood in Utah and the early years of her marriage to Floyd. The pages are chock-full of asides relaying the couple's inside jokes and sentimental scenes depicting their love, with Floyd humorously choosing cheap decor for their Brooklyn apartment or cheering her on as she plunged into her job at Bonwit Teller.

Hortense came to see her career as a consolation prize. Perhaps it was an offering that Floyd extended in the hopes that it would ease her sadness at the breakdown of their marriage, or to distract her while he carried on his affair. A part of him might also have hoped to empower Hortense in the way that he supported Jackie and her flying ambitions. At first, Hortense had taken to her role at Bonwit Teller with enthusiasm, relishing the work and feeling exhilarated and engaged by store life, even voicing pride at her achievements. To ease the discomfort that she felt at being depicted as a career woman, Hortense recast the job so that it fit neatly within a paradigm that made sense to her, one that was consistent with her self-image. She perpetuated the notion that being the president of a department store drew on the same skills as the wifely duties that she so cherished, only writ large. Welcoming shoppers into Bonwit Teller, she maintained, was akin to a hostess gracefully receiving her husband's business associates into their home for dinner.

But over the years, it became impossible to keep up the facade. With Floyd married to Jackie, and her sons moving away, Hortense was left with only her job as cold comfort. She decided that a career was never something that she had wanted, but rather something that was foisted on her. And as she reflected on the decade that she had devoted to Bonwit Teller as adviser, then president, and finally board chairwoman, Hortense felt an intense hatred for what had befallen her, a seed of regret that grew over time into fully bloomed animus. Hortense decided that she had played the fool, and she began to vociferously, and publicly, decry women's work.

"I don't say anything that I don't *know* myself," she told one journalist. "When a woman takes a job, she gets too cocky and independent," she said, adding that her husband "loses confidence in himself. And he begins to think: 'Well, she doesn't need me anymore.'" In expressing such views, Hortense was hardly alone. While disparagement of women's work outside the home was temporarily paused during the war years, once the fighting ended, the narrative resumed, as exemplified by the 1950s ethos that glorified women's role as homemaker. "America is overemphasizing business careers for women in a way that threatens the country's good," Hortense declared. "Too many women are beginning to regard household work as drudgery. They need to be shown that a woman's greatest contribution to the world is to stay at home and rear her children right."

In the coming years, her son Stanley's painful decline into alcoholism would add to Hortense's sense of regret. Unable to persuade him to stop drinking, Stanley's long-suffering wife finally divorced him. In February 1957, on Stanley's forty-first birthday, Floyd sent his elder son a birthday check, as was his habit. He also wrote him a note. "This is the age when, according to many, life begins," Floyd wrote, "I hope that for you." He added, encouragingly, "the future years will pale into insignificance the years to date." But it wasn't to be. Just a few weeks later, Stanley was hospitalized in New York. Floyd instructed the doctors to spare no expense at making his son well and warned his young grandchildren to stay away so that their father could rest. But rest wasn't what Stanley desired; it was drink, and a steady march to self-annihilation.

Hortense and Floyd rarely corresponded following their divorce. What little interaction they had was limited to unavoidable topics, like family finances or issues regarding the children. And it was usually conducted through lawyers and other intermediaries. If Floyd did reach

out to Hortense directly, he dictated an impersonal missive to his secretary, who typed it up and sent it along. But when Stanley was hospitalized, Hortense penned a rare personal note to her ex-husband. "Dear
Floyd, Do not hesitate to contact me if you wish to—all is forgiven in
our hour of mutual love and concern," she wrote, on stationery from
the Drake Hotel, where she lived. Turning toward the faith in which
she had been raised, Hortense wrote of their son, "I know the life
within him is God life—perfect life—and I know God never forsakes
us—and never fails—if we keep tuned into the one presence and the
only power." Hortense signed the letter, "Love always, Tenny." There
is no record of whether Floyd responded. Ten days after entering the
hospital, Stanley died from complications caused by alcoholism.

When she stepped down in 1940, Hortense left behind a store
that was at the top of its game, with sales of $10 million, or
nearly $210 million today. It was a record, surpassing Bonwit Teller's
previous high, reached in 1928, at the peak of the heady Jazz Age. It
was also a 185 percent increase over its sales when Mr. Bonwit was in
charge. Yet competition from discount chains and other industry pressures began driving down Bonwit Teller's profits. In the 1950s, there
was an increased emphasis on efficiency as new technologies that were
developed during wartime to speed up production were applied to the
civilian sphere. Retailers consolidated and merged, and at America's
best-known department stores a series of executives cycled through,
holding leadership posts at one store, then moving on to another, then
even a third. In the decade that followed Hortense's tenure as president,
Bonwit Teller, like its competitors, underwent several transitions at the
top, with a revolving door of executives, some of whom stayed a few
years, others only a few months.

In 1956, Maxey Jarman, Geraldine's mentor at Henri Bendel, took
ownership of Bonwit Teller. The store's reputation had devolved since
the time that Hortense was in charge there, and it had overexpanded,
opening dozens of branch locations, many of which were operating at
losses. Maxey watched with dismay as new executives came and went,
none able to improve the store's outlook. The one bright spot was

the Bonwit Teller stores in Philadelphia, which were outperforming the other branches and were overseen by a female executive, Mildred Custin. Finally, in 1965, Maxey recruited Mildred to come to New York and take over the Bonwit presidency. "It wasn't more than 24 hours before the changes began," reported Eugenia Sheppard, the fashion columnist. First, Mildred closed most of Bonwit Teller's traditional departments to reassemble them anew. She opened the Espresso Shop, with affordable clothes for younger shoppers, the Safari Room for avant-garde customers, and the Designer Salon for affluent women looking for elegant evening wear.

Mildred, like Geraldine, had a knack for spotting design talent, and she placed the first major order for clothing by the then-unknown Calvin Klein. He was so new he was "wheeling the rack of clothes up Fifth Avenue on a Saturday morning" himself, Klein later recounted to *The New York Times*. "It wasn't even a collection; it was just fall coats and dresses. She was so supportive to me in those early years." Mildred also introduced America to André Courrèges, placing an enormous initial order for two thousand of the French designer's far-out dresses and coats. "Ours is a business of risk and if you don't take the risks, you don't get the gains," Mildred said. Perhaps her most radical change was in 1966, when she opened the Pierre Cardin men's boutique at Bonwit Teller. The store introduced "the French couturier's neo-Edwardian silhouette for men, the double-breasted blazer and other notions then deemed radical or effeminate," reported *The New York Times*, adding it "heralded the men's fashion revolution in the United States." The East Fifty-Sixth Street side of Bonwit Teller became known as a men's shopping mecca, with not only the Cardin boutique but also a Bill Blass shop and an outpost of the haberdashery Turnbull & Asser of London. "I had a strong feeling it was time for men to become fashion oriented and that if they weren't ready, their wives would urge them on," Mildred said.

After nearly five years in the job, Mildred, who was five feet three and famous for speaking in a soft, little-girl voice, had grown Bonwit Teller's sales to $85 million, or nearly $680 million today, from just $58 million when she joined. When she was still in Philadelphia, her fellow merchants had named Mildred "Man of the Year"—presumably not ironically. She never married and was unapologetic about her single status.

"There isn't room for a husband and children in the kind of job I have," she told *Time* unequivocally. "Retailing is a full-time job." In 1970, after turning the business around, Mildred left Bonwit Teller. Once again, the store was rudderless, cycling through an astounding eight different leaders in just nine years. None could achieve what Hortense, and then Mildred, had, and Bonwit Teller once again began to slide into a decline.

In 1979, Maxey was no longer in charge at Genesco, and the conglomerate was facing its own financial and leadership crisis. To shore up its losses, the company began unloading money-losing assets, including the unprofitable Bonwit Teller. Allied Stores Corporation, a department store chain, acquired every Bonwit Teller store—save for the flagship location on Fifth Avenue and Fifty-Sixth Street. That building, with its famed Art Deco flourishes, situated on a prime block in the center of New York's most exclusive shopping area, was sold separately. The buyer was a brash thirty-two-year-old real estate developer, Donald J. Trump. For Trump, the old building held little appeal, and he announced plans to demolish the structure to make way for a $100 million, sixty-story gleaming new condominium, what would become Trump Tower.

The news came as a shock to many. For thirty years, Sylvia Fabricant had awoken most mornings to dress, eat breakfast, read the morning paper, then leave for her job as a saleswoman at Bonwit Teller. One morning, however, she was perusing the news when she discovered that the store had been sold and that it would soon be closing. "That's how we found out about it," she told *The New York Times* on one of her last weeks on the job. "Honestly, it was heartbreaking." With Bonwit Teller's impending closure, the department store held a massive sale, and its once-tidy aisles and organized shelves quickly devolved into chaos, with items thrown in jumbled piles, customers pawing through them in search of steals. "The interior of the venerable department store has a desolate air, despite the frenzy generated by clearance sales," *The New York Times* reported. "It's become more like a bargain basement, rather than a high-class, sophisticated place for the elite to shop," said Wendell Hodge, a shoe salesman there. "It's pathetic!" cried Janet Oseroff, a young shopper who was wandering around, stunned at the store's diminished state. "Bonwit's was part of my upbringing. There are certain things I always imagined would be here to show my own children, and it's so sad to see good solid things go away."

This was not to be Bonwit Teller's final humiliation, however. The famed building featured several architecturally significant embellishments, particularly the stone bas-relief sculptures on the building's facade, which stood fifteen feet high and were situated between the eighth and the ninth floors. They depicted a pair of stylized women, their figures partly draped with fabric, and when Trump announced his purchase of the building, he offered to donate them to the Metropolitan Museum of Art. Trump also offered to donate the distinct fifteen-by-twenty-five-foot grillwork of interlocking geometric designs that had decorated Bonwit Teller's entryway ever since Mr. Bonwit hired the architect Ely Jacques Kahn to redo the original Warren & Wetmore details in a restrained, modernist style.

But one afternoon, construction workers climbed up the facade and began destroying the female figure bas-reliefs. "They were just jack-hammered in half and pulled down in such a way that they shattered," said a shocked Robert Miller, a gallery owner who was staring out his eleventh-floor window directly across from Bonwit Teller when it occurred. "I really couldn't believe my eyes," added Peter M. Warner, a researcher at an architectural firm whose window was also opposite the building and who witnessed the destruction.

"The merit of these stones was not great enough to justify the effort to save them," a Trump spokesman, John Baron, told the papers. (In fact, "John Baron" was an alias of Trump's, a fake alter ego he cloaked himself with when calling reporters.) The bas-reliefs were "without artistic merit," he said, and worth less than $9,000 in "resale value."

"How extraordinary," responded Ashton Hawkins, secretary of the Board of Trustees of the Met, when he heard. "Can you imagine the museum accepting them if they were not of artistic merit? Architectural relief of this quality is rare and would have made definite sense in our collections. Their monetary value was not what we were interested in." By then, the grillwork, which had been successfully removed from the facade, had also disappeared.

The controversy intensified, with angry editorials and letters to the editors and newspaper headlines. "John Baron" doubled down, arguing that it would have cost the developer $32,000 to have workmen chip away by hand to remove the bas-reliefs from their concrete and steel beds, not to mention the added cost of delaying the demolition. But the outcry would not abate, so, finally, Trump was forced to answer the critics himself. "Mr. Trump, who said he had been out of the city for four days and thus had been unable to respond to the criticisms, said last night that the $32,000 cost of removal had not been an important consideration," reported *The New York Times*. "I contribute that much every month to painters and artists—that's nothing," Trump told the paper. The real reason for the destruction of the bas-reliefs, he insisted, "was the safety of the people on the street below." The sculptures were cracked and weathered and weighed two tons. "If one of those stones had slipped, people could have been killed."

While the Bonwit Teller building was demolished and replaced with Trump Tower, the store itself was resurrected, albeit temporarily. Two years after it disappeared from Fifth Avenue, news broke that a new, reduced-sized Bonwit Teller was set to open a few hundred feet away, as a retail anchor for Trump's gleaming new condominium. Trading in its characteristic restrained Art Deco style for flashy pink marble, the new Bonwit Teller location was about one-third of its original size and in a shifting retail landscape struggled to succeed. It changed hands several times until, in 1990, after losing a staggering $30 million in just three years, Bonwit Teller was dismantled and the Fifth Avenue store at Trump Tower shuttered. Like many of its competitors in the ensuing years, the once-proud retailer that Mr. Bonwit had dedicated so much of his life to building dwindled and diminished until finally it was vanquished.

In the years following Stanley's death, Hortense too began to disappear. She receded ever further into herself, her relationship with her surviving son and her grandchildren increasingly estranged. "It was a very distanced family, with big spaces between people," said Bruce's son, Brian Odlum. Hortense occasionally flew to California to see Bruce and his children, but there could be years-long gaps between such visits. "She was an absent sort of person," said Brian of his grandmother.

"The fact that she wasn't around was the most obvious sign of the quality of the relationship." While Bruce and his family were in California, Stanley's ex-wife and his children lived in a New York suburb and, growing up, saw slightly more of their grandmother. Every year at Christmastime, their mother would drive the children to Hortense's apartment at the Drake Hotel in Manhattan, where they gave her an obligatory hug, then stood around awkwardly, without much to say to one another. "It was ghastly," recalled Stanley's oldest son, Stanley Jr., describing his grandmother as "one of those cold fishes."

As Hortense aged, her health began to fail, and she suffered from heart problems and later dementia. It fell to Bruce to care for his mother. At the time, he was living on a large plot of land at Floyd and Jackie's California ranch, with his second wife and daughter. Seeing no other option, Bruce decided to have a small house built nearby on the property for his mother. "Tenny had to go somewhere, and my dad felt responsible for her," said Wendy Odlum, Bruce's daughter, who grew up on the ranch. Hortense's new home was a few hundred yards from her son's house, and less than a mile from Floyd and Jackie's home. Perhaps being in such proximity to her ex-husband, combined with her diminished memory, proved too confusing for Hortense. While Bruce hired caregivers, Hortense frequently grew agitated and had to be restrained from venturing out to try to find Floyd. Despite her attempts, Hortense never did manage to see her ex-husband. "Tenny was on my father's part of the ranch, and Floyd never went over to see her," recalled Wendy. "I couldn't even imagine them using the word 'hi' with each other."

Hortense died in early 1970, at age seventy-eight. Bruce called the undertaker to take her body away. "When my grandmother died, I remember my father saying something along the lines of 'Well, the old witch is finally dead,'" said Brian. "There was no sense of loss or pain, just a great relief that he had discharged his duty as a good son. . . . There just wasn't a lot of love lost." Several newspapers, including *The New York Times*, published obituaries citing Hortense's many achievements. But there was no funeral service. Hortense was cremated and there is a grave marker, a few miles from Floyd's ranch, that reads, simply, "Hortense Odlum, 1893–1970." The marker, which inexplicably put her birth year as two years later than it actually was, is placed next to a similar one for her son Stanley.

Hortense reluctantly shattered norms and unintentionally paved the way for others. Without a road map, she rebuilt the struggling Bonwit Teller until the business employed fifteen hundred people, from maintenance staff to powerful buyers to fellow executives, answering to an all-male board of directors and commanding a budget with sales in excess of $200 million in today's figures. Hortense was forced to navigate changing cultural norms as she searched for an elusive happiness, trying to establish her footing amid the quicksand of history. While she was desperate to love and to be loved, she kept those closest to her at bay. In the end, she was both a perpetrator and a victim of her era's societal rules and the expectations that governed women.

Chapter 14

Geraldine Meets Her Match

One evening in 1964, Geraldine was running late. It was a perpetual problem for which she was infamous, and her hostess, the legendary fashion publicist Eleanor Lambert, wasn't terribly surprised. Just as Eleanor's guests were sitting for dinner in her antiques-filled dining room, in rushed Geraldine, throwing off her coat. "I'm so sorry," she said, grateful that at least this time she had a proper excuse. "The hair salon caught on fire!" Most of the guests barely looked up before continuing with their chatter, but her seatmate, a debonair British art dealer, David Gibbs, gave her a bemused smile. David, forty-two and tall, with shaggy hair and a slightly overgrown goatee, assumed Geraldine was a beautician, given her excuse for being tardy. "I didn't know Geraldine was a career lady at all when we met," David said. "I thought she worked in somebody's beauty parlor as an assistant." Geraldine, who was forty, with stylish hair worn in a curly pixie cut and her uniform of formfitting Sonia Rykiel sweater and slacks, fell into an easy, flirtatious rapport with her neighbor. As they talked, Geraldine dished on the day's drama at Manhattan's chicest department store and David was quickly disabused of his initial impression.

It had been seven years since Geraldine left I. Miller for the challenge of running Henri Bendel, and during this period she had been focused and ambitious, allowing herself little freedom to pursue romance. But after a dozen years on the analyst couch, spending significant time confronting what Geraldine later described as the "enormously damaging" effects of her strict Catholic schooling, she felt in tune with her psyche and ready for a relationship. While her education had provided training for "discipline and control and performance," she said, it also made her a "tap dancer," a woman who was high achieving, but above all obedient. "I wanted to perform for the authorities in my life," Geraldine said. "I wanted to please my mother, the Mother Superior, and the Mother Church, in that order."

In addition to being a people-pleaser, Geraldine was also taught to be self-effacing. "I was raised . . . in a series of convents where nuns were second echelon to priests, and I grew up in a patriarchal family," she said. Despite such realizations, her hours spent in analysis could not reverse certain stubborn tendencies, in particular, Geraldine's chronic habit of running egregiously late. But in terms of romance, she came to believe that it wasn't her career that was preventing her from having a boyfriend, but rather her own skewed perspective. "As I got more deeply into my analysis, I began to understand that my problems had nothing to do with my professional viewpoint but my personal viewpoint of being a woman—this second-class citizen." Geraldine had paramours over the years, including Condé Nast's inscrutable owner, Si Newhouse Jr. But none of her relationships were very serious. "There were men who regarded me as a sex object and not as a total person, and that made me very angry," Geraldine said. "Then there were men who were in competition with me, but I found that boring and usually the feeling of competition existed only in very immature men."

When Geraldine met David that night at Eleanor Lambert's dinner party, there was an immediate electricity between them and they both fell, hard. "He reminded me a bit of her father, tall and thin and soft-spoken," said Ellen Hopkins, Geraldine's niece. "She was vivacious, and he was British." David, who worked as an art dealer representing the estate of the Abstract Expressionist Jackson Pollock, loved America. To David, the country represented freedom, a place where he could be far from his domineering mother and from the horrors of World War II, where he had witnessed intense fighting as a member of the Welsh Guards. David also loved American women. "They are more in touch with themselves than most of the Europeans," he said. "They are really alive."

But for all of David's positives, he also carried significant baggage,

Paul J. Bonwit
in 1934.

The Art Deco
entrance of
Bonwit Teller,
designed by the
architect Ely
Jacques Kahn.

Saleswomen for the St. Luke Emporium in 1905.

From left to right: Hortense; her elder sister, Zella; and her younger sister, Laura Marie.

Hortense with her grandchildren Brian (left) and Chris (right) in September 1967, at the Beverly Hills Hotel.

Floyd, digging a car out of the mud at his ranch in California, while Amelia Earhart looks on.

A young Dorothy, far right, with several friends in New York.

Dorothy (seated) with Elsie and her paintings, as featured in *Harper's Bazaar* in March 1946.

A rare photo of the Little Shavers Shop that Dorothy and
Elsie opened on Forty-Seventh Street in 1919.

An undated snapshot of Dorothy.

Geraldine with
James Jarrett Jr.,
the Henri Bendel
doorman known
as Buster.

Geraldine at her desk at
Henri Bendel in 1963.

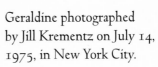

Geraldine photographed
by Jill Krementz on July 14,
1975, in New York City.

An illustration by
Andy Warhol that
adorned a feature
edited by Geraldine
in *Glamour* in 1949.

Miriam Marshall on a buying trip in Kashmir,
purchasing items for her Henri Bendel boutique Port of Call.

A contact sheet of Geraldine and David, with an unidentified friend, while on vacation in Jamaica in the 1960s.

Geraldine (in white cap) standing with some of her favorite Henri Bendel designers, including (from left to right) Don Kline, Lee Bailey, Viola Sylbert, Dick Huebner, Ralph Lauren, Holly Harp, and Carlos Falchi.

A Christmas window at Henri Bendel,
designed by Robert Rufino.

Geraldine and David attending a party
at the home of Donald Brooks in 1974.

most notably a wife and two elementary-school-age daughters back in London. He was a Peter Pan, charming, with a sharp, dry sense of humor, but resistant to responsibility. David won the prestigious, and lucrative, assignment to sell Pollock's work after coming to America and seducing his widow, the painter Lee Krasner. Seventeen years David's senior, Lee was besotted with the young Brit and hoped he would divorce so they could marry. Within a year of his winning the Pollock assignment, however, the relationship petered out, and Lee's friends considered him alternately "an ambitious careerist" or merely "a bit of a fancy boy, but not a villain, or cruel." When he met Geraldine, the relationship with Lee was over. "They fell in love and started having an affair, and my mother told him, 'Either you go and get it out of your system, or we get divorced,'" recalled Emma Turner, David's eldest daughter. "So, my father left to live with Geraldine in New York."

In 1965, after a year of dating, Geraldine and David were married in a country church in Connecticut. Back in the city, Geraldine's close friend, the clothing designer Donald Brooks, hosted a reception for the newlyweds at Delmonico's. "Because Bendel's president Gerry Stutz is so well liked, her romance with English painter, David Gibbs, was

Geraldine (third from left) having lunch at La Côte Basque with (left to right) Nancy White, former editor of *Harper's Bazaar*; Eugenia Sheppard, the fashion columnist for the *New York Herald Tribune*; and Sally Kirkland, the retired fashion editor at *Life*, photographed by Jill Krementz on July 29, 1980.

one of the best kept secrets in history," wrote Eugenia Sheppard in the *New York Herald Tribune*. After the wedding, David gave up art dealing to pursue painting full time, and the pair lived in Geraldine's East Sixty-Fourth Street duplex, on the top two floors of Donald Brooks's brownstone. David quickly fell in with Geraldine's celebrity crew, the newlyweds hanging out with the theater producer Hal Prince and the performer Bobby Short, and were regulars at Elaine's, the famed eatery on the Upper East Side. They had cocktails with the likes of fashion editor D.D. Ryan and socialite Lee Radziwill, both of whom were loyal Bendel customers, lunched at Orsini's with the gossip columnist Liz Smith, and attended social gatherings, like a book party for Truman Capote at the home of Gloria Vanderbilt and Wyatt Cooper. As part of her job publicizing the store, Geraldine frequented society hot spots and hosted events, such as a birthday party for the singer Diana Ross, the guest list full of celebrities like Bianca Jagger and Lauren Bacall.

"My father loved Jerry's success and the access to that life," said Emma, noting that "his own career went alongside hers."

To find a respite from so much entertaining, Geraldine and David purchased a two-hundred-year-old country home on a rambling eight-acre estate in rural Connecticut. They enlarged and modernized the house, filling it with a comfortable mix of Welsh furniture from David's mother and modernist glass-and-chrome touches. The couple had no staff there, and since neither enjoyed cooking, they brought fresh produce and prepared food with them from New York City to eat through the weekend. David was a passionate gardener, a pastime that Geraldine also learned to love. Geraldine called herself "a maker," and gardening was an active pursuit, "the first thing I've found other than fashion which uses my perceptions of form and color," she said.

The socialite C. Z. Guest persuaded Russell Page, the famed landscape architect, to advise Geraldine on the sloping property, which bordered the Shepaug River and looked out onto the dramatic cascades of the Roxbury Falls. The elderly Brit, whose clients included the Duke of Windsor and King Leopold III of Belgium, agreed on the condition that Geraldine pick him up promptly at 9:00 a.m. at the Carlyle hotel and return him by 7:00 that evening. Geraldine managed to appear at the appointed time, pulling up to the hotel on Madison Avenue to find waiting the seventy-three-year-old Page, a "tall man in exactly the right kind of worn corduroy and gum boots with an easy jacket and a scarf twirled twice around his shoulders, wearing a beret because it was raining," said Geraldine. "He was like a tree who had been out against the elements." When they arrived at her house, "he takes his umbrella out of the backseat, raises it, hands it to me, and without a word takes off," Geraldine later relayed. She spent the next two hours traipsing through the mud, past the wild daylilies that ran along the riverfront, and pointing out the small cottage that dated from the 1740s and was once the town post office and now served as the garden shed. The pair explored in absolute silence, Geraldine holding the umbrella above Page's head—no easy task given that he was six feet seven—while he picked up leaves and examined the soil. Afterward, Page sent Geraldine a ten-year gardening plan, which she dutifully followed.

Living with Geraldine in America, David rarely saw his daughters. It wasn't until 1966, a year into their marriage, that Geraldine met his children. The plan was for David to leave from London and Geraldine from New York and to meet his daughters in Malta. To soften the blow, David's mother planned to join them, as did David's sister, brother-in-law, and their children. Geraldine was running behind schedule, as per usual, and had to stay in New York to finish the all-important Bendel Christmas catalog, which had become big business for the store. When she finally arrived, she had terrible jet lag. "My father went to pick her up at the airport, and for three days after, we didn't meet her. All we saw were room service trays set outside the door," Emma recalled.

Finally, Emma, who was ten years old, was told that she could go in the room and meet Geraldine. Emma had envisioned her as "Cruella de Vil, the wicked stepmother who took our father away." But when she opened the hotel room door, Geraldine was standing there smiling, and the first thing she said was, "Have you ever seen floating soap?" She took Emma conspiratorially by the hand and led her into the bathroom, where she had filled the enormous tub to overflowing with a mountain of bubbles. "She said, 'Get in and try and find the soap!' And I just loved her. I just absolutely loved her from that moment until the day she died," said Emma. "Jerry just had a way about her with young people. She wasn't maternal, she never tried to be my mother, but she was great fun."

In the early years of Geraldine's marriage, New York was a city in flux, where high and low were meeting and melding and social movements were taking form. Andy Warhol created high-priced artwork from everyday objects like Brillo boxes, while the composer Leonard Bernstein hosted fundraising parties for the Black Panthers. There was a burgeoning gay liberation movement, spurred by the Stonewall uprising in Greenwich Village; second-wave feminism and the accompanying sexual revolution; and the increasingly powerful civil rights movement. Geraldine relished the moment and reflected it back at Bendel, creating a similar fabulous amalgam at the store, burnishing its reputation as a magnet for the high tastes of uptown society women even as it was a cool draw for the downtown party crowd.

One way Geraldine pushed Bendel into this progressive, boundaries-defying mood was through its display windows. Windows were always the public face of the department store, and under Geraldine they became so famous as to be an art form all their own. Robert Currie, a twenty-five-year-old seminary school dropout, was the genius behind the Bendel windows, creating displays that were notable for being always original, usually humorous, and occasionally shocking. As ever, Geraldine had a knack for finding a singular talent. One day, she was walking down Madison Avenue and happened to look up. There, in a second-floor window, she spotted what looked to be an entire construction site—orange-and-white-striped street barricades, tall funnels where steam usually emits from pipes below the streets, a series of stop signs. It was a window display for the designer Norma Kamali, who was just starting out in the fashion business. Robert wanted a way to draw attention to the upstairs location of her store, and without much budget to play with, he had gone out in the night and stolen the items from the street. When Geraldine found out who had created the windows, she immediately called Robert and offered him a job.

Within weeks of starting at Bendel, in 1973, Robert became a key architect of a new window display aesthetic. Dubbed "street theater," it was the practice of using store merchandise to depict a dramatic narrative, often one that was confrontational or jarring. Every Thursday after Bendel's 6:00 p.m. close, Robert and his staff would begin deconstructing the previous week's windows and installing a new creation. The windows soon became happenings, crowds gathering Friday morning to see what perverse psychodrama the windows revealed. It might be a mannequin who was sprawled out on the floor, her arms splayed, a vial of poison spilled beside her, as a group of fellow mannequins looked on, the sign above them reading, "Who Dunnit?" Or it could be a mannequin clad in the latest Jean Muir, clawing desperately at a wall covered in delicate floral wallpaper, her face smeared with makeup, her fingernails broken and raw, the sign above declaring, "You'll Go Mad over Muir." One window featured mannequins drinking at a lesbian bar, another, mannequins in preppy blazers surrounded by piles of garbage. One tableau, of ladies of the night garbed in lingerie and stretched across a bed, elicited so much attention that one customer even purchased the bed. But there were also limits put on Robert's creations. When he told Geraldine that he planned a window with a coffin and a funeral scene, she quipped, "Over my dead body."

Another window artist lent Bendel his creativity, and eventually became famous in his own right. Twenty-two-year-old Joel Schumacher was designing windows for Lord & Taylor and Saks, when, in 1961, he was plucked from obscurity by Geraldine. For four years, Joel, who would go on to become a Hollywood director of such blockbusters as *St. Elmo's Fire* and *Batman Forever*, attended Parsons School of Design by day and worked nights designing Bendel's windows. In 1965, Joel graduated from school and quit Bendel to open Paraphernalia, a mod clothing boutique featuring go-go dancers in the windows, where Edie Sedgwick was a regular and the Velvet Underground played gigs. But that same year, Joel's mother died, and his casual dabbling in drugs grew into a full-blown addiction. "I lived on speed," he recalled. "I was shooting up speed six times a day. I had lost five teeth. I was down to 130 pounds." Geraldine recognized Joel's talent, and even after he left the store, the two were in regular contact. As Joel's addiction grew increasingly severe, Geraldine came to his rescue, hiring him back at Bendel. Joel called Geraldine "my mentor, savior, discoverer and best friend," noting, "I rebuilt my entire life there, at Bendel."

Joel repaid the favor to Geraldine by introducing her to one of Bendel's most important discoveries, a twenty-six-year-old fashion designer named Stephen Burrows. Joel was a regular in the party scene, hanging out with the beautiful set at Max's Kansas City and dancing until morning at The Loft in SoHo. Stephen was enmeshed in the same world and was gaining an avid following, dressing the young models and artists in his fringed leather and body-conscious clothes. Joel arranged for Geraldine to meet Stephen at her office one morning. He arrived dressed in one of his designs, a wraparound coat that closely resembled a bathrobe. Geraldine immediately asked to see the item and, trying it on, took a twirl. She gave Stephen an enormous grin and, her internal alarm bell for talent blaring, offered the rookie designer his own boutique.

Stephen Burrows and models wearing his designs, posing
in front of Bendel in 1977 with the store's famous doorman,
James Jarrett Jr., better known by his nickname, Buster.

Geraldine gave Stephen an unused room on an upper floor of Bendel
to use as his atelier, even supplying him with his own pattern maker.
In the fall of 1970, Stephen Burrows World opened on the third floor.
To celebrate, Geraldine hosted a packed fashion show, with Stephen's
friends, fashion buyers, and the press forming a crush, the runway
marked by dressing room lights that had been laid on the floor. Some
models wore Afros, some wore their hair slicked back in a bun, and
one had a shaved head. The clothing was exciting and different—black
leather gaucho suits with nail-head trim, patchwork, appliqué, and
leatherwork in rainbow hues. As the models pranced and smiled, the
crowd grew rowdy, stamping their feet and stretching out their hands
to touch the clothes, and when the designer himself walked down the
runway, dressed in black leather, "they became a bloodcurdling roar,"
wrote *The New Yorker* in a review. Geraldine, costumed in one of Stephen's simplest outfits, a knee-length black jersey with canary collar,
hem, and dickey, presided over the fashion show with "the uneasy
poise of a permissive mother at a birthday party when the jellies start
to fly." *The New Yorker* declared that "Burrows' clothes are made for the

fashionable lives and bodies of Bendel's people," noting, "Henri Bendel is really a department store for women, but its principles are those of the successful boutique and its concerns the exclusive, the transitory, and the young designer in his prime. . . . Only a fool or an eccentric would visit the store if she were fat, dowdily dressed, or accompanied by someone who will not pass for the right accessory."

As Stephen's name caught on and he grew comfortable with his perch at Bendel, he began focusing on dresses made of draped jersey, in bold monochromatic colors and slinky metallic mesh, and his unique "lettuce edge" technique of leaving the garment unfinished to create a ruffled effect. As the 1970s proceeded, a Stephen Burrows dress became nearly a requirement for entrance into Studio 54 and the disco nightlife that was dominating New York, with stars like Liza Minnelli, Farrah Fawcett, and Barbra Streisand draped in his designs. Mick Jagger supposedly flew to Bendel for a private fitting, and *People* magazine dubbed Stephen the "Fashion King of the Sexy Cling." In one of Bendel's advertisements for the designer, the copy read "Stephen Burrows . . . Stephen Burrows . . . How does your garden grow? With clothes that cling like secondskin and rainbows all in a row." In 1973, Stephen was the youngest, and the only African American, to participate in the Battle of Versailles, the famous fashion show that Eleanor Lambert helped create and that pitted American designers, who also included Halston, Oscar de la Renta, Bill Blass, and Anne Klein, against a team of French rivals made up of Yves Saint Laurent, Pierre Cardin, Givenchy, and others. That same year, Stephen became the first African American to win a Coty American Fashion Critics' Award, his first of three.

Stephen was such a phenomenon that when Pat Tennant, who oversaw Bendel Studio, came to Geraldine with the idea of creating a separate company to manufacture Stephen's designs, Geraldine not only said yes but also personally invested in the endeavor. The company, Pat Tennant Inc., manufactured Stephen's clothing and sold it across the country; in New York they were available exclusively at Bendel. But while his popularity soared, Stephen struggled with productivity, frequently choosing to spend his nights dancing with his celebrity clientele, which

Geraldine (left) and Jean Muir (right) in 1975, attending a Zandra Rhodes fashion show at Henri Bendel.

made it challenging for him to spend his days designing at his drafting table. Eventually, Stephen was wooed away by a competing manufacturer. He felt so sheepish about abandoning the women who had championed him that instead of informing Geraldine in person, Stephen slipped a note under her office door.

During these years, being able to boast exclusivity for coveted designers was a backbone of Bendel's business, and the store's buyers, including Jean Rosenberg, combed little shops and dressmaking studios from Chinatown to Tokyo in search of undiscovered talent, just as they had once canvassed the streets of Europe. In addition to Stephen Burrows and the French designer Sonia Rykiel, another mainstay among Bendel's shoppers was the British designer Zandra Rhodes.

In 1969, Zandra, known for her printed textiles and use of holes and safety pins, was introduced to the legendary editor of *Vogue*, Diana Vreeland. "I entered her office in New York exotically made up wearing a flowing headscarf and a gorgeous printed chiffon kaftan together with high white Biba boots," recalled Zandra. "Diana adored my clothes." She decided to use Zandra's designs for a *Vogue* photo shoot with the actress Natalie Wood. When the shoot finished, Natalie "picked up the phone to Geraldine Stutz," Zandra said, the actress telling the department store president that she should carry Zandra's designs. "I immediately went there with my clothes over my arm." Not long after, Zandra and Geraldine struck an exclusive deal for Bendel to carry her line. The so-called princess of punk quickly garnered a fan base that ranged from Freddie Mercury to Joan Rivers, and Mica Ertegun to Chessy Rayner.

Jean Rosenberg (left) and Marion Greenberg (right)
when they were both buyers at Henri Bendel.

Marion Greenberg, a young buyer for Bendel's Fancy, the evening-wear shop, was in charge of maintaining relationships with designers, including Zandra. Marion, who grew up in New York City, was, like many of Geraldine's buyers, a dark-haired beauty with a canny fashion sense. Marion understood that exclusives with designers were critical to Bendel's success, and she took care with the relationship, letting Zandra store her clothing trunks in her Bendel office when she went on a cross-country road trip. When Babe Paley, who was a Zandra fan, was sick in the hospital, Marion accompanied the designer to the socialite's private suite at Memorial Sloan Kettering. "I carried over two garment bags, and we gave Babe her own showing. It was quite emotional," Marion said. But despite these overtures, three years into Zandra's exclusive arrangement with Bendel, a Zandra Rhodes boutique opened in Bloomingdale's. "Someone called and told me that Bloomingdale's was carrying her clothes," said Marion, who was in London at the time. Geraldine was also in London, staying at her favorite hotel, the Connaught, and invited Marion to have lunch and commiserate. "Don't worry," Geraldine told her. "There are hundreds of Zandra Rhodes, but there's only one Marion Greenberg."

Unheralded designers clambered to be featured at Bendel, the chicest of stores, knowing that the platform was almost certain to result in coverage in fashion bibles like *Vogue* and *Women's Wear Daily*. But like

Stephen Burrows and Zandra Rhodes, once these designers became established, Bendel lost them to larger competitors. While the store's small size provided customers with finely curated, selective merchandise, on the flip side there was less space to exhibit clothes, less money to play with, and less ability to scale up. For example, Joseph Cicio, a merchandiser at Macy's at the time, was lunching with the designer David Leung, who relayed his excitement that Bendel had placed an order for his crepe de chine shorts. "I said to him, 'That's great, how many did they buy?' expecting David to give me some number in the hundreds," said Joseph. "Instead, he said, 'They bought six: two small, two medium, and two large.' I thought to myself, 'Wow. You couldn't do that anywhere else but Bendel's.'" In any other store, such a minuscule order would have been lost among the racks of clothes on offer, but at Bendel six pairs of shorts could stand out.

Bendel's biggest threat came from Bergdorf Goodman, its rival around the corner on Fifty-Eighth Street. Ira Neimark was Bergdorf's president, an experienced hand who had started his career as a bellhop at Bonwit Teller when Hortense Odlum was in charge and attended business school on a scholarship provided by the *Polly Tucker* book. In 1975, Neimark was appointed president of Bergdorf's, and he immediately recruited his protégée Dawn Mello, whom he had known since his days working for Beatrice Fox Auerbach in Connecticut, as the fashion director of her department store, G. Fox. Neimark and Mello went to excessive lengths to steal exclusives from Bendel. For instance, in the spring of 1976, as part of a clandestine effort to attract the Italian brand Fendi, the pair arranged a secret meeting with the five Fendi sisters in Rome. The plan was for them to slip unnoticed onto a flight to Italy following the close of Paris Fashion Week. But they hadn't prepared for Charles de Gaulle Airport to be overrun with fashion insiders making their way back to New York from the shows. In particular, Neimark and Mello were desperate to avoid being spotted by John Fairchild, the powerful publisher and editor of *Women's Wear Daily*, who happened to be sitting at his gate, waiting for his Pan Am flight to JFK. "If he saw us boarding a flight to Rome instead of New York, he would have been the one most likely to put the pieces together," said Neimark. To shield himself from Fairchild's powerful gaze, Neimark jumped into a nearby telephone booth. With Mello in the booth next to him, they pretended to be in mid-conversation, although it was only with France Télécom's dial tone.

Neimark and Mello eventually boarded the plane and made it to their rendezvous, a grand palazzo near the Colosseum. There, over a lunch of calamari and fresh pasta, they tried to persuade the women to end their exclusive agreement with Bendel and come to Bergdorf instead. At first, the Fendi sisters were noncommittal, but when Neimark promised them fashion shows, advertising campaigns, and prominent placement in their Fifth Avenue windows, they acquiesced. "Once Dawn Mello arrived at Bergdorf Goodman's, she was always trying to hire away Bendel staff and take our designers," said Koko Hashim, a Bendel buyer at the time. "Bergdorf's was trying to figure out what was the Bendel magic, what made the store so special." Its chicness was an intangible factor, nearly impossible to replicate. "The thing about Bendel's is there would be these amazing women who would come in, Gloria Vanderbilt, Cher, Barbra Streisand, and nothing would change—no one would miss a beat," said Jacqui Wenzel, who was a twenty-five-year-old buyer for Bendel's Fancy at the time. "It was just elegant and understated, and everyone was treated with the same care."

Publicly, Geraldine took the high road, refusing to beg when brands like Fendi left. "A couple of seasons ago, it was very clear that exclusivity was no longer possible, and it really doesn't matter," Geraldine told a reporter. "It's the story of our life, kiddo. I'm not at all worried about Bendel's spot in the world." Yet privately, Geraldine was in a state of constant anxiety that Bendel's might become passé, that she might lose her touch, and that the store would age along with her. Through the 1970s, however, Geraldine's Bendel maintained its cool edge.

In 1973, *New York* magazine described the difference between women who shop at Bendel rather than at Bergdorf. "Unlike the Bergdorf, the Bendel is not born, but made," it quipped. "Covered in Stephen Burrows inside-out chicness or resplendent in Chloé blouses tucked into skinny jeans tucked into $400 boots, she has never underestimated the power of a beautiful thing. She knows, without her yoga instructor's telling her, that size 4 is the size that's right for her. The Bendel is subtle and a little shy—she hides her Penelope Tree eyebrows under oversized sunglasses; her swinging straight hair under turbans and berets; her freshly manicured toenails beneath oversized clogs as she looks for the simple throw-on at $275. The Bendel does not eat during the day, except for an occasional asparagus. She prefers her store's boutiques with their maximum of chic and minimum of stock. The Bendel woman is methodical and thinks ahead, and if she has stayed past the sensible 3:30, thank God for Buster, who will get her a taxi."

As Geraldine kept her focus on maintaining Bendel's position as the chicest of New York department stores, her marriage with David began to falter. "My father was very good-looking, but emotionally unavailable," said Emma. While Geraldine was undoubtedly the more financially successful of the two, David insisted that Geraldine's career did not bother him. "I thought it was a great compliment to me that she loved me," he said. "I didn't feel threatened by her work." His feelings were likely more nuanced. "He loved the fact she was successful," said Emma, but Geraldine was the breadwinner, paying for David's art studio, and for their lifestyle, and his career as a painter never quite took off. David did exhibit at a SoHo gallery in 1966, where Maxey Jarman and his wife purchased one of his works, titled *57th Street*. And in 1971, he had a one-man show at the Richard Feigen gallery. But around town and among their friends, David was known as Mr. Jerry Stutz. As the 1970s continued, the tensions between Geraldine and David mounted. "One summer I went to visit them," said Emma. "It felt like walking on eggshells."

In 1976, after eleven years of marriage, Geraldine and David separated. There were rumors that he had a much younger girlfriend, but publicly, the former couple remained cordial. "It's a test of sorts," reported the *Daily News* of their split. "They want to see if living apart works out better for them than living together." It turned out that it did work better living apart, and by the following year Geraldine and David were divorced. "I was deeply saddened by the failure of my marriage," Geraldine later said. "I don't like to fail any more than anybody else, particularly in something important. . . . But I had a good marriage for a brief period of time." While divorce was privately painful, Geraldine was never one for public displays, and she insisted that all was well. "David and I had one of those amicable no-contest divorces. Neither one of us wanted to marry anyone else. It was just, at the end, nothing was working out for us." While David would go on to marry again, Geraldine never did. She seemed resigned, and at peace, with this decision. "Listen, I wouldn't have missed my marriage for anything and there were lots of terrific things about it, but it did not endure," Geraldine said simply. "Quite possibly, she loved Bendel's more than she loved him," said Emma.

In 1970, while still married, Geraldine and David gave an interview together to *New York* magazine, where they discussed their meet-cute story and the topic of feminism. "I think women's liberation is a good, healthy movement," said David. "But I don't think there is equality of the sexes. Male and female are equal but different. The greatest harm the movement can do is to lump the sexes together." Geraldine seemed to agree. "I think women's liberation may overstress the need to get rid of differences," she responded. "There is a difference of needs, not just a difference of penis and vagina. As for me, I wish to be loved romantically, affectionately, all those ways. . . . I know human beings are all alone, but what was lonely about my life has vanished since I met Davie." Following the divorce, Geraldine seemed more at ease without a consistent romantic partner. "The best life is one you share happily with another person," she told her friend Helen Gurley Brown, author of the bestseller *Sex and the Single Girl* and editor in chief of *Cosmopolitan*, "but living peacefully alone is better than living wretchedly with a partner."

The Friday Morning Lineup

Number 52 turned a bright shade of red and let out a squeal. To an outside observer it might have looked as if she had just supplied the winning question on *Jeopardy!* But for the twenty-four-year-old costume designer turned pocketbook maker, it was something far better. Anne Leibensperger, as number 52 was known in regular life, had just been awarded $250 and a coveted spot to show off her shoulder bags at Henri Bendel. "It was like a dream come true," Anne said a few minutes later, regaining her composure. It was her second attempt at the Friday Morning Lineup, as the weekly open call that Jean Rosenberg had begun at Bendel in the early 1960s, was known. At 8:30 on Friday mornings, silk-screen artists, coppersmiths, leather tanners, and knitters came from as near as Queens, New York, and as far as Queensland, Australia, to line up along the West Fifty-Seventh Street service entrance for a coveted moment to present their creations to a Bendel buyer. That morning, standing behind Anne was an Argentinian accountant who also fancied himself a pocketbook designer, a pregnant mother who ended up waiting two hours, only to discover she had lined up for the wrong buyer, and a grandmother who made leather garter belts. For some it was their first audience, while others were Friday regulars, appearing each week, stubbornly undaunted by the rejections. There were sportswear designers with hanging bags over their shoulders, jewelers clutching small attaché cases, fabric makers lugging great zippered containers, and at least one accessories creator who toted her goods in an oversized laundry bag. Friday mornings were an abundant pipeline for new merchandise: 15 percent of the items in the store were discovered during the lineup.

When Bendel finally opened at 10:00 a.m., the hopefuls filed in under the watchful eye of Buster, the store's famous doorman, taking their places along a narrow, overheated corridor adjacent to the freight elevators. There they were handed tickets on a first-come, first-served basis and waited their turn. If they were lucky, they found a folding chair to sit on; otherwise, they crouched on the floor or leaned against the walls, some politely chatting and admiring one another's wares, others quiet, nervously biting their nails or staring off into space. Friendships were formed in the line, business partnerships, even romances—one couple who met on the line later tied the knot. There was tedium, and to a degree humiliation, waiting hours for an audience that could last as little as ninety seconds. "I thought, 'Do I really want to subject myself to this?'" said Ilene Danchig, who ended up successfully selling her fabrics to the store. For Anne, there was no doubt. Despite the hours-long wait, the potential rejection, the crowded conditions, and the fifty-one tense people ahead of her, "yes, yes, and most emphatically yes" she would do it again, she said.

It was Geraldine's hope that the parade of amateur clothing and accessory designers, so many talented and untried, would continue flocking there on Friday mornings, despite the downsides. "That back door is a lifeblood to the store," Geraldine said, adding that Bendel needed "clothes all our own, otherwise, we would end up being a baby Bonwit's or a mini-Bergdorf's." For Geraldine, Friday mornings were the very essence of Bendel. "Businesses are getting so big, aren't they?" she asked. "The commercial market is consolidating big business. On the other end of the stick is this very lovely world of small, personal businesses that work today out of lofts and cellars. . . . On Fridays anybody can come in and show anybody anything. It's that infusion of fresh young ideas that keeps the store fresh."

Friday mornings weren't always easy for the Bendel buyers, who were made to wade through dozens—sometimes more than eighty—designers over several hours. "I take every single one seriously, you never know who the next terrific designer will be," Claire Nicholson, a thirty-one-year-old accessories buyer dressed in a Kenzo shirt and creamy white harem pants, with serpentine bangles adorning her wrists, told *The New York Times* one Friday. "I have an appointment to see Claire Nicholson," said a willowy blonde to the guard as she took her ticket. "So does everyone," called out a voice in the crowd, causing laughter to ripple down the corridor. Armed with a calculator and a million ways to politely say no, Claire met an average of forty-five designers any given week, although her record was eighty-eight. She "wrote an order," or said yes to, one in five, she said. Claire told the rest some version of "These are wonderful but they're not for me," or "I'm sorry but I've finished with the leaf motif," or "It's very pretty but it's too junior for the Bendel customer," or "I'm staying away from quilted fabrics," or "I'm not buying metal this season." She would often lavish praise, despite declining to buy. "They really look delicious," she told a designer of brass bracelets. "They are absolutely charming," she said to a designer of ceramic pins, but were too breakable for the store's heavy floor traffic. "They do look quite, quite wonderful," she assured another, trying to soften the blow. Of course, there were the occasional catastrophes. One woman threw a two-pound necklace at her after being rejected. Another woman collapsed in her office and asked that she phone her psychiatrist. Claire, whose husband was a well-known songwriter with hits like "The Lion Sleeps Tonight" ("Aweem away, aweem away"), heard all manner of shtick. "Hello, these are my little friends," said one lady, presenting a series of crocheted hair combs. "I'm late for my dentist's appointment in Chinatown and this is all I have to show," said another, before presenting Claire with a single ostrich feather. When she had first been hired, Geraldine had given Claire a directive that became her guiding principle: "Buy only what you would wear personally. Buy only if you're drooling for it and forget about what will sell."

Jean, despite overseeing all the store's merchandise, still liked to partici-pate in Friday mornings. One morning, she was considering a handful of colorful sweaters by a lineup hopeful. "Could you make something special for us?" Jean asked the designer, always angling for an exclusive. Usually, the purchases were modest, maybe just two of a kind, or possibly half a dozen. But while the orders might start out small, if the items proved popular with customers, they could lead to larger reorders. At first, Bendel ordered only a few of Mira de Moss's evening-wear designs after meeting her at a Friday lineup. Soon, she was getting reorders worth $100,000, or $300,000 in today's dollars. The handbag designer Carlos Falchi was discovered at a lineup, eventually earning his own boutique at the store. There was also Ted Muehling, a jewelry designer who took a shoebox of his sculptural work to the lineup and won a Coty Award just six months later. It was the same with the hat designer Don Kline, also a Coty Award winner, who called the Friday lineup experience "nerve-wracking." And Patricia Underwood, a milliner and Coty Award winner, remembered the lineup as "pure showbiz," adding that she fielded one offer to become an importer and two opportunities to start a partnership while on the line.

After Geraldine and Jean were long gone from Bendel, there were attempts to copy the store's Friday Morning Lineups. In August 1995, *Paper* magazine rolled out what it dubbed a Fashion Mobile, a mobile home that was filled with fashion editors and stylists, parking it in a lot near Manhattan's Union Square. The editors and magazine writers welcomed a steady flow of designers throughout the day, including Serena Da Conceicao, who offered a single outfit designed to attend a rave, and Gaetano Cannella, who brought an entire runway show worth of clothes, including a bridal gown for his finale. Jeremy Scott, before he became famous, made an appearance, accompanied by his muse, the model and 1990s club kid Jenny Dembrow, who was dressed in one of his designs, a hot-pink sheer organza dress. In 2009, Bendel, in a later, and very different iteration, tried to revive its own tradition after it had fallen off, promising it would become a twice-yearly affair. Designers spent a sleepless night holding their spot on a midtown sidewalk, braving the March cold, to meet the store's representatives. The first in line was a student from Parsons School of Design who had hair accessories to sell, and his endurance was repaid with a promise of a future appointment with a buyer, although no sale. Also lucky was a jeweler who specialized in snakeskin cuffs that had reportedly been worn by Rihanna, and a swaggering designer who arrived with a gaggle of models sporting his bubbly neon skirts. A thirteen-year-old girl in a plaid dress and braces played hooky from school for the chance to show off jewelry that she had been working on "all her life," and Bendel selected a few rings. Others were less fortunate. The creator of "peeky socks," which lacked toes, and were meant to be worn with flip-flops, garnered a quick no. The designer of "Kamelflage"—a triangular piece of fabric that went inside a thong to avoid unseemly lines when wearing tight pants—was also rejected. (The designer was undeterred, telling one newspaper reporter that his life's goal was to "wage war on the front lines.") But these modern reincarnations were poor approximations. The original, legendary Friday Morning Lineup under Geraldine and Jean had a status of cool and promise. It was "like Camelot, a brief moment in history," one buyer recalled. When the formula changed, the magic was lost, and so was a venue for artistic discovery and the next fashion innovation.

Chapter 15

⧁⧂

Geraldine, Department Store Owner

Geraldine had always been able to count on Maxey Jarman's support. The head of Genesco believed in her abilities, trusted her judgment, and nearly always backed her decisions. Geraldine called her longtime boss "fair, generous, demanding." Maxey had taken his father's small-town shoe shop and transformed it into one of the country's largest retail conglomerates, snatching up shoe wholesalers, department stores, and fragrance businesses. But as the 1970s got under way, the Vietnam War was roiling the country, high inflation was wreaking havoc on the economy, and an oil embargo was causing an energy crisis. Meanwhile, Maxey was forced to step down as chairman of Genesco's board, the result of a company-wide policy that he instituted years earlier of mandatory retirement at age sixty-five.

Maxey installed his son, Franklin, to replace him, but he retained his leadership of Genesco's powerful finance committee. While Maxey was no longer chairman, he was still in control of the company's finances, and Franklin, unhappy at being just a figurehead, began to revolt. A father-and-son power struggle played out in the press, and Genesco was further destabilized. Finally, in 1973, the company's once-high-flying stock reached a nadir and Franklin engineered a coup, using a secret ballot to oust his father from the $1 billion conglomerate that he had built up over more than three decades.

But Franklin was not cut out to be a chief executive. While Maxey was a cunning salesman with the charming wiles of a genteel southerner, Franklin could be aloof—a whiz with numbers, but lacking social acumen. In one of his first meetings as head of Genesco, Franklin doled out gifts to his senior lieutenants. Inside each box was a hangman's noose made from real rope, as well as a brass belt buckle engraved with the same grisly image. A note inside read "Tighten Your Belt, Not Your Noose." The tone-deaf gesture, along with other perceived management missteps, led several executives to mobilize against Franklin, and a three-inch dossier was circulated, filled with allegations that he was mentally unstable, irrational, and paranoid. Following a contentious eight-hour board meeting, Franklin was fired, and for the first time in Genesco's history outsiders were hired to run the business. The new chief executive was a "corporate hatchet man, the fellow who cuts the cancer out," and he slowly began to dismantle the company, selling off subsidiaries in an effort to drive down costs and drive up profits.

With Maxey and Franklin sidelined at Genesco, Geraldine was left to fend for herself. It was clear that the new honchos running the company felt little of the loyalty that she had enjoyed with the Jarmans, and the two sides settled into a détente. "Bendel is no problem to them, and is an ornament to the empire, so they've left us alone," said Geraldine. "And I've left them alone." She did do one thing: she requested that if the company ever received an offer for Bendel that she be given the first right of refusal—an opportunity to meet the price and buy the store herself. "I don't think we could sell it without you," the Genesco boss told her, and agreed to the deal.

For the next few years, Geraldine dug in her heels and maintained a tight focus on the Bendel bottom line. The store continued performing well, but in early 1979, Geraldine received news that shook her out of her sense of complacency. Genesco was selling Bonwit Teller, and the historic Art Deco building, located just around the corner from Bendel, was destined for the garbage heap, designated for demolition to make way for Trump Tower. She realized that it was only a matter of time before she got the call from Genesco that they were also selling her store. And one morning in May 1980, her hunch proved true when she arrived at her office to discover a memo on her desk. It was from Genesco, informing her that Barneys, a menswear shop, had offered $8 million, or $28 million in today's dollars, to buy Bendel as part of its effort to transform itself into a full-fledged department store. Geraldine had thirty days to match the offer.

The clock had started, and with only a month to put together a deal, the most stressful weeks of Geraldine's life began. "Because I had run the store for 20 years as if it were my own, I somehow—I felt from the beginning that it was my own," Geraldine told a reporter for *Newsday* a few months later, as she puffed on a Carlton. "Tireless, she nevertheless looks tired," the reporter wrote, noting that the department store president had dropped 12 pounds from her already thin 110-pound frame, unable to eat from the anxiety. "When she stands, her black wool culottes hang loosely from hips even leaner than usual."

Luckily, Geraldine had met someone several weeks before the Barneys offer had surfaced whom she felt confident could help her raise the money within the allotted time frame. Linda Beltramini was a European sophisticate who lived with her Swiss psychiatrist husband in an Upper East Side town house. She was also a savvy investment banker. *The New York Times* ran a profile of the thirty-four-year-old beauty, who lunched at the high-society temple La Côte Basque and drove around town in a chauffeured Mercedes. "One of the toughest and sharpest of a new breed of financiers in the city," the newspaper called her. Linda was a member of a "secretive cadre" of bankers responsible for importing foreign capital into New York City, boasting a Rolodex thick with the names of wealthy European and South American businessmen. But the identities of these investors were mysterious, as was Linda herself. According to *The New York Times*, Linda's biography verged on the unbelievable. Raised in Brazil and England, she conducted business around the world, selling Fabergé eggs to a central African dictator and traveling through war-torn Beirut disguised as an Arab. "She says she once filled a Ugandan order for 10,000 hand hoes after buying the type of hoe needed in Britain, carrying it on a flight to Brazil in her Gucci bag, having 10,000 hoes made there, and shipping them to Kampala at $1 each under the British price," *The New York Times* reported.

Yet while Linda's stories sounded fantastical, and the identity of her contacts was unknown, the money was real. Linda and Geraldine spent the next several weeks working the phones and hosting meetings. Linda "seems to be coolly indifferent to the notion that there is anything

unusual about a woman wheeling and dealing in the most traditionally masculine fields," wrote *The New York Times*. "I never think about
that," she responded. "If you think you're a woman in a man's world,
you're dead." Working with Linda to raise the money, Geraldine realized the precariousness of her situation. Particularly one night, when
it looked as if a deal might not happen. "I woke up and sat up in bed
and thought, 'My God, I have gone along for 20 years under the con-
viction that it was my business, when in reality, at any minute, I could
have lost it.' I had never even thought about it," she said. "I thought,
'I don't own it—and that's been true all these years!' Perhaps it would
have demolished me."

The women emerged from their weeks of hard work with the financing that Geraldine needed to usurp Barneys and buy Bendel herself.
Under the terms of the deal, Geraldine would put in a "minute" share
of the $8 million all-cash purchase price, the remainder financed by a
group of anonymous European investors. In return for her investment,
and in recognition that she would run the store, Geraldine would be
given a 30 percent ownership stake in Bendel. Her European partners
would own the remaining 70 percent of the department store. The deal
structure was dizzying, a spiderweb of tax shelters and shell companies
stretching from Panama, to the Netherlands Antilles, to Switzerland.
The names of the investors were so shielded that even Geraldine didn't
know all of their identities. These investors were more interested in the
transaction as a real estate play and less interested in the retail business. General Electric Pension Trust owned the Bendel's building and
had a long-term lease with the store, and as part of their deal the new
investors had an option to purchase the building at any time during
the life of the lease.

Linda "is a brilliant conceptualist," said Geraldine after the deal was
announced. "She sees the creative possibilities in an investment faster
than anyone I've ever worked with." As for the anonymous investors,
"They are the perfect partners, in my opinion. They know nothing
about retailing and do not want to," Geraldine said. "Geraldine Stutz
was 'Gerry Who?' when she took over as president of Bendel 23 years
ago," wrote *The New York Times*. "She was, in her own words, 'very
young, very inexperienced, and a woman.' . . . She is now, with the pos-

sible exception of family firms, the first woman to own a major fashion specialty store." Geraldine was ecstatic. She had replaced Genesco with another wealthy partner who would give her freedom to run the store as she wished. "Isn't it true that in the most marvelous moment of your life, you're in a state of shock?" she said months later. "The full impact that the store was mine, all mine, didn't hit me for a while, and perhaps, even now, still hasn't."

As the first woman owner of a major Fifth Avenue department store, Geraldine became even more intertwined with Bendel. "I am Henri Bendel; this is what I realized from my point of view—I am the store," she said. "If there are papers and Coca-Cola cans in the planters in front of the store, I think, 'My slip is showing!' It's that kind of identification." But ownership, and the lessons learned from Genesco's demise, had, perhaps subconsciously, altered the way that Geraldine carried on the business. "The reality is that there is an enormous difference between being a hired hand and being the managing partner," she said.

While competitors like Bonwit Teller and Lord & Taylor pursued branch stores as a growth strategy, Geraldine had long operated on the assumption that there simply weren't enough women outside New York who abided by the Bendel Look for that type of expansion to make sense. But growth was necessary, so Geraldine began researching how she might open freestanding Streets of Shops in luxury areas like Beverly Hills. In the end, however, the idea went nowhere. "I came to the conclusion that money being what it is and costs being what they are, it would be so expensive," she said. Besides, when Geraldine started at Bendel her concept had been unique, but now specialty stores like hers had become hopelessly common. "You trip on a cluster of lustrous names every time you go out on the highway," she said. Instead, Geraldine struck upon a different means of expanding—mail orders.

Pat Tennant, whose business manufacturing Stephen Burrows's clothing was forced to close after the designer left for a competitor, was hired back by Geraldine and put in charge of what became a juggernaut—the Bendel Christmas catalog. These were beautifully crafted square booklets, only a few inches wide, filled with clever copy and delicate line drawings. The items had the telltale Bendel's cool and were exclusive to the store. Merchandise included a leather key caddy in purple suede or tomato-red calfskin, a John Kloss–designed shirt robe in diamond-patterned cotton jersey, and a child's lunch pail in skipper-blue plastic, the child's name penciled in red, and jam-packed with an assortment of root beer candies, fruit sticks, fizz mints, and bubble gum coins. At first, the catalogs were sent only to Bendel's charge accounts, which numbered twelve thousand, but as demand grew, so did the number of addresses and the frequency of the catalogs. To Geraldine's relief, the Bendel's catalog business became exceedingly profitable and far cheaper to produce than new brick-and-mortar stores.

Despite making inroads, Geraldine was still plagued by the exodus of designers to larger rivals. To stem the losses and increase profitability, Bendel stopped selling menswear and limited its children's clothes from infants to age six. Geraldine also turned to the tried-and-true method of refurbishing the physical space. She enlarged the store's windows, which were relatively small, having been built by Mr. Bendel to display the store's hats, and installed a fresh new Bendel awning. And while other retailers were busy aping the success of tiny boutiques, with buzzy intimate spaces, Geraldine, ever original and counterintuitive, went in a new direction. She combined and enlarged the store's third and fourth floors, connecting them via a sweeping staircase to create a new loftlike department called 4 Plus 3.

"The new floors are kind of the opposite of the boutique concept, because it's just all out there," said Geraldine. "I wanted an evocative kind of contemporary look, neither modern, post-modern nor period." The clothing was organized by type, with sweaters in one area and shirts in another, instead of the more traditional method of grouping the clothes by designer. To eliminate clutter, Geraldine had only a single size of each item on display, and to show off the merchandise, she eschewed mannequins and used hangers attached to wall panels to exhibit them. The reviews for 4 Plus 3 were mixed. *Women's Wear Daily* called the new layout "confusing and puzzling," noting there was "more space than clothes" and adding that it felt "as quiet as a temple for fashion nuns." *The New York Times* described it as "an innovative high-class understated look" with clothes "jauntily displayed," creating "a relaxing way to shop."

F ar more important than confronting the physical layout of the store was the emergence of a new threat that would soon force Geraldine to rethink Bendel's entire merchandising strategy. The early 1980s brought a punishing recession, but, even more troublesome for Geraldine, it brought the dawn of the mall era. Mall culture, with its celebration of conformity and its embrace of brands like Benetton and the Gap, was not in step with Geraldine and her emphasis on unusual fashions and exclusivity. The public clamored for Izods, but Bendel loyalists "wouldn't be caught on a back road in this year's safe preppy look," noted the *Daily News*. Geraldine's worst fear was realized as the store appeared out of step, its fashions feeling stale. "Bendel: Small but Not Quite as Sassy," blared a headline in *Women's Wear Daily* in 1984, the article quoting anonymous designers who called Bendel "not as slick as it used to be" and "not as innovative." Geraldine did have noted successes, such as her embrace of avant-garde Japanese fashion, opening the first American boutique for Comme des Garçons, for instance. But for perhaps the first time in her career, Geraldine seemed to be missing the mark. Critics "feel she has made compromises, now that she is part owner, that she wouldn't make if the store was owned by someone else," *Women's Wear Daily* reported, adding that "her willingness to gamble or experiment seemed to diminish." She addressed the shift in her responsibilities only obliquely, telling one interviewer, "I adore my career. It stretches every physical, emotional, and intellectual muscle I have. Plus, I've invested all my money in this. It's called taking a chance on love."

In January 1985, once again the ground shifted beneath Geraldine. She received the unwelcome news that her anonymous partners had executed their option to buy the Bendel building and, having achieved the primary reason for their investment, wanted to sell the store. "Our intention was always to sell the business," said Ronaldo de Souza, the representative in America of Geraldine's largest investor, a Brazilian construction firm. "We always had a good relationship with Jerry," he added, "we just couldn't help her because we essentially weren't planning to fund the business." Geraldine couldn't afford to buy the remaining 70 percent of Henri Bendel from her partners, so she found herself once more on the market for new investors. It was either that or forfeit the store.

One weekend in the spring of 1985, de Souza stumbled upon a possible solution to the Bendel's quandary. He was perusing a magazine when he read a feature story on Leslie Wexner, a forty-seven-year-old retailer from Ohio whose cheap, trendy sportswear was dominating the market. With brands like the Limited and Victoria's Secret, Wexner's company claimed to produce 200 million garments a year, or roughly three items for every woman in America. "I said to myself this is a very good potential buyer for Bendel's," said de Souza, who began reaching out to his business network to find a common contact who could make an introduction. Two days later, Wexner arrived at de Souza's office for a meeting. It was 8:30 in the evening, and the enigmatic Wexner stayed for three hours. "You cannot read him," said de Souza afterward, "but my gut feeling was he wouldn't have stayed that late talking about generalities." De Souza was correct; Wexner was interested.

Through the summer, the two sides began hammering out a possible sale of the store, and by early August they had the outlines of an agreement. There were other bidders, most notably Leonard N. Stern, the billionaire developer who wanted to purchase the 70 percent stake and let Geraldine keep her 30 percent, and relocate Bendel's to a new building he was developing at Sixty-First Street and Madison Avenue. Geraldine liked the idea, but Stern eventually backed out when it became clear that Wexner was willing to pay far more.

With Wexner the lead buyer, de Souza decided it was time that Geraldine meet the mall merchant, particularly since her contract required that she approve the sale. Wexner, de Souza, and Geraldine met in August for lunch at Wexner's apartment in Manhattan. "If the chemistry hadn't worked between her and Wexner there would have been no deal," said de Souza. The lunch went well, even though Wexner was his typically cryptic self. "I am difficult to read," he admitted. "I look and smile and do not tell you what I think." While the entrepreneur's intention was difficult to discern, Wexner could be convincing when he wanted. He assured Geraldine that he appreciated and respected her achievements at Bendel and had no plans to transform the store into a highbrow version of the Limited. He also wooed Geraldine with the promise of future investments, telling her that he planned to spend upwards of $50 million to carry out a national expansion of the Bendel brand. "We'll come in every once in a while, just to say hello and see how things are going," he told her. "We're not wheeler-dealers."

Geraldine was hopeful that Wexner might finally replace Maxey as a man who understood and supported her vision, albeit one with extensive financing and the infrastructure to see it through. "She wanted to believe," said Miriam Marshall, who ran Port of Call on the Street of Shops. "She was at a crossroads, and he told her what she wanted to hear." Geraldine said a sale felt "like I'm putting up my child for adoption," yet at the same time there was some relief at shedding the onerous responsibilities of ownership. As much as she loved the store, there were perks to being a hired hand. Some of Geraldine's closest friends also urged her to sell and move on. "I think you are tired of Bendel's," the gossip columnist Liz Smith wrote her friend. "Sell it and seek new worlds. How about taking over for Mrs. Vreeland? Or go into politics? Or become creative director of Lincoln Center? You could do anything."

There were numerous red flags that Wexner was not Maxey and that their relationship would not follow the same pattern. First, there was the obvious difference in taste and approach, with Bendel's focus on the unusual and the chic and the Limited's focus on broad, commercial appeal. Second, there was the noted difference in personalities. Geraldine addressed every Bendel employee, from senior buyers to the maintenance staff, as "Mr." and "Miss" and was famous for giving personalized gifts, often beautifully curated baskets of Bendel's famous soap, to her vast circle of friends and acquaintances. At the Limited, Wexner called his employees "associates," and the gift he was best known for doling out was company stock options, which had allowed some longtime workers to retire as millionaires. Geraldine was fully ensconced in the New York celebrity scene, with an array of famous friends and a deep commitment to civic and cultural groups, sitting on boards including Carnegie Hall and the Fifth Avenue Association. Geraldine proudly appeared in the first celebrity advertisement for the American Foundation for AIDS Research, standing next to such close friends as the designer Perry Ellis. Oscar de la Renta called Geraldine "Mother Teresa."

Wexner, meanwhile, was of a different type altogether. In several interviews he heralded the fashion philosophy of Revlon's founder Charles Revson, who famously claimed to know what women want. "He'd go off and watch hookers to see how they dressed," Wexner said. "Revson said women all hope they get laid, and I agree. They're sensuous. They're different from men. They dress to please men," he told *Fortune* in August 1985, the month that he had his first lunch

Jacqueline Kennedy Onassis and Wexner at a charity dinner at Henri Bendel in 1991.

with Geraldine. "You're not selling utility," he said of fashion. "That's why uptight women stockbrokers will put on a G-string when they get home. Like Revson said, we're selling hope in a bottle." This attitude toward women was not only troubling; it was in absolute contrast to Geraldine's own viewpoint. At Bendel, fashion was not about seducing men; it was a tool for women to find the best expression of themselves.

It was during these years that Wexner hired Jeffrey Epstein, the notorious sex trafficker and sexual predator, as his financial adviser and close confidant, eventually giving him power of attorney. But back then, Wexner was mostly known for his boyish energy and his astounding success. The same month that *Fortune* ran its article with Wexner quoting Charles Revson, *New York* magazine also published a profile of him. It was a cover article, and it showed Wexner with his arms around two models, beneath the headline "The Bachelor Billionaire." In that piece, Wexner was characterized as "wanting approval and at the same time suspicious of others," relishing "all the pretty girls who never noticed him but now stand very close and knot their fingers behind their back when they talk to him and look wham into his mournful eyes."

Geraldine decided not to heed these warning signs. She was not ready to cut ties with the store, so she agreed to the sale and signed a five-year employment contract to stay on board as a paid employee. Wexner paid a total of $3.2 million, or the equivalent of $8.5 million in today's dollars: a discount compared to what Geraldine and her investors had paid several years earlier, although the building lease added another $25 million, or $67 million today. There are no public records of exactly how much Geraldine earned as a return on her investment, but when she died two decades later, her gross estate, including the value of her Connecticut country home, was in excess of $10 million.

As soon as the deal was finalized, there was a sense inside Bendel that something had gone terribly wrong. On his first day as the store's new owner, the diminutive Wexner made a speech introducing himself to the staff, standing atop the stairwell leading from the main floor. He reassured the sophisticated, well-adorned buyers and chic saleswomen that nothing would change under his tenure. "That man stood there looking down on us, telling us that Bendel's was the jewel in his retail crown," recalled Pat Tennant, furious, even decades later. "He said that we shouldn't worry, that he wasn't going to change a thing." But later that week, Pat opened *Women's Wear Daily* and read an article declaring that the Bendel catalog, which she oversaw, was being shut down. Not only that, but Pat was also out of a job. She wasn't alone. Suddenly changes were everywhere.

A parade of "associates" from the Limited, dressed just like their boss in khakis and blue button-downs, flew in from Ohio and began appearing at Bendel in droves. The store was one of the few in New York that still used pneumatic tubes, a quaint throwback, but out of seemingly nowhere computerized cash registers were installed on the floors, and baffled saleswomen struggled to use them. In the stationery nook, where tasteful leather-bound books and writing styluses were once displayed, stacks of cashmere sweaters started appearing, with large, garish signs announcing they were on sale. The amusing, clever windows that Bendel was long known for were replaced with new displays. One tableau, styled like a pajama party, featured a mannequin dressed in a garter belt and dark stockings, positioned so she was lying flat on her back with her legs propped up on a couch. Along the Street of Shops, more tawdry mannequins began appearing, cheapening the ambience.

One day, Jacqui Wenzel, a lingerie buyer, was wearing an outfit from Bendel mainstay Comme des Garçons, including a military-style jacket and army boots. She was in a buyers' meeting, showing off some Italian-made pajamas, when Wexner, who was sitting in on the group, suddenly interrupted. "Do you know what eroticism is? Can you explain erotic?" he asked. Jacqui, who was twenty-seven, was humiliated by the line of questioning from her much-older new boss. Flustered, she tried to explain that the Bendel woman was more "Lauren Bacall than Victoria's Secret," more at home in men's silk pajamas than an overtly sexy push-up bra. When the meeting ended, Jacqui retreated to the ladies' room, where she burst into tears. "Geraldine would never have treated me that way and never would have made me cry," she said. Karol Kempster, who oversaw the store's cosmetics business, one of its most profitable departments, tried twice to quit the store after Wexner arrived, but both times he increased her paycheck. Finally, Karol hit a breaking point. "I went to meet Les in Geraldine's office," she said. "He told me that he wanted me to design soaps that had phallic shapes." Karol assumed that Wexner was joking and began to laugh. But he was serious. "I thought, 'I am going to be sick,'" said Karol, who walked out of that meeting and called Revlon, who quickly hired her away.

It was like watching a car accident in slow motion. Geraldine loyalists on one side, newcomers from Middle America on the other, and a head-on collision as the most glamorous store in America crashed into the largest mass-market purveyor of 1980s retailing. Observers began wondering what Wexner's endgame was. The year before buying Bendel, Wexner had tried and failed to purchase the Carter Hawley Hale Stores chain, which owned Bergdorf Goodman. Was Wexner a sore loser, "determined to show snooty New Yorkers how retailers from Columbus, Ohio, can squeeze huge profits from even the most specialized of specialty stores?" wondered *New York* magazine. Perhaps it was simply an unintended blunder, "that Limited zealots, high on the gospel of Systems, didn't know they were destroying the identity of the store they'd come to help."

While Geraldine was bewildered and angry, she never publicly criticized Wexner. Nevertheless, rumors began to circulate that she was unhappy and looking for an exit. There were stories that Geraldine might take the helm at Harrods in London and that she was considering an editorship at *Vogue*. And she did speak to the press, through her proxies. "I don't think one can expect the brilliant woman who single-handedly, out of her own creativity, built up the most unique store in America, to smile contentedly while a conglomerate decides to merchandise it as a chain!" wrote Liz Smith in her column for the *Daily News*. "But Stutz is nothing if not circumspect, polite, and tactful," she added, noting that her friend "has never been one for half measures, for suffering fools gladly, for accepting the dimmed visions of others," and was "impervious to the blandishments of mere money and sordid commercialism."

Away from the public eye, Geraldine tried reaching Wexner repeatedly, hoping to uncover the meaning behind the changes. But in the ten months that Geraldine worked for him, Wexner did not reply, not even once. Finally, she went to Europe for a two-week break. While there, Geraldine wrote her boss a final note. It was a request that he buy out her contract. That message Wexner immediately returned, and the sides began negotiating a release from Geraldine's employment. As news leaked that she was leaving, Geraldine's lawyer remained discreet. "She has had some difficulties with regard to the way some things were being done or not being done with the store," he told the press. In July 1986, less than a year after Geraldine sold Bendel to the Limited, just days before her sixty-second birthday, and some twenty-nine years after she first arrived, she walked down the back stairs of Henri Bendel and out the service entrance. Geraldine never returned—not once—her focus set firmly ahead.

Afterword

After walking away from Henri Bendel, Geraldine contemplated what she called her "Walter Mitty dream." She returned to her editorial roots, starting her own book imprint, which she aptly titled Panache Press, where she published cookbooks, a tome on the interior designer Elsie de Wolfe, and several volumes of Andy Warhol's artwork. Geraldine spent her weekends in Connecticut, gardening and watching old movies, many of which starred her famous friends. Then, in 2004, she hosted a series of grand luncheons at her country estate. Though she failed to inform her guests, the elegant parties were her goodbye; the cancer that plagued Geraldine as a young woman had returned. In early 2005, as she became increasingly ill, Geraldine retreated to her Upper East Side town house, where she refused to see anyone but her nurse. Instead, she communicated exclusively by telephone, ringing up her inner circle with her trademark "Darling, it's Geraldine." In April 2005, the eighty-year-old who had for half a century defined what it meant to be a chic New Yorker died peacefully at home.

Meanwhile, Henri Bendel continued. Under Wexner's helm, it relocated to Fifth Avenue, into a new building that was four times the size of its old space, catty-corner from Trump Tower, where Bonwit Teller once stood. Bendel also opened a string of suburban stores, including in a Paramus, New Jersey, mall and off a highway in Newton, Massachusetts. None took, and in 2009 the legendary department store stopped selling clothes. The upper stories of its New York flagship closed, and the main floor was transformed into a bastardized Street of Shops, filled with rows of bins piled high with plastic hair clips, cheap lip glosses, and Bendel-branded key chains. The store limped along in this diminished state until the winter of 2019, when the once-dignified retailer finally met its unavoidable end.

Just weeks before, Lord & Taylor suffered a similar fate. Since the early years of the twenty-first century, the home of Dorothy Shaver and the first American-branded designers struggled to remain profitable. The Fifth Avenue store was sold to WeWork, and after a fire sale to off-load its remaining merchandise, the building was converted into a maze of glass-walled cubicles, Ping-Pong tables, and cold-brew taps. When WeWork imploded, the internet overlord Amazon took its place. Floors that once vibrated with the frenzied energy and chatter of generations of saleswomen and shoppers now ring with the clacking of keyboards as coders execute billions of online sales, moving everything from designer dresses to groceries to electronics from the cloud to warehouses to your front door. Not long after the Fifth Avenue store closed, Lord & Taylor's remaining locations also shuttered, and in 2021 America's oldest department store emerged from bankruptcy as a website.

I grew up during the tail end of the department store era: too young to experience Hortense's heyday, Dorothy's legendary run, or Geraldine's Street of Shops. My first department store memory is inextricably linked to my favorite second-grade outfit, a birthday present that I opened while sitting cross-legged in my grandparents' bedroom in Brooklyn, pulling apart the white Lord & Taylor box with its giant rose insignia to reveal a palm-tree-covered shorts-and-shirt combination, the height of elementary school fashion. My other department store memories involve a late-summer road trip to Manhattan with my mother to shop for school clothes at Bloomingdale's and persuading her to splurge on button-fly, acid-washed Guess jeans that I had long coveted. And recollections of lining up along Seventeenth Street in Chelsea, waiting for the doors to open at the annual Barneys Warehouse sale, then diving headlong into the elbowing mass of bargain hunters to snag a nip-waisted DKNY denim blazer and a Dries Van Noten button-down that I still wear.

Today, when I take my daughter school shopping, we don't drive an hour and a half from New Jersey to Bloomingdale's; we walk a few steps to my laptop, where we scroll through $23 pleated tops from Zara and $15 joggers from H&M. And when my son shares his birthday wish list with his grandparents, he texts them a series of Amazon links, and presents arrive at our doorstep in anonymous brown cardboard, covered in tape and barcodes. Sure, there's still Bergdorf Goodman standing majestically on the corner of Central Park, or Saks Fifth Avenue across from Rockefeller Center. Dallas is known for Neiman Marcus, and Seattle, Nordstrom. But in most cases, that ephemeral glamour, the atmosphere of luxury and excitement that was once integral to the department store, has evaporated.

Would Hortense, Dorothy, and Geraldine mourn these changes?

I don't think so. Department stores once provided invaluable opportunities for ambitious women; I focus on three here, but there are many more whose stories deserve similar attention. Yet for all their positive attributes, department stores were also citadels: hierarchical organizations that kept out as many as they allowed in. Now American fashion is more democratized, with Etsy shops and social media channels enabling most anyone to start their own brand. And while there remains more work to be done, every year new pathways to success open for female leaders. In 2018, the Fortune 500 list of largest companies included only twenty-four female CEOs, a paltry 4.8 percent of the total. Five years later, that number has more than doubled to fifty. And the industries where women can thrive are similarly expanding. While fashion companies are represented, of those fifty female CEOs women helm both CVS and Rite Aid, lead the aerospace giant Northrop Grumman, and oversee the financial powerhouses Citigroup and Fannie Mae.

Even though Hortense, Dorothy, and Geraldine never joined forces, I always felt as if they were in conversation with one another, speaking through time, building on each other's achievements. I also was a part of this conversation, serving as their translator and moderator. When I began to write this book, at the height of the pandemic, the topic of women and work was foremost in many minds, including my own. I found myself without any child-care system, with two young kids, with a job I had no time to perform. As I dug into my research, the struggle that each of my three subjects faced to find balance between her career and her personal life was thrown into sharp relief.

I wrestled most with my portrayal of Hortense, who voiced frequent regret about her role at Bonwit Teller. As a working mother myself, I was made uncomfortable by her views. It was only after many months, and valuable feedback from trusted readers, that I was able to summon the empathy that she deserved, and better contextualize her plight. It was much easier to connect with Dorothy, to feel in awe of her singular focus and envious of her ability to recognize and pursue her desires, unfettered by self-doubt. I most related to Geraldine, a modern woman who wished to succeed on her own terms, who fought norms and broke molds, yet who was still plagued by an internalized sexism—expressed through her favoritism of thin customers, for example, or her power dynamics with men—an issue that many of us also contend with.

Department stores were a brief idyll, a safe space where women who wanted a more dynamic life, who wished to explore their ambition without ridicule, could find reprieve and support. And while I look back on this period with admiration, and even a tinge of romance, I am grateful that I came of age now. While there is undoubtedly a mountain of obstacles women in the workforce must continue to overcome, I have more options than these pioneering women ever did, and I am optimistic that my daughter will have even more choices than I've had.

Acknowledgments

Despite there being just a single author's name attached to most books, the act of writing is not a singular pursuit. Yes, writers toil alone, stuck in our heads, eyes staring at a computer screen, producing a book line by (often arduous) line.

But to get to that point, where writers are doing their job of writing, a zillion hands must first contribute their part, frequently unseen. Foremost, I must thank my agent, Susan Canavan. Without her there would be no book. She came up with the first germ of the idea—a lucky talent to have in an agent—and was the first to give me the confidence to pursue it.

Another fortunate turn was that Kristine Puopolo and Carolyn Williams, a power duo of editors, liked what they read when they first saw my proposal. Editors take risks when they give us writers a shot, and we, in turn, take a chance handing our creations to someone else to help shape. It is an intimate, yet perilous, dance of mutual hazard and trust. I am eternally grateful—and hopeful—that it has paid off. Kris and Carolyn, thank you for providing me with the perfect balance of encouragement and critique, pushing me to stretch and challenge myself.

Sameen Gauhar, your talent as a fact-checker is matchless. You have helped me shepherd two books through this complex process, searching through countless files stuffed with scribbled notes, articles, and source interviews. This time, not only did you lend your diligence to the facts, but you also served as one of my first readers. Your insights and questions helped me clarify and refine my writing, for which I am eternally grateful.

To Suzanne Williams, and the intrepid Doubleday team, including Anne Jaconette, Penguin Random House's über-talented marketing manager; Kayla Steinorth and Michael Goldsmith in publicity; Peggy Samedi, production manager; Amy Brosey, production editor; Betty Lew, text designer; Emily Mahon and John Fontana, jacket designers; and Bill Thomas, publisher: Thank you for all the effort and thought that you have poured into this book.

The women featured in these pages were long since dead by the time I had the opportunity to research them. But in the case of Geraldine, many of her colleagues are still here to attest to her brilliance as a merchandiser and boss. Many chapters simply wouldn't have been written without generous assistance from Marion Greenberg, who marshaled the troops of former Bendel employees, urging them to speak with me and share their memories. Thank you to Holly Brubach, Robert Rufino, Pat Peterson, Karol Kempster, Koko Hashim, Sunny Clark, Jacqui Wenzel, and Helen Skor. Miriam Marshall welcomed me into her home and willingly answered hundreds of my pestering questions. And I spent a memorable summer afternoon with Pat Tennant and Carol Brown in Pat's beautiful Long Island home. Now age ninety-six, Pat is as fierce today as she was traipsing around Europe sourcing designers in the early 1960s. Thank you also to Joseph Cicio, John Tiffany, and the Goodman family, including Vivian, Mary Ann, and Edwin.

Geraldine's stepdaughter and her nieces and nephews were generous with their time and memory, recalling family stories and dynamics. Thank you to Emma Turner for our several Zoom calls, and to Ellen, Jim, Martha, Matt, and Elizabeth Hopkins. That breakfast in Chicago was so helpful and fun, notwithstanding my barely avoiding a parking ticket! Thank you also to Allen Greenberg for being a loyal guardian of Geraldine's personal papers.

While Hortense remained somewhat emotionally distant from her family, her grandchildren, Brian and Wendy Odlum, shared what recollections they had of her, for which I am thankful. I also learned much from David Clarke, who has written an extensive, as-of-yet-unpublished biography of Floyd Odlum. Tim Allis, author of a forthcoming biography of Henri Bendel, was also exceedingly helpful.

Archivists can be magicians, mysteriously unearthing source material that seemed impossible to find, giving us writers the illusive documents that become the nucleus around which we shape our books. I would have been lost without Teresa Orton, the director of the Daughters of Utah Pioneers McQuarrie Memorial Museum in St. George, Utah. Thank you also to the archivists at the National Museum of American History in Washington, D.C.; the Schlesinger Library at the Harvard Radcliffe Institute in Cambridge; and the Dwight D. Eisenhower Presidential Library in Abilene, Kansas. Others who assisted in my research include April Calahan at the Special Collections at the Fashion Institute of Technology; Stan Friedman at the Condé Nast Library and Archive; Ethan P. Bullard, curator of the Maggie L. Walker National Historic Site; Emma Lindsey; Elizabeth Eames; and Maria Brandt, who assisted with my research at the Bancroft Library at the University of California, Berkeley.

The Benedictine Sisters of Chicago were kind enough to invite me into the St. Scholastica Monastery so that I could view Geraldine's high school yearbooks, while the Women and Leadership Archives at Loyola University Chicago guided me through Geraldine's college papers.

I am deeply grateful to Roger Joslyn, a genealogist who managed to track down Dorothy's grandniece, Sallie Moss. And I am even more grateful to Sallie, for her willingness to welcome me to her home and give me the time to examine her extensive collection of paintings and memorabilia. Thanks to Sallie, researchers have new insight into Dorothy's relationship with Elsie, and more clarity about how these sisters carved such fascinating, independent, and fulsome lives.

My trip to Mena, Arkansas, the birthplace of Dorothy, was immensely fascinating and enriching. Thank you to Brenda S. Miner, librarian at the University of Arkansas Rich Mountain, and Harold Coogan, a keeper of the local historical record. A particular thank-you and in memoriam to Shirley "Gypsy" Manning, who embraced this project and spent several days showing me Mena and discussing its history. I am sorry that you did not live long enough to read this book.

I spoke with several professors as part of my research, and I owe gratitude to Christy Glass, professor of sociology at Utah State University, and Brian Cannon, chair of the History Department at Brigham Young University, for their assistance. A special thank-you to Hazel Clark, professor of design studies and fashion studies at Parsons School of Design, whose effort to include Geraldine's contributions in the annals of fashion history is significant and informed my research. Lorraine Hariton, president of Catalyst, a nonprofit with the important mission of building more inclusive workplaces for women, provided helpful insight.

Critical to my mental health was the support of my fellow writer friends, whose ability to relate to, complain about, laugh at, and share in the tribulations of publishing has been a source of strength. Thank you, Amanda Gordon, Fiona Davis, Greg Wands, Adam Higginbotham, Laurie Gwen Shapiro, Howard Fishman, David Oliver Cohen, and Susie Orman Schnall. Thank you, Joni Evans, for your guidance, and Ada Calhoun and Sob Sisters, for creating community. Shout-out to Alice Robb, my podcast partner, who is always game to brainstorm. Thank you also for lifelong friendship, Jerusha Klemperer, and to "mom" friends Tamar Arisohn and Andrea Aimi—middle-school girls are no joke. Thank you to my OG "mom" friends Cristi Cohen (oh, girl!) and Crystal Bock, and my friend and lawyer Jackie Eckhouse.

My family is my heart. Stuart, you are the kite flyer to my kite, and I could never soar so high without your grounding. Sophie and Jonah, I am so glad that you are old enough to share with me your insights and perspectives on my writing. You amaze me with your intelligence and kindness; thank you for forever inspiring me to be my best self. Mom and Dad, thank you for your unwavering generosity and enormous caring. Jed, I forever carry you with me. Mike, Barb, Max, Jackson, and Dylan, Beth and Rob, and Cara, thank you for always being there to cheer me on.

Notes on Research

I spent three years getting to know Hortense, Dorothy, and Geraldine—finding out what motivated them, the challenges that they faced, and how they contributed to the evolution of the department store and American fashion. I combed through archives, traveled to their hometowns, interviewed living relatives, and read mountains of published, and unpublished, materials. The most intimidating factor in starting a book project that hopes to unearth the histories of overlooked figures is a possible dearth of available materials. If the characters were not famous during their lifetime, or if their fame faded, records may not have been kept, or might have been destroyed.

Hortense was well known during her time at Bonwit Teller, but her legacy diminished over the years. There are no archives dedicated to her, and her relationship with her family was estranged, so few personal records remain. To investigate her life, I began by traveling to her hometown of St. George, Utah. The Church of Jesus Christ of Latter-day Saints is famed for its diligent genealogical recordkeeping, and I hoped I might find something there. In St. George, the Daughters of Utah Pioneers McQuarrie Memorial Museum, which Hortense helped found, had some fascinating materials, including a book that memorialized Hortense's family, given to her by old friends and neighbors. It is also fortunate that Hortense's ex-husband, Floyd Odlum, was a prominent figure. He was a close friend of President Dwight D. Eisenhower's, and Floyd's papers are archived in his presidential library, and were a useful resource. But the most pivotal document to shed light on Hortense was her own autobiography. I read and reread *A Woman's Place*, parsing Hortense's memories and stories, trying to decipher truthful depictions from those that appeared to be rosy hyperbole. Any dialogue in this book is taken directly from Hortense's own account or from interviews that she gave.

Telling Dorothy's story was somewhat more manageable, since she was among the more well researched of the women. While there is no published biography of Dorothy's life, there are several excellent dissertations that detail her many career achievements. Because Dorothy never married or had children, finding living relatives proved to be a tricky task. However, it was through a lucky turn that I met Sallie Moss, her grandniece. In one of those Aha! moments that researchers dream of, Sallie's basement was filled with boxes that were stuffed to overflowing with Elsie's drawings and stories, photographs, letters, and other family mementos. Among the treasures was "Didi and Me," a scrapbook that Elsie wrote detailing her life with her sister. My trip to Mena, Arkansas, was also illuminating. There I met eighty-year-old Harold Coogan, a local historian, who shared with me his extensive writing and research into the Shaver family. Even more fortunate was the time I spent with Shirley Manning, a self-taught genealogist. Shirley, whom everyone called Gypsy, generously spent hours driving me around her hometown and discussing its local history. Her passion and energy were infectious.

Geraldine, being the most historically recent figure in this book, was in many ways the most familiar and accessible. I was able to rely on my skills as a journalist to interview by phone, on Zoom, and in person dozens of Bendel employees and family members. From these conversations, I gleaned an understanding of Geraldine as a visionary boss, a loyal friend, and a mentor. I also came to understand her role as sister, aunt, stepmother, and wife. My trip to Evanston and Chicago, Illinois, driving through her childhood neighborhood and visiting her schools, helped fill in gaps.

Reporting is an imperfect science, and despite my best efforts, there is much that remains obscured. I wish I could understand more fully all that transpired between Hortense and Floyd, or dig further into Dorothy's romantic life, or know how Geraldine handled losing her love, Henri Bendel. But I hope that, at the very least, I have added to the historical canon, and in some way done justice to these inspirational women.

Notes

Epigraph

ix "Buying and selling": Rheta Childe Dorr, *What Eight Million Women Want* (Boston: Small, Maynard, 1910), 115.

Prologue

xiv "There's a small office": Hortense Odlum, *A Woman's Place* (New York: Charles Scribner's Sons, 1939), 63.

xiv "What would I do": Ibid.

xv boasted record-breaking sales: In 1940, Bonwit Teller sales broke a store record, reaching more than $10 million, or $209 million in 2022 dollars. This is according to the Purchasing Power Calculator by Measuring Worth, www.measuringworth.com, which is used throughout the book to convert figures into today's dollars.

xvii a tab that equated to: Mary Todd Lincoln rang up a debt of $27,000 in the summer of 1864. Wayne Fanebust, *The Missing Corpse: Grave Robbing a Gilded Age Tycoon* (Westport, Conn.: Praeger, 2005), 13.

PART 1

1 "I'm no businesswoman": Adelaide Kerr, "Utah's Career Woman . . . with a Warning," *Salt Lake Tribune*, Nov. 19, 1944, C7.

Chapter 1: Hortense Goes Shopping

3 "It was horrible": Odlum, *Woman's Place*, 8.

3 "Every way I could": Ibid., 44.

4 "I loved caring for my baby": Ibid., 45.

4 "We can't go": Ibid., 46.

5 "I knew really that it was all wrong": Ibid., 47.
5 six children: Hortense had an older sister and brother, as well as two younger sisters and a brother.
6 "a stringy straight red mane": Odlum, *Woman's Place*, 16.
7 "I had, and have to this day": Ibid., 19, 29–30.
7 "Theirs was no namby-pamby way": Ibid., 13.
7 "only marking time": Ibid., 30.
7 "a popular young lady": "Manges-McQuarrie," *Washington County News*, Dec. 26, 1912, 1.
8 "I was determined that I would not reject": Odlum, *Woman's Place*, 32.
8 "Tenny, we're moving!": Ibid., 34.

Chapter 2: Dorothy Arrives "Home"

10 "Now," she told her conspiratorially: This quotation and those following are taken from Elsie's unpublished memoir, "Didi and Me." The memoir is handwritten and includes no page numbers.
11 "Let's stay a little while": Ibid.
11 "We were here exactly one week": Ibid.
12 "From then on": Ibid.
12 "The time has come now": Dr. Anna Howard Shaw, *Women's Work and War* (The National Women's Trade Union League, Chicago, Ill., March 1919, Vol. II, No. 2) 1.
13 "Make a doll!": David K. Boynick, *Women Who Led the Way: Eight Pioneers for Human Rights* (New York: Thomas Y. Crowell, 1959), 219.
13 "You design it": Jeanne Perkins, "No. 1 Career Woman," *Life*, May 12, 1947, 120.
13 "a little wide place": Boynick, *Women Who Led the Way*, 212.
13 "The farmer paid his legal fees": Elsie Shaver, "Didi and Me."
14 "colored mammy": "Elsie Shaver and the Unexpected Exhibition," *Harper's Bazaar*, March 15, 1942.
14 the last organized Confederate force: The local Mena historian Harold Coogan, "General Robert G. Shaver," unpublished biography; *Encyclopedia of Arkansas*, s.v. "Robert Glenn Shaver (1831–1915)," encyclopedia ofarkansas.net.
15 "We must be charitable": James Shaver, in a series of letters to Dorothy and Elsie, from the personal collection of Sallie Moss, grandniece of Dorothy and Elsie, shared with author in February 2022.
15 "had no patience with intolerance": Elsie Shaver, "Didi and Me."
15 John Blake, boarded: "Seriously Injured," *Mena Star*, Dec. 3, 1901, 3; "The John Blake Affair," *Mena Star*, Dec. 4, 1901, 3.

15 "been shot, his skull": Guy Lancaster, "'There Are Not Many Colored People Here': African Americans in Polk County, Arkansas, 1896–1937," *Arkansas Historical Quarterly* 70, no. 4 (Winter 2011): 435.

15 "hundreds of curious citizens": "Hanged to a Tree," *Mena Star*, Feb. 20, 1901, 5.

15 152 Black people: Lancaster, "'There Are Not Many Colored People Here,'" 439.

16 "had nothing, nothing": Elsie Shaver, "Didi and Me."

16 "Elsie and I loved her tenderly": Boynick, *Women Who Led the Way*, 216.

17 "Good day. I am Mr. Reyburn": Ibid., 220–21.

17 "We're from Lord & Taylor": Ibid., 221.

18 "a new race of dolls": Hanna Mitchell, "'Little Shavers'—a New Race of Dolls for Young and Old," *New-York Tribune*, Dec. 14, 1919, F11.

19 "They are building up": "Little Shavers, a New York Hit," *Mena Star*, Nov. 21, 1919.

Maggie Walker's New Venture

21 "The St. Luke's Emporium opened up": "The Midas Touch in Richmond," *New York Age*, May 11, 1905, 2.

21 "contains everything that a woman": "Colored Woman's Business Ability," *New York World*, Oct. 4, 1905.

21 "If the white man insists": Maggie L. Walker, "Benaiah's Valour: An Address for Men Only," March 1, 1906, Series D: Public Addresses, box 3, folder 24, Maggie L. Walker Family Papers, Maggie L. Walker National Historic Site, National Park Service.

21 "You know the stores": Ibid.

22 "The St. Luke's Emporium has been": Ibid.

22 "If it is worth that much to them": Shennette Garrett-Scott, *Banking on Freedom: Black Women in U.S. Finance Before the New Deal* (New York: Columbia University Press, 2019), 93.

22 "Now, for what purpose": Walker, "Benaiah's Valour."

23 "St. Luke's Emporium, the negro": *Richmond News Leader*, Sept. 12 or 13, 1905, from George St. Julian Stephens to Maggie L. Walker, Sept. 14, 1905, Series C, Correspondence, box 3, folder 21, Walker Family Papers.

23 "The white man doesn't intend to wait": Walker, "Benaiah's Valour."

23 "If confidence and forethought": Fiftieth Anniversary Golden Jubilee, Historical Report of the Right Worthy Grand Council, Independent Order of St. Luke, 1867–1917, 77, Walker Family Papers.

23 In its first year: The St. Luke Emporium had sales of $32,951.90 in its first year, or more than $1 million today. In its sixth year, sales were $12,809.33, or $413,000 in current dollars.

23 "We felt, as Negroes": Journal of the Proceedings of the 48th Annual Session, Right Worthy Grand Council, Independent Order of St. Luke, Aug. 1915, 40, Maggie Lena Walker Papers, Maggie L. Walker National Historic Site, Richmond.

Chapter 3: Dorothy Discovers Art Deco

25 "I know one store": Sara Pennoyer, *Polly Tucker: Merchant* (New York: Dodd, Mead, 1946), 72.

26 "Long lines of people": "Macy and Hearn Wage Price Cutting War on Peroxide Soap," *Women's Wear*, March 21, 1919, 1.

27 America counted eight thousand: Susan Porter Benson, *Counter Cultures: Saleswomen, Managers, and Customers in American Department Stores, 1890–1940* (Urbana: University of Illinois Press, 1988), 23; Sara Smith Malino, "Faces Across the Counter: A Social History of Female Department Store Employees, 1870–1920" (PhD diss., Columbia University, 1982), vi.

27 "A fat well-dressed woman": "The Autobiography of a Shop Girl," *Frank Leslie's Popular Monthly*, May 1903, 53–61.

28 They had their own slang: Benson, *Counter Cultures*, 245.

30 "You would be very much surprised": Malino, "Faces Across the Counter," 128.

30 "The employment department of the store": Frances R. Donovan, *The Saleslady* (Chicago: University of Chicago Press, 1929), 4.

31 "My first sale completed": Ibid., 24–25. Traditionally, department store clerks like Flossie hand wrapped each purchase in paper and tied it with a string, but after 1870 machines that made paper bags came into use. Not only were the bags cheaper and more efficient, but they also proved a quick and easy method of store advertising.

31 "As a customer I had considered": Ibid., 61–62.

32 "To the very poor": General Theodore A. Bingham, "The Girl That Disappears," *Hampton's Magazine*, Nov. 1910, 559–74.

32 "Sales girl aged 17": Department Store Investigation, Macy's, Nov. 1911 to April 1912, Committee of Fourteen Records, box 39, Manuscripts and Archives Division, New York Public Library.

33 "Women Forced to": "Women Forced to Underworld by Low Wages," *Atlanta Constitution*, March 16, 1913, 1.

33 "Mr. Lord had an aptitude": *The History of Lord & Taylor, 1826–2001* (New York: Guinn, 2001), 11.

34 "too man-made": Dorothy and Elsie Shaver, "Confidential Memorandum," Jan. 17, 1921, from the personal collection of Dorothy's grandniece, Sallie Moss. The memorandum, which was authored by both Dorothy and Elsie, indicates that the sisters were advising Mr. Reyburn some three years before Dorothy officially came on board at Lord & Taylor.

34 "I believe homes would be": "Samuel W. Reyburn Predicts Women's Field in Business Will Increase," *Women's Wear*, Nov. 7, 1924, 1.

35 "The idea of 'comparison' struck me": Alvin H. Goldstein, *St. Louis Post-Dispatch*, June 20, 1943.

35 "We should spend less time": S. J. Woolf, "Miss Shaver Pictures the Store of Tomorrow," *New York Times*, Jan. 5, 1947, 151, 161.

36 "Ambitious in scope": "'Modern Art' Gains Ground in Retaildom— Lord & Taylor's Exposition of French Art," *Women's Wear Daily*, March 3, 1928, 1.

36 "A magnificent exposition": Helen Johnson Keyes, "Decorative Art at the Lord and Taylor Exhibition—Jean Dunand," *Christian Science Monitor*, March 16, 1928.

36 "Surely this will bring you": Chase to Dorothy Shaver, Feb. 29, 1928, Dorothy Shaver Papers, Archives Center, National Museum of American History.

36 "an expression of the age": "Modern Art in Industry: An Attempt to Find Out Whether We Should Point with Pride or View with Alarm," Blackman Company, 1928, Shaver Papers.

36 "to help guide a new movement": "Decorative Art to Be Shown Here," *New York Times*, Jan. 23, 1928, 18.

36 "Look, I have to be up": Alvin H. Goldstein, *St. Louis Post-Dispatch*, June 20, 1943.

Chapter 4: Hortense's First Job

38 "I had done my share": Odlum, *Woman's Place*, 1–2.

39 "come along and have your dinner": Ibid., 2.

39 "I can't understand it": Ibid., 4–5.

40 "hunger marchers": "'Hunger Marchers' Arrive at Capitol," *New York Times*, Dec. 5, 1932, 1.

41 "There are approximately 10 million": Norman Cousins, "Will Women Lose Their Jobs?," *Current History and Forum*, Sept. 1939, 14.

41 "Is it necessary for you": George W. Mullins, acting dean, in his commencement address, *Columbia University Quarterly* 23 (1931).

41 In 1893, the liberal magazine: Clare de Graffenried, "The Condition of Wage-Earning Women," *Forum*, March 1893, 68.

41 "our job-bent women": Poppy Cannon, "Pin-Money Slaves," *Forum*, Aug. 1930, 98.

42 "one of those girls about": Jane Allen, "You May Have My Job: A Feminist Discovers Her Home," *Forum*, April 1932, 4.

42 one-third of married women: Alice Kessler-Harris, *Out to Work: A History of Wage-Earning Women in the United States* (New York: Oxford University Press, 2003), 256.

43 "Art is the most jealous": Sarah Comstock, "Marriage or Career?," *Good Housekeeping*, June 1932, 32–33, 156–60.

44 When the Great Depression arrived: This was an oft repeated fact, but may have been hyperbole. See David Clarke Jr., "Wall Street Gothic: The Unlikely Rise and Tragic Fall of Financier Floyd B. Odlum, Part Five," 9.

45 "Mrs. Odlum, come in and sit down": Odlum, *Woman's Place*, 6–9.

46 "I know what you're up to": Sydney Guilaroff, *Crowning Glory: Reflections of Hollywood's Favorite Confidant* (Los Angeles: General Publishing Group, 1996), 50–51.

47 "While the playwright was herself": Ibid., 100.

49 "severe, almost unornamented": Christopher Gray, "The Store That Slipped Through the Cracks," *New York Times*, Oct. 3, 2014, RE11.

50 zero value: "The Atlas Story," 8, box 2, folder 1, Floyd B. Odlum Papers, 1892–1976, Dwight D. Eisenhower Library.

50 "Jobs were hard to get": Floyd Odlum, marked-up, untitled document, 7, box 2, folder 1, Odlum Papers.

51 "There isn't a dress": Odlum, *Woman's Place*, 72.

51 "I suppose it does seem possible": Ibid., 73.

52 "I never did anything": Nov. 16, 1934, box 4, folder 5, Gladys Tilden Papers, BANC MSS 88/229 c, Bancroft Library, University of California, Berkeley.

52 "out of the spirit of adventure": Odlum, *Woman's Place*, 92.

52 "I consulted the buyer": Ibid., 93.

53 "The benefits of its location": S.F., "Alertness Keynote of Bonwit Millinery," *Women's Wear Daily*, Jan. 20, 1938.

Bessie Harrison Becomes a Buyer

54 "I remember the morning well": This and all following quotations are from "From Dust-Rag to Buyer's Desk (the Story of a Working Girl)," *Forum*, July 1917, 81–90.

Chapter 5: President Hortense

59 "never held a job before": "Mrs. Odlum Heads Bonwit Teller's," *New York Times*, Oct. 9, 1934, 14.

59 "A woman of vivacity": Ibid.

59 "combined the candor": "Mrs. Odlum Is New Head of Bonwit Teller," *Women's Wear Daily*, Oct. 9, 1934.

59 "A small woman": "Woman Saved Store When Men Failed," *Boston Globe*, Jan. 11, 1938, 3.

59 "she THINKS": Dorothy D. Lovatt, "Ideas Behind Careers," *Women's Wear Daily*, May 29, 1935, 3.

60 percentage of employed women who worked: Linda Keller Brown, "Women and Business Management," *Signs* 5, no. 2 (Winter 1979): 267.

60 "I didn't feel like a president": Odlum, *Woman's Place*, 106.

60 "retired because of ill health": "Mrs. Odlum Heads Bonwit Teller's."

61 "was, literally, a morgue": "Mrs. Odlum Brings Warm, Human Quality to Daily Retail Contacts," *Women's Wear Daily*, Jan. 11, 1938, 6.

61 "There was nothing to do": Ibid.

61 "I brought to my new job": Odlum, *Woman's Place*, 105.

61 "fresh take": "Bonwit—A Woman's Place," *New York Times*, October 1, 1939, 5.

61 "a woman's sixth sense": "There's that Sixth Sense Again . . . ," *New York Times* (advertisement), October 15, 1939, 5.

61 "I worked, I think, twenty-four": Odlum, *Woman's Place*, 117–18.

62 "With Mr. Holmes to divide with me": Ibid., 120–21.

62 "To be a charming and successful hostess": Ibid., 113–14.

63 "the average human being's aversion": Ibid., 89–91.

63 "My office is a court": "Mrs. Odlum Brings Warm, Human Quality to Daily Retail Contacts."

63 "I had spent all my free time": Ibid.

63 "I did little else during store hours": Odlum, *Woman's Place*, 121.

63 "If I were at home": Ibid., 160.

64 "There was an enormous market": Ibid., 96.

64 "There are sign posts": Ibid.

64 "Look, Mrs. Odlum": Ibid., 87.

65 "High class but not high hat": "Mrs. Odlum Heads Bonwit Teller's."

65 "I knew I was criticized": Odlum, *Woman's Place*, 110.

65 Monsieur Leon: "Beauty Salon to Open," *New York Times*, Oct. 14, 1934, 30. Sydney Guilaroff, the hairdresser at Antoine's, claimed in his autobiography that he was the first hairdresser at Bonwit Teller. He might have worked there, but it is unlikely that he was the first.

65 "from a crowd of frantic": "SRO Sign Marks 721 Club Party at Bonwit Teller's," *Women's Wear Daily*, Dec. 3, 1937, 2.

65 "the only place you can get a decent drink": Bern Adine Morris, "Christmas Shopping Services for Men Only Turn Coed," *New York Times*, Dec. 7, 1971, 58.

66 a $3,000 gold lamé: That is the 2023 value.

66 550 horsepower: "Mrs. Odlum Launches New Bonwit Teller Air-Condition Plant," *Women's Wear Daily*, May 24, 1938.

66 "In a jiffy": "Bonwit Teller Goes on the Air (Cool)," *Women's Wear Daily*, May 24, 1938.

66 "Our Mercury Goes *Down*": *New York Herald Tribune*, June 12, 1938, 6.

67 "Polly Tucker is the ideal": Emma Bugbee, "Sara Pennoyer Finds Fashion Industry Is Woman's Best Friend," *New York Herald Tribune*, Sept. 27, 1937, 6.

67 "But tell me, Lyda": Pennoyer, *Polly Tucker*, 45.

68 "Don't you have to be dazzlingly": Ibid., 240.

68 "designed to play a dual role": "Polly Tucker Ensemble," *New York Herald Tribune*, Jan. 11, 1943, 9A.

68 "any night course in any school": "Book Notes," *New York Herald Tribune*, March 15, 1938, 15.

68 "She has her own specialized bailiwick": Hortense Odlum, foreword to *Polly Tucker*, by Pennoyer, x.

69 "an interesting book": "Fifth Avenue Shop," *New York Times*, Oct. 22, 1939, 32.

69 "fashion is a frame of mind": "Bonwit Teller's Tonic Sessions on Style Opens," *New York Herald Tribune*, Sept. 20, 1938, 22.

69 "Attempts are being made": "Store Talks to Go On," *New York Times*, March 23, 1938, 40.

69 "I have a proboscis": "Will Kallie Foutz, Ugly Today, Be Scarlett O'Hara Tomorrow?," *Women's Wear Daily*, Aug. 17, 1938.

70 "Bonwit representatives sadly reported": Ibid.

70 "She's had plastic surgery": *New York Herald Tribune*, Oct. 9, 1938, 33.

71 "We have been building within": "Mrs. Odlum Cites Sharp Sales Gains," *New York Times*, Sept. 30, 1937, 32.

71 "essentially feminine, presenting none": "Woman Saved Store When Men Failed."

PART 2

73 "I'd far rather": Comstock, "Marriage or Career?," 160.

Chapter 6: Dorothy's American Look

75 "like something dragged out": Dorothy Roe, "Decadent Styles from France Cause Flurry in New York Marts," *Washington Post*, April 21, 1944, 14.

75 "If these are truly French": Tom Twitty, "Nazis Promoting 'Parisian' Styles in New York Market," *New York Herald Tribune*, April 18, 1944, 1.

76 "daring propaganda plot": Ibid.

77 "It is medieval": Elizabeth Hawes, *Fashion Is Spinach: How to Beat the Fashion Racket* (New York: Random House, 1938), 18.

77 By 1880, there were more: Roy Helfgott, *Made in New York: Case Studies in Metropolitan Manufacturing* (Cambridge, Mass.: Harvard University Press, 1959), 49.

78 "Fashion had gone democratic": Morris de Camp Crawford, *The Ways of Fashion* (New York: G. P. Putnam, 1941), 52.

79 "spellbound by the phrase": Dorothy Shaver, untitled typed document, 2, Shaver Papers.

79 "In New York in 1928": Hawes, *Fashion Is Spinach*, 112.

80 "We began to realize": Dorothy Shaver, untitled typed document, 5, Shaver Papers.

80 "This stuff is no good": Hawes, *Fashion Is Spinach*, 113.

80 "We whose work it is": Dorothy Shaver, untitled typed document, 4, Shaver Papers.

80 "America had no designers": Dorothy Shaver, "The Best Advice I Ever Had" (draft of text prepared for *Reader's Digest*), box 14, folder 6, Shaver Papers.

81 "We still doff our hats to Paris": Hawes, *Fashion Is Spinach*, 195, quotation from "Style Display 100% American," *World-Telegram*, April 13, 1932.

81 "Lord & Taylor recognizes a new trend": *New York Times*, April 17, 1932, 16.

82 "Women came into the store": Tiffany Webber-Hanchett, "Dorothy Shaver: Promoter of 'the American Look,'" *Dress*, Jan. 2003, 84.

82 As part of the promotion: Rebecca Arnold, *The American Look* (London: Bloomsbury Publishing, 2009), 112–13.

83 "For the next few years": Hawes, *Fashion Is Spinach*, 193.

84 "Paris is a city of brooding": Crawford, *Ways of Fashion*, 9.

84 "for decades, our garment industry": Stanley Marcus, "America Is in Fashion," *Fortune*, Nov. 1940, 81.

86 "A lot of people seem to think": Alvin H. Goldstein, *St. Louis Post-Dispatch*, June 20, 1943.

86 "Fur-edged parkas": "Army Nurses to Wear Khaki," Box 9, folder 6, Shaver Papers.

86 "The Army Nurses Corps threw": Ann France Wilson, "Army Nurses Wear Slacks," *New York World-Telegram*, Feb. 2, 1943.

86 "If anybody thinks that a woman": Alvin H. Goldstein, *St. Louis Post-Dispatch*, June 20, 1943.

86 "In a tribute to the largest women's army": *Women's Wear Daily*, March 8, 1943.

87 Between 1940 and 1945, the male labor force: Claudia Goldin and Claudia Olivetti, "Shocking Labor Supply: A Reassessment of the Role of World War II on Women's Labor Supply," *American Economic Review* 103, no. 3 (May 2013): 257.

88 Black-owned department stores: Traci Parker, *Department Stores and the Black Freedom Movement: Workers, Consumers, and Civil Rights from the 1930s to the 1980s* (Chapel Hill: University of North Carolina Press, 2019), 38–39, 57.

88 "When I saw this girl": Richard Dier, "New York's Lord & Taylor Hires 4 Colored Salesgirls," *Afro-American*, Jan. 1, 1944, 2.

88 By 1947, fourteen major New York: Lillian Scott, "N.Y. Stores Hire Negro Clerks and Business Goes on as Usual," *Chicago Defender*, Nov. 15, 1947, 13.

89 "It seems to me that it is only fair": Dier, "Lord & Taylor Hires 4 Colored Salesgirls."

89 "that certain kind of American figure": "What Is the American Look?," *Life*, May 21, 1945, 88.

89 "How's about doing a favor": "The American Look," leather-bound book, Shaver Papers.

Fashion Is Spinach

92 "I became sufficiently trusted": Hawes, *Fashion Is Spinach*, 41.

92 The book's title: The quotation became a catchphrase, calling something "spinach" becoming shorthand for calling it nonsense or rubbish. willyorwonthe.wordpress.com/2020/01/31/i-say-its-spinach/.

93 "She was about fifty-five": Hawes, *Fashion Is Spinach*, 43–44.

93 "The workgirls had gone home": Ibid., 44–45.

93 "The situation among American buyers": Ibid., 52–53.

94 "All the houses knew perfectly well": Ibid., 56.

94 "Every time one of them": Ibid., 57.

94 "his showrooms were vast": Ibid., 58.

95 "the battle cry of the world": Ibid., 60–61.

95 "Clothes were lying in tired piles": Ibid., 62.

96 "One day, during my third": Ibid., 63.

Chapter 7: Geraldine at *Glamour*

97 "My dear, you are too young": Marylin Bender, "Elizabeth Howkins, Editor, Dies," *New York Times*, Jan. 12, 1972, 46.

97 "I didn't know beans": Sheila John Daly, "A Female Bearcat Named Stutz," *Saturday Evening Post*, April 13, 1963, 62.

98 "just what the Girl-with-a-Job": Jerry Stutz and Betty Olmstead, "Two on the Aisle," *Condé Nast Ink*, Aug. 1948, Conde Nast Archives, New York.

98 "For the girl with a job": When *Glamour* debuted, it was called *Glamour of Hollywood* and was intended to be a down-market companion to *Vogue*, also owned by Condé Nast. The original tagline had been "The Hollywood Way to Fashion Beauty and Charm." The tagline was changed twice more until, by 1949, it was "For the girl with a job." Kathleen L. Endres and Therese Lueck, *Women's Periodicals in the United States: Consumer Magazines* (Westport, Conn.: Greenwood Press, 1995), 108.

98 a special conference room: Chelsea L. Payne, "*Glamour, Incorporating Charm*: Two Fashion Magazines for Working Women, 1939–1959" (master's thesis, Fashion Institute of Technology, 2021), 18.

99 "A job has become more than": Elizabeth Penrose, "We Can Take It with Us," *Glamour of Hollywood*, May 1941, 27.

99 "straight from the hinterlands": Karin Lipson, "The Warhol Party Goes On . . . ," *Newsday*, Oct. 5, 1988, 150.

99 "In so many ways, Andy": *Sunday Times Magazine* (London), Feb. 18, 2007, 54.

99 "extraneous, spur-of-the-moment": Jerry Stutz, "Fashion Fundamental No. 2: Accessories," *Glamour*, Feb. 1950, 89.

100 rarely spoke of him: Geraldine later said that her father greatly admired her mother but felt defeated by her, unable to live up to her expectations, while her mother was exasperated by his "weaknesses." Kathy Larkin, "Gerry Stutz—Innovative Fashion Retailer," *Gazette Telegraph*, May 14, 1984.

100 "I know she had 12 people": Shirley Clurman, "Gerry Stutz Is Hardly Just Window-Dressing at Bendel's—She Owns the Store," *People*, Nov. 3, 1980, 120.

100 "She held herself like": Mathew and Martha Hopkins, interview by author, Evanston, Illinois, May 10, 2022.

100 "always wanted to be president": Daly, "Female Bearcat Named Stutz," 60.

102 "I quite literally fell": Video of Geraldine Stutz interviewed by Dorothy Hanenberg, at Henri Bendel offices, Nov. 13, 1979, Special Collections Archive, Gladys Marcus Library, Fashion Institute of Technology.

103 "Don't try to strengthen people": Fred Smith, "Something I Learned from Maxey Jarman," *Christianity Today* (Winter 1981): 87.

103 "It just never dawned on me": Georgia Dullea, "On Ladder to the Top, a Mentor Is Key Step," *New York Times*, Jan. 26, 1981, B6.

104 "That was a very tough thing": Phyllis Stewart, "Geraldine Stutz: The Miracle on 57th Street," *Newsday*, Oct. 21, 1980, 8.

104 "At one point, I felt I couldn't cope": Clurman, "Gerry Stutz Is Hardly Just Window-Dressing at Bendel's."

104 "I had just embarked on psychoanalysis": Larkin, "Gerry Stutz—Innovative Fashion Retailer."

104 "I'm paid awfully, awfully well": Phyllis Lee Levin, "Shoe Business a Glass Slipper for Miss Stutz," *New York Times*, May 4, 1957, 24.

104 "They took a little winning": Ibid.

105 "There is nothing too expensive": "Henri Bendel: He Has Proved That American Women Want 'Values,'" *Women's Wear*, March 27, 1914.

106 "and carrying the accounts": Ibid.

107 "My purpose," Mr. Bendel said: "$1,800,000 of Stock to Go to Employees," *New York Times*, June 20, 1923, 30.

107 "faithful employee": "Henri Bendel Left $200,000 to an Aide," *New York Times*, April 1, 1936, 14.

107 "old and conservative": Virginia Pope, "Bendel Wollens Bring Admiration," *New York Times*, Dec. 4, 1940, 31.

107 "distinction rather than so-called": Winifred Spear, "Fashion Mirrors Wartime Demand," *New York Times*, March 4, 1943, 14.

Chapter 8: Hortense Has a Rival

108 "the decapitated head": "Dali's Display," *Time*, March 27, 1939, 193.

109 "hired to do a work": "Police Called to Quell Surrealism Run Amok," *Globe and Mail*, March 17, 1939, 1.

109 "unquestionable genius": Odlum, *Woman's Place*, 168.

109 "I really have tremendous sympathy": Ibid., 166–67.

109 fined $500: Sara K. Schneider, *Vital Mummies: Performance Design and the Store-Window Mannequin* (New Haven, Conn.: Yale University Press, 1995), 15.

109 "These are some of the privileges": "Dali's Display," 193.

110 one-third of all sales: Jan Whitaker, *Service and Style: How the American Department Store Fashioned the Middle Class* (New York: St. Martin's Press, 2006), 113.

110 L. Frank Baum: William Leach, *Land of Desire: Merchants, Power, and the Rise of a New American Culture* (New York: Vintage Books, 1993), 57–61.

111 exempted from military service: Whitaker, *Service and Style*, 117.

111 During an unseasonably warm winter: "Snowstorm in Store," *New York Times*, Nov. 13, 1938, 69.

113 "the most beautiful skin": Doris L. Rich, *Jackie Cochran: Pilot in the Fastest Lane* (Gainesville: University Press of Florida, 2007), 25.

114 Jackie's young life carried on: Ibid., 1–21.

114 "the most interesting person": Jacqueline Cochran, *The Stars at Noon* (New York: Little, Brown, 1954), vii.

114 "Every orphan dreams of marrying": Jackie Cochran and Maryann Bucknum Brinley, *Jackie Cochran: The Autobiography of the Greatest Woman Pilot in Aviation History* (New York: Bantam Books, 1987), 56–57.

115 "but this time it made sense": Ibid., 57.

115 female aviators were still rare: In January 1933, there were 588 women fliers in America, and Jackie was one of only 57 women who boasted transport licenses, according to Rich, *Jackie Cochran*, 31.

115 "He didn't want me to talk about him": Cochran and Brinley, *Jackie Cochran*, 61–62.

115 "extreme cruelty": Hortense McQuarrie Odlum, Plaintiff v. Floyd Bostwick Odlum, Defendant, Douglas County, Nevada, Oct. 7, 1935, Decree of Divorce.

115 "nothing but a manicurist": Stanley Odlum Jr., telephone interview by David Clarke Jr., May and June 2006.

115 thrown out of Dartmouth: Clarke, "Wall Street Gothic," part 5, chap. 2, 6.

116 "a one-way trip": Stanley Odlum Jr., telephone interview by David Clarke Jr., May and June 2006.

116 constant stream of celebrity guests: Rich, *Jackie Cochran*, 59, 64.

117 "If my strange ability": Cochran, *Stars at Noon*, 91.

117 a feature that queried readers: *Woman's Day*, Aug. 1940, 48.

118 "I am alone now": Donald L. Pratt, "Mrs. Odlum Regards Discourtesy as Stores' Public Enemy No. 1," *Women's Wear Daily*, Sept. 30, 1937.

118 "It still breaks my heart": "Around Town: Mrs. Odlum Says a Woman's Place . . . ," *PM*, Nov. 2, 1944, 12.

119 "misrepresented his financial": "Mrs. Odlum Asks Decree," *New York Times*, March 17, 1938, 52.

119 who spied for the Americans: Rhodri Jeffreys-Jones, *In Spies We Trust: The Story of Western Intelligence* (Oxford, U.K.: Oxford University Press, 2013); "Mrs. Odlum Remarried," *New York Times*, Nov. 17, 1954, 37.

120 "I know it was Tenny's interest": Floyd to Rulon J. McQuarrie, June 23, 1953, box 23, folder 9, Odlum Papers.

120 "Women executives in the field of retailing": "Mrs. Odlum Cites Sharp Sale Gains," *New York Times*, Sept. 30, 1937.

120 "hard boiled": "Store Head Backs Women in Business," *New York Times*, Dec. 8, 1938, 51.

120 "I never had the least desire": Donald L. Pratt, "Never Had a Desire to Be a Business Woman," *Women's Wear Daily*, September 29, 1939, 2.

120 "When I came to Bonwit Teller": "Mrs. Hortense M. Odlum Retiring as President of Bonwit Teller," *New York Times*, Oct. 11, 1940, 17.

121 In a filing with the Securities: "Bonwit Teller Salaries Filed," *Women's Wear Daily*, May 6, 1941.

121 When Holmes was elected president: "65% of Bonwit Teller's Volume Done by Store's 90,000 Charge Accounts," *Women's Wear Daily*, Nov. 4, 1943.

121 "loathed": "Around Town: Mrs. Odlum Says a Woman's Place . . . ," 12.

121 "We all know that in back": "Mrs. Hortense Odlum Urges Roosevelt Defeat," *New-York Tribune*, Oct. 23, 1940, 15.

122 was likely drunk: Clarke, "Wall Street Gothic," part 5, chap. 2, 5.

122 "I feel completely lost": "Around Town: Mrs. Odlum Says a Woman's Place . . . ," *PM*, Nov. 2, 1944, 12.

The Real Rachel Menken

124 "Mrs. Auerbach brooks no opposition": Virginia Hale, *A Woman in Business: The Life of Beatrice Fox Auerbach* (self-published, XLibris Corporation, 2008), 98–99.

124 a single worker: Ibid., 11.

124 "G. Fox is one of the few department stores": Marjorie Greene, "Fair Employment Is Good Business at G. Fox of Hartford," *Opportunity*, April–June 1948, 58.

125 "She was a tiny little thing": Cramer, telephone interview by author, Dec. 8, 2022.

125 "One thing you can be certain of": John Ingham and Lynn Feldman, *Contemporary American Business Leaders: A Biographical Dictionary* (New York: Greenwood Press, 1990), 17.

126 One customer placed a $25,000 order: Robert Hendrickson, *The Grand Emporium: The Illustrated History of America's Great Department Stores* (New York: Stein and Day, 1979), 165.

127 "It is no longer the fashion": Ibid., 179.

128 "women of larger proportions": Ibid.

128 "It's a miracle": "Lane Bryant's New Store Will Open Monday," *New York Herald Tribune*, Jan. 30, 1947, 14A.

Chapter 9: President Dorothy

129 "As she sweeps across": Perkins, "No. 1 Career Woman," 117.

130 "Don't give me dits and dats": Allene Talmey, "No Progress, No Fun," *Vogue*, Feb. 1946, 196.

130 "Of course, I don't have": Perkins, "No. 1 Career Woman," 118.

130 "I will never give an ultimatum": Dorothy Shaver, "Miss Shaver's Remarks for Executive Training Class," March 11, 1957, 5, series 3, box 16, folder 3, Shaver Papers.

130 "Darned if I know": Talmey, "No Progress, No Fun," 159.

130 "I always knock on wood": Alexandra Kropotkin, "A Woman Who Takes Her Husband Shopping," newspaper clipping, series 3, box 14, folder 5, Shaver Papers.

130 "Her friends say she is a diplomat": Talmey, "No Progress, No Fun," 198.

130 "only a quarter of the sum": Perkins, "No. 1 Career Woman," 117.

131 "I refused to talk about myself": Woolf, "Miss Shaver Pictures the Store of Tomorrow."

131 "Miss Dorothy Shaver, whose personality": Christine Frederick, "Successful Business Women: Dorothy Shaver," Shaver Papers.

131 "Success is a pitfall": Alice Hughes, "A Woman's New York," syndicated column, May 19, 1947.

131 "The typical career woman": Perkins, "No. 1 Career Woman," 118.

131 "I am tired of hearing": Woolf, "Miss Shaver Pictures the Store of Tomorrow," 161.

132 "You said 'American businessmen'": *The Tex and Jinx Show*, May 21, 1950, WNBC, box 3, folder 9, Shaver Papers.

132 "carefully and painstakingly separated": Perkins, "No. 1 Career Woman," 125.

133 New York's first department store lunch counter: Sandra Lee Braun, "Forgotten First Lady: The Life, Rise, and Success of Dorothy Shaver, President of Lord & Taylor Department Store, and America's 'First Lady of Retailing'" (PhD diss., University of Alabama, 2009), 87.

133 "How many women who are customers": Dorothy Shaver remarks, executive training class, March 11, 1957, box 3, folder 22, Shaver Papers.

133 Dorothy hired the artist: Braun, "Forgotten First Lady," 94.

134 "We're selling style": Perkins, "No. 1 Career Woman," 125.

134 "Why sell one pair of slippers": Talmey, "No Progress, No Fun," 198.

134 "My, it's good to see you again": Boynick, *Women Who Led the Way*, 209.

134 Puritan, who was being sawed: Braun, "Forgotten First Lady," 95.

134 "You Know Who": Ibid., 96.

135 duplex penthouse: Eleanore Roberts, "Her Rag Dolls Started Her on Road to Riches," *Boston Sunday Post*, Feb. 3, 1946; "Penthouse in Painters' Colours," *Vogue*, Nov. 15, 1938, 80–81.

137 "Being completely feminine": Elsie Shaver, "Didi and Me."

137 "the other would apparently": Correspondence between Agnes Shaver and the Mena historian Harold Coogan; Harold Coogan, "From Mena to Fifth Avenue: Dorothy Shaver, President of Lord & Taylor," *Mena Star*, Sept. 13, 1987, 5.

137 "I have always maintained": Dorothy Shaver to Mrs. Nicholas Jourdan Gantt, Feb. 28, 1950, Shaver Papers.

139 "at the risk of life and limb": Isabella Taves, *Successful Women and How They Attained Success* (New York: E. P. Dutton, 1943), 147.

140 "If you want the most complete mental bath": Dorothy Shaver to Reyburn from Paris, Hôtel Westminster, July 20, 1930, from the personal collection of Dorothy's grandniece, Sallie Moss.

140 "I believe so deeply": Dorothy Shaver, "This I Believe" Speech, *This I Believe*, March 14, 1955.

141 "spreading passion for conformity": "Conformity Held Peril to Freedom," *New York Times*, April 14, 1954, 21.

141 "She spoke of the paradox": "Miss Dorothy Shaver on Fear of Nonconformity," editorial, *Hartford Courant*, April 15, 1954.

Chapter 10: Geraldine's Street of Shops

142 "Even the stockroom roof": Larkin, "Gerry Stutz—Innovative Fashion Retailer."

142 "a beautiful old name": Lucile Preuss, "Young Executive Emphasizes Personality," *Milwaukee Journal*, 1963.

142 "Financially speaking": Hannah Southern, "How Fashion Is Sold," *Cosmopolitan*, Feb. 1960.

142 "I knew—and he knew I knew": Larkin, "Gerry Stutz—Innovative Fashion Retailer." In today's dollars, this would be $8.45 million in annual revenue, with a loss of $2.82 million; the reality was likely far worse, because it took Geraldine five years to turn her first profit.

143 "all so wrong!": Ibid.

143 "I want five years": Daly, "Female Bearcat Named Stutz," 62.

143 "a clever psychologist": "Behind the Bendel Phenomenon: The Imagination of Geraldine Stutz," Plaza newsletter (Winter 1982–83): 1.

143 "I had just been installed": Larkin, "Gerry Stutz—Innovative Fashion Retailer."

143 "I had the advantage only a woman": Betsy Holland Gehman, "Geraldine Stutz: Bendel's Bearcat," *Promenade*, June 1965, 34.

144 "What we want is something intimate": Stutz, interview by Hanenberg, 1979.

144 "I almost died": Helen Dudar, "Trading Up," *Daily News*, Aug. 26, 1980, 1.

145 "I was struck dumb": Stutz, interview by Hanenberg, 1979.

145 "Until two days before": Ibid.

146 "Well, you've got guts": Enid Nemy, "Geraldine Stutz: The Woman Who Bought the Store," *New York Times*, July 21, 1980, 15.

146 "the Street of Flops": Pat Peterson, telephone interview by author, May 17, 2021.

146 "Jerry's Folly": Enid Nemy, "Geraldine Stutz: The Woman Who Bought the Store."

146 "nice girl": "Super Salesmen," *Women's Wear Daily*, April 11, 1963, 14.

146 "Many men did expect": "Living with Liberation: Geraldine & David," *New York*, Aug. 31, 1970, 34.

147 "Although many stores have 'prettified'": Emmett Davis, "Street of Shops Is a Novel Idea," *Daily American*, Sept. 26, 1959.

147 "Won't you come in": *New York Times*, Sept. 13, 1959.

148 "is like being inside a fabulous": "Diary of a Window Shopper," *Women's Wear Daily*, Sept. 27, 1960, 12.

148 "soft-spoken, wise": Gloria Emerson, "Lipsticks and New Luxury," *New York Times*, Sept. 21, 1960, 41.

149 "Women who are interested": "Bonwit's Lady Boss," *Time*, Jan. 22, 1965.

149 "Maxey Jarman is famous": Eugenia Sheppard, "Maxey and the Girls," *New York Herald Tribune*, Jan. 14, 1965.

149 "You can't help soaking up": Eugenia Sheppard, "The First Hundred Pages Are the Hardest," *New York Post*, June 30, 1971.

150 "Jerry charmed Maxey": Kempster, telephone interview by author, May 24, 2021.

150 "Bridget wore her success": Van Slyke, *The Rich and the Righteous*, 156.

150 "When I came to Bendel": Geraldine Stutz, "Buster of Bendel's," *New York*, Dec. 21, 1987, 68.

150 "He trots out to the curb": Nan Robertson, "Buster, Long a Doorman, Still Plies 57th St. Trade," *New York Times*, Jan. 18, 1956, 35.

150 "Over the years, his role": Enid Nemy, "That Buster Is a Doll," *New York Times*, Nov. 10, 1978, A22.

150 "bell-boy chic": "Bell-Boy Chic to Cap Holiday Heads," *Tobé Report*, Aug. 30, 1978, 66.

151 "He carried his celebrity": Stutz, "Buster of Bendel's," 68.

151 "From the beginning": Estelle G. Anderson, "Identify Your Affinity and Pursue It," *Boot and Shoe Recorder*, April 15, 1962.

151 "a serene atmosphere": Southern, "How Fashion Is Sold," 84.

151 "Our customer is big-city": Gehman, "Geraldine Stutz: Bendel's Bearcat," 34.

151 The Bendel Look was "elegant, chic": Southern, "How Fashion Is Sold," 84.

152 "Correctly pronouncing the name": "Behind the Bendel Phenomenon," 2.

152 75 percent of the clothing: "Management Looks at Sportswear," *Sportswear Merchandise*, May/June 1962, 26.

152 "The dresses were mostly": June Callwood, "The Incredible Women of Madison Avenue—What It Costs to Out-man Men," *Maclean's Magazine*, Nov. 5, 1960, 78.

152 In the 1940s: In the 1980s, American clothing manufacturers started

employing so-called vanity sizing, inflating sizes so that larger apparel was sized smaller, to flatter, and presumably lure, customers. Increasingly, new sizes like 0 were introduced, and even 00, as is common today.

152 At Bendel, within four years: Callwood, "The Incredible Women of Madison Avenue."

152 " 'dog whistle' fashion": Jesse Kornbluth, "The Battle of Bendel's," *New York*, Feb. 23, 1987, 29.

153 "At Bendel's there is no special": Geraldine Stutz, *Glamour*, Oct. 1963.

153 "The talented should be given": Jean Campbell, "New York Newsletter: Gerry Gets £14,000 to Mind the Shop," *Evening Standard*, Dec. 6, 1961, 7.

153 "When he was getting ready to leave": Marshall, interview by author, Chappaqua, New York, July 27, 2021.

153 "My flight landed at 6:00": Ibid.

154 "He opened up this blanket": Ibid.

154 "Bendel's has just gone from red": Daly, "Female Bearcat Named Stutz."

PART 3

157 "What's wrong with a woman": "Can Women Succeed in Retailing by Really Trying," *Clothes*, April 1, 1971.

Chapter 11: Dorothy Branches Out

159 selling at the equivalent of $220: This is today's dollars; the perfume cost $20 an ounce in 1955.

160 The Philadelphia outpost also boasted: "Unusual Decorations Will Enliven Opening of New Lord & Taylor Store," *Suburban and Wayne Times*, Feb. 22, 1955, 1.

160 For the staff of more than three hundred: "Swanky New Lord & Taylor Brings Deft Fashion Touch to the Main Line," *Main Line Times*, Feb. 17, 1955, 18.

160 "Lord & Taylor moved in": *Time*, Feb. 28, 1955.

161 In 1945, the country had: State Motor Vehicle Registrations, by Year, 1900–1995, U.S. Department of Transportation, Federal Highway Administration, www.fhwa.dot.gov/ohim/summary95/mv200.pdf.

161 suburban populations grew: Vicki Howard, *From Main Street to Mall: The Rise and Fall of the American Department Store* (Philadelphia: University of Pennsylvania Press, 2014), 134.

161 Between 1954 and 1963: Ibid., 139.

161 Between 1940 and 1947: Will Lissner, "48 Branches Set Up by City's Big Shops," *New York Times*, June 11, 1949, 15.

162 "abnormally high cost": "Lord & Taylor Puts Off a Move Farther Up-town," *New York Times*, Oct. 15, 1952, 46.

163 "Not having their money tied up": "Retailing: Everybody Loves a Bar-gain," *Time*, July 6, 1962.

164 In 1958, discounters made up: Howard, *From Main Street to Mall*, 169, 171.

165 Some 80 percent of workers: Ibid., 174.

165 worth $40 million: "Retailing: Everybody Loves a Bargain."

166 Doodie and Schmultzie: Ibid.

166 in 1990, Walmart was: Job Stobart and Vicki Howard, eds., *The Routledge Companion to the History of Retailing* (New York: Routledge, 2019).

166 "Welcome Assistant Managers": Nelson Lichtenstein, "Wal-Mart's Authoritarian Culture," op-ed, *New York Times*, June 21, 2011.

167 "complete fatigue": "Dorothy Shaver Resting in Hospital," *Women's Wear Daily*, Dec. 5, 1958, 8.

167 "I was shocked": Sulzberger to Elsie Shaver, June 29, 1959, Shaver Papers.

167 "Terribly distressed": Rockefeller to Elsie Shaver, wire, June 29, 1959, Shaver Papers.

167 "remarkable": Nixon to Elsie Shaver, June 30, 1959, Shaver Papers.

167 "Although we knew": Fashion Group newsletter, 15, box 1, folder 6, Shaver Papers.

167 "I prize your message": Custin to Dorothy Shaver, April 23, 1958, Shaver Papers.

168 "I always wanted": Elsie Shaver, "Didi and Me."

168 "If she were here": Ibid.

168 "The fact that I happen to be": Woolf, "Miss Shaver Pictures the Store of Tomorrow."

169 "in the act of voting": Perkins, "No. 1 Career Woman," 126.

169 it was still $25,000: Wilma Soss, "Feminist Tribute to Dorothy Shaver," *Pocketbook News*, NBC, July 6, 1959.

169 "I am not an artist": Taves, *Successful Women and How They Attained Success*, 143.

169 "I wouldn't change places": Marjorie Farnsworth, "Woman of the Week: Sharing a Sandwich with Dorothy Shaver," Dorothy Shaver Papers.

Chapter 12: President Geraldine

170 "There must have been maybe 20": Rosenberg, interview by Hazel Clark and Lauren Sagadore of Parsons School of Design, transcript, Nov. 21, 2014.

170 "Go to Europe": Ibid.

170 "charming little bits and pieces": Ibid.

171 "Next to a bad cold": "Store's Imported Fashions Next Best Thing to One-of-a-Kind," *New York Times*, Sept. 19, 1959, 26.

171 "We couldn't compete": Mary Krienke and June Weir, "Two Fine Heads," *Women's Wear Daily*, May 6, 1965, 4–5.

172 "It is unsound": "H. Bendel Skips Paris Openings," *Women's Wear Daily*, July 25, 1961.

172 "not a need for bigger": "Management Looks at Sportswear."

172 "stumbled across a shop": Jean Rosenberg, guest lecturer at Fashion Institute of Technology, video, 1981, www.youtube.com/watch?v =wd4avSJ5KbA.

172 "Jean Rosenberg, the brilliant fashion": "Behind the Bendel Phenomenon," 2.

173 "Bendel's fashion conscience": Stutz, interview by Dorothy Hanenberg (FIT), Henri Bendel offices, New York, 1976.

173 John the Baptist: Clurman, "Gerry Stutz Is Hardly Just Window-Dressing at Bendel's," 119.

173 "There was a symbiotic": Rosemary Feitelberg, "Jean Rosenberg, Retail Pioneer and Ideal American Size 6, Dies at 97," *Women's Wear Daily*, June 19, 2022.

173 "Geraldine always said": Rosenberg, interview by Hazel Clark and Lauren Sagadore of Parsons School of Design, transcript, Nov. 21, 2014.

173 "I want our own stuff": Tennant, interview by author, Cutchogue, New York, June 12, 2021.

173 "Fashion says, 'Me Too'": "Style Belongs to Leaders, Not Followers," *Austin American–Statesman*, E6.

173 "We went with tape measures": Tennant, interview by author.

174 "It was probably partly my fault": Rosenberg, interview by Hazel Clark and Lauren Sagadore, 2014.

174 "Geraldine always insisted": Tennant, interview by author.

174 "Inconsistency of fit": Marylin Bender, "Shops Look to 7th Ave., Not Europe," *New York Times*, June 19, 1963, 63.

174 "made an adventure": "Biography of Geraldine Stutz," Bendel press release, 1958, Geraldine Stutz Henri Bendel collection, New York Public Library.

175 "Throughout the past eighteen months": "French Imports, Adapted Designs, and Boutique Fashions Are Shown," *New York Times*, March 11, 1957.

175 "We had to start to sneak": Tennant, interview by author.

175 "New York buyers": Marylin Bender, "European Ready-to-Wear Attracts New York Stores' Buyers Abroad," *New York Times*, Dec. 31, 1959, 14.

175 "It's becoming almost as easy": "Management Looks at Dresses," *Dress and Costume Merchandiser*, Feb.–March 1964.

175 "We almost had exclusivity": "Henri Bendel Sets Goal of 15 Crimpers Units," *Women's Wear Daily*, July 10, 1969.

175 "exclusivity is absolutely essential": "Management Looks at Dresses."

175 "Considering the dollar volume": "Retailing: The Henri Bendel of Geraldine Stutz," *Clothes*, March 1, 1967.

176 "a new economy nourished": "Young Fashion Areas Enjoy Growing Pains," *Women's Wear Daily*, Jan. 21, 1963, 1.

176 "I'm not just talking about": "Beauty Is What's Happening in Fashion," interview with Geraldine Stutz at the Cosmetic Meeting of the Fashion Group, Feb. 10, 1966.

177 "I'm wild about the young kids": Gehman, "Geraldine Stutz: Bendel's Bearcat," 32.

177 "Starting at 11 a.m.": John Weitz, "The Young Goddesses," *Cosmopolitan*, March 1967, 66.

178 "She's simply the best dressmaker": Sinty Stemp, *Jean Muir: Beyond Fashion* (Suffolk, U.K.: Antique Collectors' Club, 2007), 157, 115.

178 "contemporary custom": "Bendel Revives Made to Order," *New York Herald Tribune*, Oct. 4, 1961, 18.

179 "deluged with requests": "Custom Orders Gain Popularity," *New York Times*, Nov. 28, 1961, 43.

179 "perhaps the first": "Henri Bendel to Dress in Own Fashions," *Women's Wear Daily*, Feb. 7, 1967, 1.

180 "a traditional Catholic marriage": Clurman, "Gerry Stutz Is Hardly Just Window-Dressing at Bendel's," 120.

180 "Now, honey": Jim Hopkins, telephone interview by author, April 7, 2022.

180 "I was totally aligned": Larkin, "Gerry Stutz—Innovative Fashion Retailer."

180 "used to think of fashion": "Beauty Is What's Happening in Fashion," interview with Geraldine Stutz, 1966.

181 "the underground, swinging hairdresser": Marylin Bender, "Bendel's President Sees Herself as Customer," *New York Times*, May 10, 1965, 37.

181 "I hate sitting in bullpens": H. McKim Glazebrook, "Bendel's Great Big Garden Gazebo," *Interiors*, July 1965, 69.

181 "important people": Priscilla Tucker, "Universal Reformer Comes to Bendel's," *New York Herald Tribune*, Oct. 10, 1965.

181 "Considering herself unable": "Retailing: The Henri Bendel of Geraldine Stutz."

182 "The store was run by": Brown, telephone interview by author, May 20, 2021.

182 "I am the father": Marylin Bender, "When the Boss Is a Woman," *Esquire*, March 28, 1978, 37.

182 "Everyone loved Charlie": Tennant, interview by author.

182 "But, Marjorie!": Bender, "When the Boss Is a Woman," 35–38.

183 "an amazing esprit de corps": "Retailing: The Henri Bendel of Geraldine Stutz."

Adel's Mannequins

185 "as much for those dolls": Catherine Houck, "The Artful Business of Making Mannequins," *Cosmopolitan*, Jan. 1976, 149.

185 These early versions: Schneider, *Vital Mummies*, 70.

186 "I could have wept": Odlum, *Woman's Place*, 162–63.

186 "One night, escorted": Lester Gaba, *The Art of Window Display* (New York: Studio Publications, 1952), 11.

187 "I sit at the piano": "A Girl Needs a Background," *House & Garden*, Dec. 1941, 75.

188 "When the fiberglass dummy": Houck, "Artful Business of Making Mannequins," 149.

188 first Black mannequin: Gaba, letter to the editor, *New York Times*, Dec. 17, 1980, C8.

188 American department stores "were frightened": Michele Ingrassia, "A Model for Her Industry," *Newsday*, June 30, 1983, D2.

188 "For a long time, mannequins": Ibid.

190 "She leads a short life": Angela Taylor, "They Find Right Face—Then Create a Mannequin to Resemble It," *New York Times*, Nov. 28, 1977, 51.

190 "brash and particular": Joshua David Stein, "Kevin Arpino Plays to a Silent Audience," *New York Times*, Dec. 12, 2012, E7.

Chapter 13: Hortense on Her Own

191 "Careers, careers": "Around Town: Mrs. Odlum Says a Woman's Place . . . ," 12.

192 "Mrs. Odlum added": "Mrs. Odlum Finishes Year as Store Head," *New York Times*, Oct. 4, 1935, 32.

192 "As I told my husband": "New York Department Store, Run by Woman, Is Success," *Daily Home News*, Oct. 13, 1935, 5.

193 "I don't say anything": "Around Town: Mrs. Odlum Says a Woman's Place . . . ," 12.

193 "America is overemphasizing": Adelaide Kerr, *Salt Lake Tribune*, Nov. 19, 1944, C7.

193 "This is the age": Floyd Odlum to Stanley Odlum, Feb. 13, 1957, box 62, folder 3, Odlum Papers.

194 "Dear Floyd": Hortense Odlum to Floyd Odlum, box 62, folder 3, Odlum Papers.

195 "It wasn't more than 24 hours": Eugenia Sheppard, "Fifth Avenue's First Lady," *Hartford Courant*, Jan. 21, 1969.

195 "wheeling the rack": Anne-Marie Schiro, "Mildred Custin, 91, Retailer, Made Bonwit's Fashion Force," *New York Times*, April 1, 1997, B10.

195 "Ours is a business of risk": Marylin Bender, "Miss Custin Bids Adieu to Bonwit's," *New York Times*, Dec. 12, 1969, 68.

195 "the French couturier's": Ibid.

196 "There isn't room": "Bonwit's Lady Boss."

196 "That's how we found out": Leslie Bennetts, "Bonwit's Final Sales: Chaos and Sadness," *New York Times*, April 23, 1979, 19.

197 "They were just jackhammered": Robert D. McFadden, "Developer Scraps Bonwit Sculptures," *New York Times*, June 6, 1980, A1.

197 "The merit of these stones": Ibid.

197 "How extraordinary": Ibid.

198 "Mr. Trump, who said": Ibid.

198 "It was a very distanced family": Brian Odlum, telephone interview by author, Dec. 1, 2021.

199 "It was ghastly": Stanley Odlum Jr., telephone interview by David Clarke Jr., May and June 2006.

199 "Tenny had to go somewhere": Wendy Odlum, telephone interview by author, Nov. 18, 2021.

199 frequently grew agitated: According to an interview that Doris L. Rich conducted with Judith Odlum, Bruce's second wife, in October 2000, as per her book *Jackie Cochran*, 217.

199 "Tenny was on my father's part": Wendy Odlum, interview by author.

199 "When my grandmother died": Brian Odlum, telephone interview by author, Dec. 1, 2021.

Chapter 14: Geraldine Meets Her Match

201 "I didn't know Geraldine": "Living with Liberation: Geraldine & David," *New York*, Aug. 31, 1970, 34.

201 "enormously damaging": Ibid.

202 "discipline and control": Dudar, "Trading Up," 1.

202 "He reminded me": Ellen Hopkins, Zoom interview by author, Jan. 24, 2022.

202 "They are more in touch": Eugenia Sheppard, "Anything but Stripes," *New York Post*, May 7, 1971.

203 "an ambitious careerist": Gail Levin, *Lee Krasner: A Biography* (New York: HarperCollins, 2011), 344.

203 "They fell in love": Emma Turner, Zoom interview by author, June 3, 2021.

203 "Because Bendel's president": Eugenia Sheppard, *New York Herald Tribune*, Sept. 13, 1965.

205 "My father loved": Emma Turner, interview by author.

205 "a maker": Ellen Hopkins, Zoom interview by author, Jan. 24, 2022.

205 "the first thing I've found": Rea Lubar Duncan, "Garden Secrets," *Connecticut*, March 1985, 24.

205 "tall man in exactly": Senga Mortimer, "The Garden Page," unidentified publication (Archive of Garden Design: RP/5/1/11), 130, gardenmuseum.org.uk.

206 "My father went to pick her up": Emma Turner, Zoom interview by author, May 9, 2023.

207 "Who Dunnit?": Deborah Sue Yaeger, "Chic Shops' Displays No Longer Are Just Window Dressing," *Wall Street Journal*, Sept. 9, 1976.

208 "Over my dead body": Rosemary Kent, "Drama Department: Comedy, Sex, and Violence in Store Windows," *New York*, May 24, 1976, 85.

208 "I lived on speed": Bernard Weinraub, "Visual Flair, a Hip Sensibility, and a Past," *New York Times*, June 11, 1995, H15.

208 "my mentor, savior": Joan Kron, "Home Beat," *New York Times*, June 2, 1977, 51.

208 "I rebuilt my entire life": Weinraub, "Visual Flair, a Hip Sensibility, and a Past," H15.

209 "they became a bloodcurdling roar": Kennedy Fraser, "Feminine Fashions," *New Yorker*, Oct. 10, 1970, 165, 167, 171.

210 "Stephen Burrows . . . Stephen Burrows": *New York Times*, March 1, 1971.

211 In 1969, Zandra: Rhodes, email interview by author, Aug. 9, 2023.

212 "I carried over two garment bags": Greenberg, telephone interview by author, June 1, 2022.

213 "I said to him": Cicio, telephone interview by author, May 18, 2021.

213 "If he saw us boarding": Ira Neimark, *Crossing Fifth Avenue to Bergdorf Goodman* (New York: Specialist Press International, 2006), 167.

214 "Once Dawn Mello arrived": Hashim, telephone interview by author, May 24, 2021.

214 "The thing about Bendel's": Wenzel, telephone interview by author, June 1, 2021.

214 "A couple of seasons ago": June Weir, "A View from the Ritz with Geraldine Stutz," *Women's Wear Daily*, April 4, 1977.

214 "Unlike the Bergdorf": Joni Evans and Carol Rinzler, "The Bendel," *New York*, March 5, 1973, 58.

215 "My father was very good-looking": Turner, Zoom interview by author, June 3, 2021.

215 "I thought it was a great compliment": "Living with Liberation," 34.

215 "He loved the fact": Turner, Zoom interview by author, May 9, 2023.

215 "It's a test": "Suzy: Versailles Is Still for Royalty," *Daily News*, Nov. 30, 1976, 12.

215 "I was deeply saddened": Stewart, "Geraldine Stutz: The Miracle on 57th Street."

216 "David and I had": Larkin, "Gerry Stutz—Innovative Fashion Retailer."

216 "Listen, I wouldn't have missed": Dudar, "Trading Up," 98.

216 "Quite possibly, she loved": Turner, Zoom interview by author, June 3, 2021.

216 "I think women's liberation": "Living with Liberation," 34.

216 "The best life": Helen Gurley Brown, "A Woman Can Have It All," *Santa Ana Register*, Nov. 18, 1982, C1.

The Friday Morning Lineup

217 "It was like a dream come true": Andy Port, "Trauma Time at Bendel's: 'Oh God! It's Friday!,'" *Women's Wear Daily*, Feb. 19, 1978, 15.

218 "I thought, 'Do I really want'": Sandra Salmans, "Dozens Wait in Line on Fridays," *New York Times*, Jan. 29, 1982, D1.

218 "yes, yes, and": Port, "Trauma Time at Bendel's," 15.

218 "That back door": Kathy Larkin, "Back Door to Fashion," *Daily News*, Sept. 12, 1977.

218 "clothes all our own": June Weir, "Bendel's New Role: Fashion in Living," *Women's Wear Daily*, Sept. 21, 1973.

218 "Businesses are getting so big": Constance Daniell, "An Executive with Class," *Milwaukee Journal*, Sept. 11, 1977, 5.

218 "I take every single one seriously": Salmans, "Dozens Wait in Line on Fridays," D1.

219 "These are wonderful": Ibid.

219 "Hello, these are my little friends": Port, "Trauma Time at Bendel's," 15.

219 "Could you make something": Salmans, "Dozens Wait in Line on Fridays," D1.

220 "nerve-wracking": Port, "Trauma Time at Bendel's," 15.

220 In August 1995: Amy M. Spindler, "They Called for Talent. They Got It," *New York Times*, Aug. 8, 1995, B8.

220 In 2009, Bendel, in a later: Armand Limnander, "At Henri Bendel, Wannabes Welcome," *New York Times Style Magazine* blog, March 31, 2009.

220 "like Camelot": Sharon Edelson, "Honorees Eleanor Lambert Award," *Women's Wear Daily*, May 2006, 32.

Chapter 15: Geraldine, Department Store Owner

221 "fair, generous, demanding": Thomas Moran and Allen F. Richardson, "Genesco's Billion-Dollar Dream Fades," *Women's Wear Daily*, Nov. 1, 1977, 1.

222 "Tighten Your Belt": Lynn Langway, Barbara Graustark, and Frank Sutherland, "A Noose for Jarman," *Newsweek*, Jan. 17, 1977, 70.

222 mentally unstable: Philip Greer and Myron Kandel, "Dossier a Weapon in Genesco Coup," *Newsday*, Feb. 3, 1977, 37.

222 "corporate hatchet man": Tony DeStefano, "The Company Bendel Left Behind," *Women's Wear Daily*, July 21, 1980.

222 "Bendel is no problem": Ibid.

222 "I don't think we could sell it": Lisa Barat Anderson, "Geraldine Stutz: Thinking Big for Bendel," *Women's Wear Daily*, Oct. 8, 1980, 14.

223 "Because I had run": Stewart, "Geraldine Stutz: The Miracle on 57th Street," 1.

223 "One of the toughest and sharpest": Ann Crittenden, "She's a New Kind of Financier," *New York Times*, Feb. 20, 1981, D1.

223 "seems to be coolly indifferent": Crittenden, "She's a New Kind of Financier," D1.

224 "I woke up": Linda Ashland, "Geraldine Stutz," 73–74, newspaper

clipping, New York Public Library, Geraldine Stutz Henri Bendel scrapbooks.

224 "is a brilliant conceptualist": Crittenden, "She's a New Kind of Financier," D1.

224 "They are the perfect partners": Anderson, "Geraldine Stutz: Thinking Big for Bendel," 14.

224 "Geraldine Stutz was": Nemy, "Geraldine Stutz: The Woman Who Bought the Store," A15.

225 "Isn't it true": Dudar, "Trading Up."

225 "I am Henri Bendel": Ashland, "Geraldine Stutz," 73–74.

225 "I came to the conclusion": Lisa Anderson, "Bendel's Puts Stamp Back on Mail Orders," Women's Wear Daily, June 17, 1982, 6.

226 "The new floors": Suzanne Slesin, "At Bendel's, Innovative Displays on 2 New Floors," New York Times, April 30, 1985, C10.

226 "confusing and puzzling": Pete Born, Women's Wear Daily, July 1, 1985, 1.

226 "an innovative high-class": Slesin, "At Bendel's, Innovative Displays on 2 New Floors," 61.

227 "wouldn't be caught on a back road": Dudar, "Trading Up," 97.

227 "not as slick as it used to be": "Bendel: Small but Not Quite as Sassy," Women's Wear Daily, March 20, 1984, 29.

227 "feel she has made compromises": Ibid.

227 "I adore my career": Clurman, "Gerry Stutz Is Hardly Just Window-Dressing at Bendel's," 122.

227 "Our intention was always to sell": Peter Wilkinson, "The Brazilian Connection at Bendel Discusses Plots," Women's Wear Daily, Nov. 6, 1985, 42.

228 200 million garments: Julie Baumgold, "The Bachelor Billionaire," New York, Aug. 5, 1985, 32.

228 "I said to myself": Wilkinson, "Brazilian Connection at Bendel Discusses Plots," 42.

228 "You cannot read him": Ibid.

228 "If the chemistry": Ibid.

229 "I am difficult to read": Baumgold, "Bachelor Billionaire," 36.

229 "We'll come in": Kornbluth, "Battle of Bendel's," 28.

229 "We're not wheeler-dealers": Janet Key, "The Limited: Bold Designs for a New Brand of Store," Chicago Tribune, Nov. 27, 1985, B1.

229 "She wanted to believe": Marshall, telephone interview by author, May 11, 2021.

229 "like I'm putting up my child": Ellen Hopkins, Zoom interview by author, Jan. 24, 2022.

229 "I think you are tired": Smith to Stutz, Dec. 7, 1984, from her personal papers, provided to the author by Allen Greenberg.

230 "Mother Teresa": Kornbluth, "Battle of Bendel's."

230 "He'd go off and watch": Brian O'Reilly, "Leslie Wexner Knows What Women Want," *Fortune*, Aug. 19, 1985.

231 "wanting approval": Baumgold, "Bachelor Billionaire," 28.

231 There are no public records: I contacted Geraldine's former law firm, Phillips Nizer, as well as her accountant, Allen Greenberg, to uncover documents related to Wexner's purchase of Bendel's. Neither party had kept its files on the decades-old transaction. The press never reported on Geraldine's personal windfall. The value of Geraldine's estate upon her death was provided by Allen Greenberg, an executor of her will.

232 "Do you know what eroticism is?": Wenzel, telephone interview by author, June 1, 2021.

232 "I went to meet Les": Kempster, telephone interview by author, May 24, 2021.

233 "determined to show snooty": Kornbluth, "Battle of Bendel's," 28.

233 "I don't think one can expect": Liz Smith, *Daily News*, June 26, 1986, 10.

233 "She has had some difficulties": David Moin, "Stutz's Future with the Limited Is Being Discussed by Attorneys," *Women's Wear Daily*, July 17, 1986, 2.

Afterword

237 In 2018, the Fortune 500 list: Data is as of September 2023, as collected by Catalyst, a global nonprofit promoting gender equity and workplace inclusion.

237 While fashion companies: As of September 2023.

Index

Page numbers in *italics* refer to illustrations.

Etsy, 237
Eugénie, Empress of France, 76
European ready-to-wear
	designers, 170–75
Evangelista, Linda, 189
*Exposition of Modern French Decorative
	Art* (Lord & Taylor), 36

Fabricant, Sylvia, 196
Fairchild, John, 213
Falchi, Carlos, 219
Falkenburg, Jinx, 131–32
Famous-Barr, xix
F&R Lazarus, 125
Fannie Mae, 237
Farley, James A., 167
Fashion Group, 84–85, 167
Fashion Is Spinach (Hawes), 92
fashion magazines, 75
Faust, Kallie (Foutz), 69–70
Fawcett, Farrah, 210
Federal Bureau of Investigation
	(FBI), 76
Federated Department Stores, 160
Feigen, Richard, 215
Feminine Mystique, The (Friedan), 183
feminism, 206, 216. *See also*
	women's liberation movement;
	women's suffrage
Fendi, 172, 181, 213–14
Ferkauf, Eugene, 165–66
Fifth Avenue Association, 230
Filene, Edward, xxi, 27
Filene's, xix, 27, 30
Fitz-Gibbon, Bernice, 25–26, 68
Five Little Shavers, 16
Forgotten Men's gulch, 40
Fortune, 230
Fortune 500, 60, 237
Forum, 41–42, 56
Foutz, Kallie (Faust), 69–70
Fox, Gershon, 124

France, 36, 83–84. *See also*
	Parisian haute couture
Franklin, Ben, 160
Freeman, Charles, 182
Friedan, Betty, 183
Furness Bermuda Line, 46

Gaba, Lester, 186–88, *187*
Gap, 227
Garden City Lord & Taylor
	branch, 159
Garment District (Seventh Avenue),
	64–65, 67, 77–79, 91, 103,
	128, 175–76. *See also* American
	garment manufacturers
gay liberation, 206
General Electric, 43
Genesco, 103, 105, 149,
	196, 221–22, 225
G. Fox, 123–25, *123*, 213
Gibbs, David (Geraldine's husband),
	201–6, *203*, 215–16
	57th Street, 215
GI Bill, 161
Gimbel, Bernard, 125
Gimbels, 26, 132, 165
Givenchy, 210
Glamour, xx, 97–99, 102–3,
	143, 148–49, 176
Glazebrook, H. McKim, 144–46, 181
Good Housekeeping, 43
Goodman, Andrew, 146
Grace, Princess of Monaco, 152
Graham, Katharine, 60
Graham, Philip, 60
Grant, Ulysses S., 14
Great Atlantic and Pacific Tea
	Company (A&P), 160
Greenberg, Marion, 212, *212*
Greene, Marjorie, 124
Greyhound, 44
Gucci, 177

Guerlain, 159
Guest, C. Z., 205
Guilaroff, Sydney, 46–47
Gump's, 125

Halston, 210
Hampton's Magazine, 32
H&M, 236
Harlem, 127, 188
Harper's Bazaar, 106, 204
Harris, Ruby, 88
Harrison, Bessie, 54–58
Harrods (London), 233
Hartford Courant, 141
Harvard University, 43
Hashim, Koko, 214
Hatch, Anne McQuarrie (Hortense's
    sister), 39–40, 45
Hatch, Boyd L. (Hortense's brother-
    in-law), 39, 44, 45, 50
Hawes, Elizabeth, 77, 79,
    82–83, 82, 91–95, 91
Hawkins, Ashton, 197
Hearn's, 25–26
Henri Bendel, 132
    Anne Leibensperger and, 217
    Bagatelle, 145
    Bag Shop, 145
    Beauty Floor, 180–81
    Bendel Look and, 151–53
    Bergdorf's vs., 213–15
    Bijoutier, 145
    Bonwit's vs., 222–23
    Buster the doorman,
        150–51, 153, 215
    buyers and, 182, 212, 214, 218–20
    Cachet sportswear
        department, 181–82
    celebrities and, 146–48, 147
    Christmas catalog, 225–26
    contemporary custom
        clothes and, 178–79

Crespin hair salon, 181
    designer collections,
        174–79, 210–14, 217
    Donald Brooks and, 178–79
    employees and, 229
    famous customers, 152–53
    Fancy shop, 211, 214
    founded, 105–7
    4 Plus 3 department, 226–27
    Freeman and finances of, 182
    Friday Morning Lineup, 217–20
    fur department, 181–82
    Geraldine as president, xx–xxi,
        143–55, 156, 182, 201
    Geraldine becomes part
        owner of, xxi, 222–27
    Geraldine retires from, 233
    Gift Shop, 145
    Gilded Cage, 148–50
    Glove Shop, 145
    Growing Up department, 148
    Jarman and, 105–7,
        142–43, 194, 222
    Jean Muir shop, 178
    Jean Rosenberg as buyer,
        170–74, 173
    Limited Editions Shop, 171–75
    mannequins and, 188–90
    Milliner, 145
    petite sizes and, 152, 174, 179
    Pilates studio, 181
    Port of Call, 153, 154, 229
    ready-to-wear and, 170–76
    Shop for Brides, 148
    Smaller Than Small Shop, 152
    staff and, 107, 153–54, 153, 183
    Stephen Burrows World,
        209–10, 209
    stock distribution and, 107
    Street of Shops, 143–48, 147,
        151, 154, 171, 177, 225, 232
    suburbs and, 155

Illustration Credits

Photo Insert

1 Everett Collection / Bridgeman Images

1 George Rinhart / Corbis via Getty Images

2 The Valentine

2 Daughters of Utah Pioneers, McQuarrie Memorial Museum, St. George, Utah

2 Brian Odlum

3 National Archives, Eisenhower Presidential Library, Abilene, Kansas

3 Sallie Moss

3 Louise Dahl-Wolfe © Center for Creative Photography, Arizona Board of Regents

4 Sallie Moss

4 Sallie Moss

5 John G. Zimmerman Archive

5 John G. Zimmerman Archive

5 Jill Krementz

6 © 2023 The Andy Warhol Foundation for the Visual Arts, Inc. / Licensed by Artists Rights Society (ARS), New York

6 Miriam Marshall

7 Geraldine Stutz Trust

7 Pierre Schermann / WWD / Penske Media via Getty Images

8 C. P. Smith

About the Author

JULIE SATOW is an award-winning journalist and the author of *The Plaza*, a *New York Times* Editors' Choice and NPR Favorite Book of 2019. A regular contributor to *The New York Times*, she has also had her work appear on National Public Radio, in *Bloomberg Businessweek*, in *Travel + Leisure*, and elsewhere. A graduate of Columbia College, she has a master's degree from Columbia University's School of International and Public Affairs. She lives in Manhattan with her husband and two children.